Dedication

This book is dedicated to the chapter authors for the rich contributions they have made to it, to my library experience, and most importantly, to the library profession.

RECREATING THE ACADEMIC LIBRARY

BREAKING VIRTUAL GROUND

EDITED BY CHERYL LAGUARDIA

THE NEW LIBRARY SERIES

NEAL-SCHUMAN PUBLISHERS, INC.
NEW YORK   LONDON

Published by Neal-Schuman Publishers, Inc.
100 Varick Street
New York, NY 10013

Library of Congress Cataloging-in-Publication Data

Recreating the academic library : breaking virtual ground /
    edited by Cheryl LaGuardia.
        p.   cm.—(New library series)
    Includes bibliographical references (p.   ) and index.
    ISBN 1-55570-293-7
    1. Academic libraries—United States. 2. Academic libraries—
    United States—Data processing. I. LaGuardia, Cheryl.
    II. Series.
Z675.U5R4425   1998
027.7'0973—dc21   98-16605
                                                       CIP

Table of Contents

Part III: In/Finite Resources

Part IV: Information Providers

Part V: Information Seekers

Afterword

Foreword

The Library as a State of Informed Mind

Richard DeGennaro

So much is up in the air about libraries these days, it's hard to make any flat-out library-related statement, no matter how bland, without being in jeopardy of being flatly contradicted—or attacked—verbally and in print. Pose a question to two or more librarians and just see how many responses you get:

Are libraries going to be completely digital?
Reply #1: Yes
Reply #2: No
Reply #3: Maybe

Do we want them to be?
Reply #1: No
Reply #2: Yes
Reply #3: Well, perhaps
Reply #4: No
Reply #5: Yes
Reply #6 given with a hazy look: Ask me again later.

Will books continue to be a major information delivery medium?

> Reply #1: Yes!
> Reply #2: No!
> Reply #3: Yes! Yes!

Will an information elite take over the management of information resources?

> Reply #1: Over our dead bodies!
> Reply #2: They already have. . . .

The list goes on.

If we pose the most basic question of all, "What *is* a library?" we will inevitably find a wide-ranging diversity of opinion about that, too. But we're willing to try to answer that question, here and now. In his poem "The Death of the Hired Man," Robert Frost defines Home as " . . . the place where, when you have to go there, they have to take you in." We define a Library as the place where, when you need information, it will be provided. That's irrespective of time, education, distance (increasingly), and financial resources (decreasingly).

As remote access, distance learning, educational consortia, and telecommuting abound, the concept of the library as a corporeal place may recede in importance in some people's minds. It happens that it does not in ours—we always think of the library as a place, a place to go. If you'll forgive another literary analogy, we liken it to Hemingway's "A Clean, Well-Lighted Place," a place of comfort and reason and sanity. But upon further analysis, that place as we define it has more to do with a state of mind, admittedly, than with a physical reality within space and time.

Despite the fact that there are no clear-cut answers, *Recreating the Academic Library* takes on some of the compelling questions and problems facing academic libraries. The chapters in "An Implicitly New Paradigm" discuss some of the directions library technology should (and may well) take, as well as some of the effects it's already had on our culture and on us as individuals. The second part, "Information's Domain," deals with the large entities currently identified as a library: the institutional organization, buildings, and fittings for those buildings that make them usable by staff and the public. "In/Finite Resources" talks about the duality of having infinite information resources available but finite resources to access, acquire, and process that information. The book's last two parts, "Information Providers" and "Information Seekers" examine issues concerning library staff and library patrons, respectively, including the possibility that a library may in future be defined more by its staff and patrons than by any entity such as a building—through remote use.

The library as a state of mind is civilization, no less. It represents the highest stages of development our culture can produce. It is that place in our consciousness that is good, and clean, and rational, and fine. And the recreated academic library, in whatever form, will be built around that as its cornerstone.

Preface

Recreating the Academic Library was originally conceived as I was transitioning between the West and East Coasts, going from the University of California at Santa Barbara (UCSB) Library to the Harvard College Library. As I was packing up my UCSB office the idea for the book emerged from among my files. Having spent the previous eight years in four different work assignments at UCSB, from Head of Interlibrary Loan, to Assistant Head of Reference, then Head of Library Instruction, and finally as Coordinator of Computerized Information Services, I had actively participated in several reorganization planning and implementation processes, during which it seemed we had made changes in practically every aspect of the Library, from the catalog to the organizational infrastructure, to numbers and kinds of collections, and especially in services.

Upon arrival at Harvard College Library, I soon realized that it had also been in the process of changing itself administratively and technologically. Major computer initiatives had been and continue to be implemented, as a rich historical resource combines with enormous electronic collection and bibliographic control capabilities in an immense, and highly complex, library environment. As different as these libraries are, I also saw distinct patterns in the kinds of changes that were being wrought. While unpacking all those boxes of file folders in Cambridge, I had another opportunity to look over the work of the past decade while planning the work I was about to undertake in my new setting.

I was struck anew by the extent of change my work and that of my colleagues in academic libraries all over the world had undergone over the past 10-15 years, and I came to believe that we were really engaged in a huge problem-solving enterprise. The problem? How to recreate our work, our institutions, and ourselves to meet the continuously changing needs of our increasingly technologically-demanding users.

So having a problem to solve, the obvious question is: How to solve it? Having spent the last 20 years attempting to write cogent program and project justifications in an accessible and convincing manner acceptable to library administrators, the questions that seemed to emerge were those answered by the basics of any good news story (or library report): who, what, when, where, why, and how. The five parts in *Recreating the Academic Library* attempt to answer these classic questions.

Part I, "An Implicitly New Paradigm," describes the essence of *what* recreating the academic library involves for those of us who must do the recreating. Clifford Lynch explores "Recomputerizing the Library: New Roles for Information Technology in a Time of Networked Information" and John Kupersmith describes two aspects of our new paradigm in "Technostress in the Bionic Library."

Part II, "Information's Domain," provides answers to both *where* and *how* we are recreating libraries and begins to describe *who* is doing it. This part of the book features Susan Lee exploring the use of leadership teams; Jim Rettig on designing effective buildings for the recreated academic library; an interview with Hazel Stamps on changes in human resource management for the academic library; and John Vasi's look at computer ergonomics for the new library's users and its staff.

Part III, "In/Finite Resources," discusses details of *what* is being created in Stella Bentley's "New Collections for Old," aspects of *when* it is happening in Liz Lane's and Barbara Stewart's "The Evolution of Technical Services to Serve the Digital Library," and more about *how* change is coming in Mary Cahill's "Access is Everything."

Part IV, "Information Providers," is a more detailed discussion of *who* is involved in the nitty-gritty shift to virtual librarianship. I have no doubt you'll recognize yourself (and many of your colleagues) in these four essays: "Making the Internet Manageable for Your Users (and Yourself)" by Abbie

Jan Basile, "Lessons Bull Durham Taught Me" by Ed Tallent, "Librarian-Teachers and the Virtual Library" by Esther Grassian, and "Virtual Library Instruction: Training Tomorrow's User Today" by Pat Ensor.

Part V, "Information Seekers," is all about the *why* of what we do, our users. Here Ilene F. Rockman looks at "Challenges and Opportunities in Reaching the Remote User" and Caroline M. Kent challenges our priorities in "Is Anyone at Home? Remembering Our Users."

My own final thoughts (for this week) on recreating the academic library appear in an Afterword entitled "The New Renaissance Librarian."

WHO IS RECREATING THE ACADEMIC LIBRARY?

The authors whose work you are about to read are a group of people I'm fortunate enough to know and have worked with during my professional life on two coasts. Having learned my profession—and kept up to date with it—from them collectively, when the time came to put this volume together I was certain their combined expertise would make for a good read. So here's a chronological account of how and why the librarians in this volume came together:

Union College

Mary Cahill and Liz Lane were colleagues at Union College in Schenectady, NY. Mary was Head of Circulation at the time, and Liz was Head of Technical Services. Liz headed up a department of some of the most knowledgeable and "user-friendly" technical service librarians it has been my pleasure to work with. Liz has gone on to a number of different positions; presently she is the Director of the New York State Library. Mary took over as Head of Interlibrary Loan when I headed for California and has created a highly-efficient, highly-automated service that is one of the busiest per capita ILL operations in New York State.

California

Ilene Rockman was head of a search committee for a job I interviewed for many years ago in California. Although I didn't take the job, when I eventually moved to California we renewed our acquaintance and have kept up through shared publishing interests and conference contacts, often swapping "transparency detail" for each other. She is a library administrator with a remarkable amount of practitioner's savvy, and the work she and her colleagues have been doing with remote users at Cal Poly San Luis Obispo has been the subject of a number of excellent, informative papers and presentations.

University of California at Santa Barbara

Stella Bentley and John Vasi were colleagues at UCSB. Actually, Stella was my boss, but for research purposes we worked together on a number of projects, including articles on electronic collections, about which she has considerable experience and great insight. She has since gone on to become Dean of Libraries at Auburn University. John Vasi has the best and most practical approach to library ergonomics of any librarian I know: we worked together on creating the first electronic library classroom at UCSB installed in 1993, and thanks to John, it worked and continues to work well for instruction. He is very knowledgeable about the larger overall design AND the day-to-day stuff nobody else thinks about (will they kick the plugs out of the sockets? etc.). John also has the greatest collection of 45s of anyone I know (including multiple versions of Hot Rod Lincoln).

While at UCSB, I met a number of colleagues at various conferences, including: Pat Ensor, who continues to be a colleague whose work I eagerly reach for to find out what's going on in the field of electronic reference; Abbie Basile, a colleague well-versed in the latest online technologies and one of the most enthusiastic—and upbeat—library instructors I've seen present; Esther Grassian, a colleague from UCLA who has one of the greatest sustained commitments to library in-

struction of any of my acquaintance and, with her considerable experience, still keeps the users' point of view upper-
most in her instruction; and Jim Rettig, who keynoted a LOEX
conference with a wonderfully cerebral yet also humorous
address and calmed the pre- and post-speech jitters of a colleague who had never before addressed an audience of over
30 (for which he will find his reward in heaven). Jim is able to
bridge the paths among life on the front lines, life in the administrative offices, and life as a library patron gracefully and
very effectively, as his piece here shows. Jim has recently become University Librarian at the University of Richmond. Also
while at UCSB, we hosted a conference titled, The Upside of
Downsizing, at which John Kupersmith presented a paper.
John is one of the most thoughtful writers and speakers on
the subject of the human costs of technology in libraries today; I highly recommend to you his Website (http://www.
greatbasin.net/~jkup/tstress.html).

In the University of California system, each year a presentation called The MELVYL Update would be given by the Division of Library Automation. And each year, the then Director of DLA, Clifford Lynch, would get up in front of his audience of 100 or so librarians from throughout the UC system,
and, without the aid of any notes or overheads or what have
you, he would deliver a remarkably incisive summary of
MELVYL developments and the future of library automation.
I met Clifford at one of these updates and have hung on to
just about every word he's written or had appear in print since,
figuring it's the way to find out the future of the electronic
library before it happens. He has gone on to become Executive Director of the Coalition of Networked Information.

Harvard University

I came to Harvard in 1994, and was nearly overwhelmed by
the research resources here, most of whom are the people with
whom I work. These include: Dick DeGennaro, the (now retired) library icon who inspired me with his articles in *Library
Journal* long before I ever got my library degree; Susan Lee,
who writes and speaks knowledgeably on a wide range of

library administrative issues and whose article here on library teams is one of the most articulate on the subject I've ever read; Carrie Kent, the Head of Research Services and the ideal person to bounce any library idea off of—Carrie can be devil's advocate and staunch supporter at the same time, a neat trick; Hazel Stamps, who has over 30 years' worth of personnel (and personal) wisdom; and Ed Tallent, who, in addition to being my partner in crime for CD-ROM reviewing, is a colleague with whom it is a joy to team-teach—he's always there to catch the ball and throw it back.

Barbara Stewart is a colleague at the University of Massachusetts, Amherst to whom I was introduced electronically by my editor at Neal-Schuman. She and Liz collaborated on their chapter long distance, a fitting close to this synopsis of "networked" connections.

No matter how distinguished or expert the authors, no one book can possibly answer all questions sufficiently unto the needs of all academic librarians: trying to be all things to all people usually means satisfying no one. I do hope that after reading *Recreating the Academic Library* you will be able to take another look at your own work and workplace, ask the classic six questions as a problem-solving exercise, and, using some of the ideas proposed by the authors here, find your own way to recreate yourselves and your libraries to best serve your clientele.

Cheryl LaGuardia
Cambridge, Massachusetts
May 1998

PART I:

AN IMPLICITLY
NEW PARADIGM

1

Recomputerizing the Library: New Roles for Information Technology in a Time of Networked Information

Clifford A. Lynch

Information technology has finally moved beyond the realm of early library computerization, when an online catalog was really just a one-for-one electronic copy of the card catalog. It will take an entirely new mindset to exploit the increased possibilities that powerful new technology offers the academic library. This "mind shift" reflects the changing needs of a networked information world no longer bound by physical space, as Clifford Lynch describes here.—CML

Library automation in the 1970s and 1980s and even into the early 1990s has been essentially a conservative and fairly predictable process (although expensive and often hard to manage). The primary objective has been to make existing, well-understood library operations and services, such as circulation, acquisitions, and the catalog, more efficient and effective by exploiting the new information technology. If anything, the "revolutionary" effects of most of this library automation effort have been somewhat overstated. They have undoubtedly reduced the rate of cost increase for library operations, and have changed many of the ways libraries operate internally and cooperate (shared copy cataloging and interlibrary loan are good examples), but, with the modest exception of the online catalog when configured as a network-based information service, they have not fundamentally changed the services that libraries have offered to their user communities. Also, until recently, the automation of the library has occurred within a relatively stable environment in terms of publishing, information services, and communications media. The relationships among libraries, their users, and information creators and distributors have remained fairly constant.

Coincident with progress in automation, we have seen a continuous, incremental growth of electronic information products and services entering libraries in various formats—diskette, CD-ROM, online (dial-up) services, and, more recently, a wide array of networked information resources. These products and services are not properly the domain of automation programs, in my view, although they share with automation efforts the need to employ and manage various forms of information technology. Rather, they represent new kinds of information content available to library users. While still a relatively small part of the overall library collections in research libraries, the quantities of electronic information being acquired are now finally starting to grow more rapidly as more and more traditionally print-based materials (the vast majority of the collection for virtually all libraries, despite their protestations of managing information independent of format) are starting to become available in electronic forms.

Libraries that have simply considered these electronic information resources as part of a library automation program because of the common reliance on information technology have probably made a fundamental mistake. The nature of this growing body of electronic information—and the choices that libraries must make about their role in its delivery and use as well as its acquisition, storage, and long-term preservation—is far more significant than the routine introduction of information technology to streamline such functions as cataloging or circulation.

This long-predicted but perhaps finally real explosion of electronic information is threatening and confusing. The road to the networked world has been longer, more gradual, and less direct than many futurists predicted back in the 1960s, 1970s, and 1980s. Many institutions such as libraries have perhaps secretly taken comfort in the slow progress toward the networked environment. They have been able to celebrate the promise and novelty of electronic information resources while still recognizing them as exciting innovations that occur around the margin of stable, well-established activities based on print collections. But as the networked information environment now begins to reach critical mass and to pervade the awareness of the general public, it is clear that a series of vast changes are in the offing. And it's my sense that once these changes begin, they will be surprisingly rapid and disruptive.

These now-immanent changes raise fundamental questions about the research library as an institution and about how libraries will operate in the future. Indeed, the impact of the transition to electronic information, and particularly to networked electronic information and communication, goes far beyond the library and promises major changes in a wide range of social, institutional, economic, legal, and political structures. These structures and institutions are so elaborately interrelated and interdependent, and so pervasively influenced by assumptions based on current print and broadcast models of information distribution and communication, that, while it is easy to recognize that something is happening, chains of cause and effect will be increasingly elusive as we try to understand the nature of the changes that are taking place.

As just one example, consider the recent debate about intellectual property in the networked environment and the controversy surrounding the Clinton administration's White Paper on "Intellectual Property Protection in the National Information Infrastructure."[1] The recommendations in this report, if implemented, will have wide-ranging cultural, social, economic, and technological implications; at the same time, they are cast as a response to massive technological, political, and economic changes. It is not clear how to separate cause and effects. At stake in the resolution of the issues raised by this report are severe constraints on the libraries' abilities to share resources or to provide the general public with access to entire categories of information that have historically been offered in printed form. The recommendations also include potentially fundamental redefinitions of the privacy of the public, and a redrawing of the boundaries between public and private space, as such scholars as Pamela Samuelson[2] have eloquently pointed out; this redrawing could have implications for new library roles.

Libraries exist within this broader social, economic, legal, political, and organizational context. Even as they are struggling to redefine their missions, roles, and strategies, this entire context is changing in ways that nobody fully understands or can forecast. Libraries do not fully control their own destinies within this shifting setting. And they are not the only institutions adrift and at risk in this uncertain environment. Publishers, for example, are already acutely aware of these uncertainties. Any number of commercial corporations have already begun to react to the changes occurring with the large-scale introduction of information technology and computer-communication networks, and, in some cases, these corporations have moved aggressively to exploit new opportunities. Others have remained passive and bewildered—as one currently fashionable metaphor has it, "rearranging the deck chairs on the Titanic"—as they watch their traditional markets and lines of business suddenly collapse. Even the higher education system and government organizations at all levels—among the most conservative and well-insulated of institutions—are beginning to recognize that the ground may be shifting under them, though there is still a great deal of denial about the extent of the threat.

The remainder of this brief paper highlights a few aspects of the transition that is occurring, and discusses their implications both for library information technology planning and library automation planning. It also considers the broader strategic issues. There is no attempt to provide a full, systematic picture of the likely, or possible, future. Indeed, the forces at work are so complex that such predictions are likely to be almost comically inaccurate when later reexamined with the clarity of hindsight.

ELECTRONIC INFORMATION AND DELIVERY TECHNOLOGIES

In electronic information resources, delivery mechanisms have become intimately intertwined with content. It's hard to say how much this relationship reflects the immature state of electronic information products and services and to what extent it is an inherent property of electronic information. As practices, technologies, and standards mature and stabilize, we may see a clearer separation between content and delivery mechanisms reemerge, and emphasis and value placed on a discipline of separation—possibly in part to facilitate the creation of content that can transcend technology changes and hence can reach more readers over a longer period of time (and also can be more easily preserved). Distinct genres may emerge. In some, content and delivery (or access) will be well distinguished, while in other types of works the inability to separate the two will become recognized as a basic characteristic of the genre. But today a complex and confusing mixture of content and delivery mechanisms is the reality for all types of electronic information.

In confronting this reality, libraries have become confused about whether they are primarily delivering content—recognizing that many patrons, at least for the present, may not be able to access or use this content effectively because they do not have access to the tools necessary to do so—or whether they need to be offering their patrons the use of access tools themselves as an integral part of providing access to content. This is the essence, for example, of much of the debate about whether libraries should offer "Internet access" as part of their services.

Some comparisons with earlier technologies that delivered content may be illuminating. Consider the telephone. Much useful information may be obtained over the telephone. Although one does not look to the phone as a primary conduit for content (recently, however, with the large-scale deployment of computerized voice response systems, it is taking on this role), early technology forecasters sometimes envisioned the telephone as a pathway through which cultural content, such as concerts or speeches, might be distributed to the general public.[3] Libraries do not typically offer free access to telephones, although, as a convenience to their patrons, they may have a few pay telephones; telephones are presumed to be universal and ubiquitous for their user community.

Television is an important source of information. One does not go to most libraries to watch television, although many libraries may have a television somewhere as a convenience and to support various programs. Libraries do not loan televisions to their patrons; it is assumed that this technology is also widely available in the user community. Broadcast radio follows the identical pattern.

Telephones, radio receivers, and television receivers are all interesting from another perspective: while library users receive a great deal of information through these channels, libraries seldom collect or preserve much of it. This information is ephemeral, disembodied; it is not housed in artifacts which can be collected, stored, and loaned. Libraries have basically defined the information that populates these channels as outside of their mainstream collections. It is also worth noting that the copyright constraints on this type of material are quite different from those on print material. I would speculate that this difference too has discouraged libraries from collecting heavily in these areas.

Many libraries do offer videotapes for circulation. These may be either recordings from broadcast media or works authored specifically for distribution on tape rather than by broadcast. As artifacts, these fit comfortably within the traditional acquisition and loan models of library operations. Libraries may also have a small number of videotape players available for convenience viewing within the library, and to provide access to video materials for those few patrons who do not have other access to the equipment. But libraries do not typically circulate videocassette recorders (VCRs). (I am told, however, that early in the VCR technology cycle, some libraries did in fact loan VCRs as well as videotapes to patrons. I consider this to be a short-term aberration that offers a very important insight on the current debate about libraries as access points to the Internet.) Again the assumption is that most videotapes and audiotapes will be played outside the library, and that playback equipment is reasonably ubiquitous within the user community.

Should other types of electronic information now coming into common use be any different? Why would libraries, for example, offer patrons Internet access on a broad scale (converting major parts of the library to computer labs), as opposed to simply subsidizing or facilitating access to selected for-fee content accessible through the Internet? Why would a library feel required to provide its patrons with access to high-end workstations or even supercomputer time to view, visualize, and analyze statistical, demographic, or complex geospatial information resources that exist in electronic formats? Should they loan computers, CD-ROM readers, and similar equipment to their patrons as part of their commitment to provide access to electronic information?

The counterargument here, of course, is that access to these new electronic information resources requires access to the appropriate technology base, and that this equipment is not yet readily accessible to the great majority of users. Thus libraries must step in and address the problem of access to the technology that makes the information usable.

To be sure, it is essential that a modest amount of access technology be readily available in the library to support librarians in performing reference functions, evaluating information resources, or simply familiarizing themselves with what is available. It is also vital for programmatic activities such as user training (which will become increasingly central to library roles in the networked information era), when one cannot assume that patrons know how to "read" electronic content in the same way that one can assume they know how to read printed materials. Such technology will provide access to what one hopes will be a rapidly decreasing number of patrons without other access to the base of technology necessary to use the content.

Library missions have been, and, in my view, should continue to be primarily involved in acquiring, organizing, providing access to, and preserving content. The information technology needed to provide patrons access to this content should be largely outside the library's mission, though assumptions about the availability of this technology to the library's patrons is certainly essential in selecting appropriate content, and in charting the transition from primarily print-based collections to collections that include substantial amounts of electronic information. And, as indicated, library staff will need to be familiar with the available electronic content and will play a vital role in training patrons to use it. The technology planning issue, as I see it, is to develop strategies and make reasonable resource allocations to bridge what one hopes will be a short-lived problem of equipment access as the needed technology diffuses throughout the user community. If we can envision a time when Internet access stations are as ubiquitous and inexpensive as telephones (including the development of the analog of the pay phone), then it becomes clear that a role as an Internet access point for patrons is not a strategic issue for most libraries in the long term.

If anything, the current focus on libraries as Internet access points is obscuring and diverting attention from much more basic and important issues. A very short-sighted and misleading public-policy discussion has grown up around such slogans as "universal access to the information superhighway." The primary goal seems to be ensuring widespread connectivity to the network as though it were some sort of power grid or telephone communication system, with little consideration that this connectivity will be related to ongoing access to a wide range of useful information resources. Through this debate, libraries are being diverted from ensuring access to a broad range of published information to ensuring access to connectivity and modest levels of communication. At the same time that guarantees of long-term public access to content are being threatened by a restructuring of the intellectual property laws, libraries are being courted in new (and ultimately far more limited) roles as network access points.

Consider the vast and continually expanding array of content accessible through the Internet. How, in the longer term, will libraries structure the relationships among themselves, this content (some of which will be for-fee, and much of which has no clear organizational or archival—much less preservation—responsibility associated with it), and their user communities? This information is intangible and cannot be readily reduced to artifacts like books or videotapes that can be acquired, stored, and loaned. Indeed libraries themselves may not even house the electronic information in question. Will the emerging library role in providing access to electronic information follow precedents from the broadcast media or print publishing, or will it be something completely different?

COLLECTIONS WITHOUT PLACE: LIBRARIES, USERS, AND CONTENT IN THE NETWORKED INFORMATION ENVIRONMENT

We understand almost nothing about the fundamental nature and practice of collections in the networked environment. In a print environment, including a work in a collection implies a number of things simultaneously: an act of selection and integration of the selected work into the library's collection; the adoption of responsibility for (and control over) the integrity of a copy of a work for as long as the acquiring library wishes to retain that responsibility; the ability to make that work available for use to anyone that the library chooses (though not, of course, to make copies of the work except under some specific, limited circumstances); and, finally, the ability to take preservation responsibility for a copy of the work if the acquiring library wishes to do so. In the print environment, most of these activities are not primarily technical; there are economic and physical actions occurring within the framework of copyright law.

In the electronic environment, each of these activities is separate, and involves distinct technical, economic, legal, and contractual issues. Further, the ability of a library to act in one of these areas does not necessarily imply its ability to conduct other related activities. For example, selecting a networked information resource as part of the library's collection may be as technically simple as including a description of it in a catalog or other database maintained by the library. This does not mean that any particular library patron may have access to it, nor does it make any statement about terms of access (for example, transactional usage fees or a requirement that usage data be collected as the resource is used). Because selection in the electronic environment is in some sense easy and doesn't represent a serious financial commitment, this type of selection raises new questions about the boundaries of a given library's collections, and how one library's collection may be differentiated from another (other than perhaps through unique, locally held materials and owned materials such as digitized special collections).

This is the further progress of a trend that began with the acquisition of abstracting and indexing databases that defined a literature rather than local holdings, with the implication that the library either held or was willing to obtain anything in the abstracting and indexing database on behalf of the user. Now these common databases have grown to include not only abstracting and indexing databases but resources such as OCLC's WORLDCAT, representing the holdings of thousands of libraries. And, as more and more of this material moves to electronic formats, it may no longer be available, due to license restrictions, through the traditional interlibrary loan mechanisms.

The integrity and continued availability of the selected resource may be under the control of some organization other than the selecting library (and, given the ability of a single network-based copy of an electronic resource to be accessed nationally or internationally, total control over the continued integrity and availability of key information resources may be centralized in a single organization—a highly disturbing situation). A library may not have the necessary permissions to take actions needed to preserve a specific information object.

Perhaps the aspect of the electronic world that is most different from the print world is that we have not developed the analogy to acquiring a copy of an electronic work and taking possession of it as a general business practice. If this problem can be resolved, many of the remaining issues will come to reflect the tactics and priorities of specific libraries. With printed works, for example, a group of libraries might choose to establish a regional storage facility and house their copies of selected works there, sharing responsibility for long-term preservation. But ultimately control rests with the owning libraries. If the ownership of copies could be solved, libraries might similarly, under some circumstances, choose to contract out the storage of their electronic copies of works, if this were economically or technically advantageous. But I do not believe that libraries would allow control of access and integrity to become dangerously over-centralized or abdicate preservation responsibilities for these works (though these preservation responsibilities might well be shared among consortia of libraries, or even contracted out).

In large part, due to uncertainties about the interpretation of copyright in the networked environment, libraries currently structure their relationships with most commercial content providers by license agreements. Libraries have not been able to negotiate these agreements from a position of strength, and a typical license agreement grants limited and specific usage rights to material by a specific, defined, and limited user community for a limited period of time. Increasingly, access arrangements also involve third-party service providers as well as primary rights-holders, further complicating the process and creating uncertainty for libraries.

These trends have been clear for some years, and I have discussed them in depth elsewhere.[4] The complex issue emerging here is the appropriate definition of collection scope for a given library, and the increasing gap between a user's ability to learn about the existence of information through a library on one hand and the library's ability to supply it on the other, in light of the breakdown of the legal underpinnings of inter-library loan for electronic content.

What does it mean to be a library user? The print scenario is surprisingly simple. There are some libraries that physically restrict access to a limited group of patrons, and a growing class of libraries that give priority service to a specific set

of users during busy periods through some form of primary
user community policy; most libraries that circulate materials place some qualifications on the people who are allowed
to borrow directly (but these same libraries are often far more
liberal in their interlibrary loan policies). But, basically, a very
large number of people have access to a very large amount of
material from a very large range of libraries, either directly or
through interlibrary loan, particularly if they are willing to
travel physically from one library to another. In the network
environment, it seems likely that this will no longer be the
case. At least for remote, network-based access, libraries will
be forced by license agreements to be quite restrictive about
who may join their user community. It is unclear that the idea
of interlibrary loan will migrate to the network access environment. Ironically, physical travel may continue to be a means
of obtaining access to electronic content at a wide range of
libraries by bypassing the user community constraints that
will govern networked remote access.

There is another side to the collections crisis in the networked information environment which has not yet received
much attention. On the network, it is possible for every author to be a publisher, and there is a large and growing corpus of "self-published" material on the network. Some of this
material is important and should be included in research library collections. We do not understand the legal and business framework and have not codified very well the custom-
ary social practice that governs the use and long-term management of this corpus of material. In the world of artifacts,
once the library has legitimate possession of an instance of an
artifact, it owns that copy; it can keep it, lend it, and preserve
it. For materials mounted on the Internet, the library's ability
to access a copy of a given object at a given point in time does
not provide it with any automatic rights to use, save, lend, or
preserve this object. Indeed, there is some question whether
the technical ability to access equates to a permission even to
view material mounted on the Internet. The number of rights-
holders who need to be contacted to provide permissions to
incorporate these self-published works properly into library
collections is vast, and specific authors will be almost impos-

sible to locate over time. Without some clarifications of these questions in a practical way, inclusion of many of the emerging riches of the network into library collections may prove to be impractical.

COHERENCE AND ELECTRONIC INFORMATION: THE USER'S DILEMMA

The publication of substantial amounts of information on CD-ROM fragmented irrevocably the information "world" viewed by the library user. The availability of significant amounts of networked information has only furthered this fragmentation, while simultaneously offering the tantalizing prospect of a renewed coherent view of what is accessible. The only (elusive) criteria are the willingness of information providers to adhere to standards rather than pursue parochial competitive advantage, the eventual maturation of such technologies as Z39.50, and the decision by various types of information providers on the network to offer only new services that somehow "fit" within assumptions about the existing genres of information resource and communication and the organizational and access apparatus that supports them. Print and the traditions of print publishing offer a great deal of coherence to the reader. From book to book and journal to journal one apprehends words printed on pages of paper in much the same way. The reading of printed pages is a common and widely understood technology; in fact, it is so commonplace and universal that we do not consider it a technology at all.

Printed works fill shelves; one removes a work from a shelf, navigates it through such tools as tables of contents and indexes, browses it by flipping through the pages, and makes connections from that work to another through the mechanisms of citation, footnote, and bibliography.

Information reaches the user through a cycle of publication; this cycle may be daily, with newspapers, or less often, with magazines or scholarly journals. The publication of a new book may be a publicized event. As material is published, it is there to be examined. One becomes aware of important new information through reviews, by word of mouth from colleagues, or simply by tracking the cycles of periodic publication on the calendar. Dissemination is relatively slow—certainly with print, and, in fact, with the distribution of any physical artifact, including CD-ROMs.

In the print environment, the literature of a discipline, a discourse, or even a culture or society is relatively consistent and coherent. The technology of print is a technology of homogeneity. There is great commonality from one literature to another. Except for certain conventions, particularly of citation and rhetorical form (such as the conventions of annotating a religious literature and its commentary, or, to a lesser extent, the practices of citation and reference not only in literature but with collected experimental data within a scientific discipline), each literature is equally accessible to the reader. There is a consistency of genre, convention, and delivery and storage mechanisms.

Each CD-ROM offering is promoted as unique. Every information resource in the highly distributed networked information environment claims to be different and unique. This is a world of distributed control, and one that honors creative differences of each provider within that world. Each information resource comes with its own navigational practices and access controls. Each has its own mechanisms of citation and reference and of publication and notification. In the networked environment, entirely new genres of communication are appearing; the fragmentation goes far beyond the superficial aspects of user interface and navigation to the existence of fundamentally new types of materials.

Literatures and discourses are being broken up into collections of autonomously managed network servers divided along lines that are inherently illogical to readers and participants (e.g., publishers, scholarly and professional societies, individual authors, and groups of authors such as academic departments within institutions of higher education) in these discourses.

This is an environment that often emphasizes speed of dissemination and distribution. While a comment from a colleague remains an important method of finding out about important new developments, such communication is being supplemented by current-awareness services, database triggers, intelligent agents, and monitoring of sites for updates and of news feeds and other telemetry-type channels for new developments. And many of these channels have been democratized: every author can be a publisher, and bring his or her personal, unique views about presentation to the act of creating content.

One model that hints at the changes now taking place, and gives a sense of the potential social dimensions of these changes, is the evolution of information about financial markets—the distribution of quotations that track, record, and illuminate the making of markets in financial instruments such as stocks. Thirty years ago a small community of "professionals" operated on relatively current information. The general public had to be satisfied with information that might already be out of date. Most people were shut out of the dialogue among professional traders who held seats on the exchanges and these people were obviously disadvantaged by this exclusion. Today, near-real-time information (typically ranging from 15 minutes online to the next day in print) is available free to the general public. Truly real-time information feeds are relatively and increasingly inexpensive and also rather broadly available—so they are within the financial and practical grasp of most people who might want them. This change in access to market information caused a revolution in the general public's investment practices, and in its perception of the integrity of marketplaces and exchanges. It created industries.

On the network, we are in the process, perhaps, of extending the use of near-real-time information (and, ultimately, perhaps, truly real-time information) from the domain of numeric information (such as market telemetry) to a broader domain encompassing text and even multimedia products (such as audio and video feeds). Consider a world in which lectures, seminars, and discussions are primary information sources along with refereed scholarly papers, and where much current information for the working scholar or interested public is obtained through these genres and mechanisms. Consider a world in which the tracings of the use of electronic collaboration environments are available for inspection, review, and replay, and in which programs charged with providing current awareness bring such materials to the screen of a workstation even as the event occurs or when the record is filed in storage. The information seeker is faced with an assault by an overwhelmingly rich array of incoherent information and events.

Users greatly desire coherence in the literature of disciplines (and even in the broader records of cultural, social, and historical dialogue and events), and they desire assistance in correlating, aggregating, and managing information from these diverse sources. What role will the libraries play in attempting to meet this user need?

THE FUTURE OF LIBRARY AUTOMATION

Library automation systems to support the existing and future print collections (and print is not going to disappear anytime soon!) are reasonably mature and well understood. There will, of course, be a routine, ongoing need to manage these systems and to modernize them as information technology changes.

But what will be the new technology in the next few generations?

- User interfaces will continue to develop and mature. Graphical interfaces to digital information collections are still in their infancy. The relationship between personal systems owned by users and systems offered by libraries will continue to be reconsidered and redefined as libraries move away from closed-system and dumb-terminal automation models and recognize that their users have local computing resources and want to draw information from a range of sources, including libraries.
- Libraries will need systems to support the acquisition of locally held electronic information resources. This is a major technical challenge if a library holds a great deal of local electronic information rather than simply providing access to it on external services. Most libraries today may receive at most two or three input streams,

typically as bibliographic or abstracting and indexing records. In the future, they may need to accommodate hundreds of input streams from a wide range of publishers and other information providers. My personal view is that this is probably beyond the capabilities of most library systems groups, and certainly beyond the capabilities of current commercial library automation systems; that it requires a more rigorous adoption of standards than we have seen in the publishing or library markets to date; and that these will be strong forces in minimizing the amount of electronic information that libraries actually hold locally.

- Libraries will need systems to support the access and management of electronic information resources that are created or developed (either directly in electronic form or by digitizing physical objects) locally.
- Libraries will have to make a fundamental decision about the objectives of their future automation systems. Either the library will be one among many providers of networked information—or the library will try to establish itself as *the* primary access point for users obtaining networked information.

Beyond these relatively predictable extensions to existing library automation activities there is a more basic question. The whole point of library automation has been to facilitate the management of library collections and their use by library patrons. It is increasingly clear that we do not yet understand what collections mean in the networked information world. Until we understand this central issue, we cannot design new library automation systems to aid in the management and use of these future collections. We can only incrementally improve library automation systems designed both to support existing (largely print) collections (which will continue to be an issue for the foreseeable future, to be sure) and to support electronic information collections that are closely modeled on these current print collections (such as locally held electronic materials, either in formats that can circulate, such as CD-ROMs, or provide ready access to a locally held electronic document, such as ASCII text that can be displayed on a screen or a digital database that can be copied to a user's machine for analysis).

CONCLUSIONS

It is both interesting and troubling that in 1991 I wrote a book chapter predicting many of the same changes from a purely technological basis.[5] In hindsight, it is clear that the most important aspects of these changes go far beyond purely technology-driven evolution. They focus on the library's relation to the changing nature of communication and publication, and the changing legal and political contexts of information access. Libraries will react to these changes; they will not drive them.

In this new environment, libraries are both immeasurably valuable and intensely vulnerable. While libraries continue to debate their roles and how to ensure their future financial, institutional, and political support, their competition is rapidly emerging. I no longer feel it is safe to assume that libraries will automatically fill the central and essential role of providing a user with a coherent view of an increasingly chaotic, incoherent, redundant, and competitive universe of information providers. If this universe is to be made coherent for users of a "literature" or for general seekers of information, new organizations must operate outside the assumptions, values, practices, and context of existing libraries.

Libraries are in the position where they must establish strategies and select roles. Some libraries will select comfortable, traditional, but increasingly marginal (though still viable) niche roles as a way of dealing with this complex, uncertain, competitive environment. These libraries will run the risk of being ever more marginalized and, while probably surviving as institutions, of becoming increasingly irrelevant to the central focus of information access and scholarly discourse in the networked information environment. It will be a great tragedy if libraries, particularly university research libraries, select this safe but uninspiring route.

Other libraries will embrace this exciting but uncertain future; they will seek to continue to select, organize, provide access to, and preserve materials broadly; they will recognize the emergence of new delivery and communication channels and new genres of information resources. They will broadly define their roles as access providers, and attempt to obtain the expensive and scarce technical resources (and supporting human resources) needed to offer a coherent view of an incoherent universe of information and to add value through organization and consistency. These organizations may be unrecognizable as libraries in another decade when viewed from traditional library frameworks and measures, such as the scope of local holdings; they will likely play an integral role in supporting programs and missions for parent universities (which are themselves becoming increasingly unrecognizable in the context traditionally used to define and evaluate universities). These libraries will not simply be extensively automated—they will not simply feature better circulation, acquisition systems, and online catalogs than today's libraries offer. Instead, information technology and electronic information access will have become a central part of the definitions of collection and access. This is where we will find the "recomputerized" library of the 21st century.

ENDNOTES

1. U.S. Information Infrastructure Task Force, Working Group on Intellectual Property Rights, "Intellectual Property and the National Information Infrastructure: The Report of the Working Group on Intellectual Property Rights." (Washington, D.C.: Information Infrastructure Task Force, 1995).

2. Pamela Samuelson, "The Copyright Grab," *Wired* 4.01 (January 1996): 134 ff.

3. Ithiel de Sola Pool, *Forecasting the Telephone: A Retrospective Technology Assessment* (Norwood, N.J.: Ablex, 1983). Communication and Information Science.

4. Clifford A. Lynch, "Accessibility and Integrity of Networked Information Collections," Background Paper, BP-TCT-109 (Washington, D.C.: Office of Technology Assessment, 1993).

5. ———, "The System Perspective," in *The Evolution of Library Automation: Management Issues and Future Perspectives*, ed. Gary M. Pitkin (Westport, Conn.: Meckler, 1991): 39–57.

2

Technostress in the Bionic Library

John Kupersmith

Life consists of a series of trade-offs and consequences: if we live here then we can't live there, if we do this work then the consequences will be that, if we get this then we must give that and compromise on the other. We're not usually conscious of the many trade-offs we make, we just live with them and move on. But in libraries there is a growing awareness of the major trade-offs that we make increasingly in the course of shifting over to new technological library standards. At the same time, technology offers us powerful possibilities and makes huge intellectual, physical, and emotional demands of us daily. Are these technological trade-offs good, bad, or indifferent? Here is John Kupersmith's informed discussion of the brave new paradigm's downside: technostress.—CML

Technostress has become a fact of life in the libraries of the 1980s and 1990s. How will it affect staff and users as libraries offer more and more information through remotely accessible electronic systems? What can designers of these systems do to reduce stress-related problems? And what can system managers do to minimize the effects of stress in day-to-day operation?

THE BIONIC LIBRARY

As readers of this volume are well aware, academic libraries are offering increasingly copious and diverse information in electronic form for local and remote access. These electronic services began with online library catalogs; have come to include bibliographic, full-text, and image databases; and, through the use of Internet tools such as the World Wide Web, are rapidly evolving into networked "information spaces" where users can identify and locate both printed and electronic items, retrieve the latter, and communicate via e-mail with expert guides (for example, the library staff).

At the same time, the physical library continues to exist and even thrive, acquiring, organizing, and serving up large quantities of material in print and other nonelectronic formats to substantial numbers of students and faculty. Thus it seems likely that academic libraries will continue to operate in both modes for some time. In coining the term "bionic library" to describe this hybrid concept, Harold Billings also alludes to the variety of reactions among potential users:

> To some scholars, the concept of an electronic library is paradise at hand; to others, it is absolutely frightening. I suggest that libraries are evolving as bionic libraries; organic, evolutionary, and electronically enhanced. Library collections will continue, perdurable with books and journals, but for some information sources available via remote workstations, the library will soon never sleep . . . The old and new library systems will become assimilated and intertwined.[1]

The library is also "bionic" in the sense that it comprises not only facilities and formats, but also the essential human elements: users and staff. The success of any library system, after all, rests not on how well the design works on paper, in the abstract, but on how readily people will accept it and how effectively they can use it. And it is the biological components of the library that embrace or reject the new technologies; fulfill or frustrate the intentions of system designers; and, especially in these times of change, experience the kind of anxiety and disorientation known as technostress.

STRESS AND TECHNOSTRESS

It hardly need be stated here that stress plays a critical and problematic role in modern life. Most modern stress theory is based on the work of Hans Selye, who defined three stages of reaction to "stressors" in the environment: alarm, resistance, and (in extreme cases where stress is serious and prolonged) exhaustion.[2] While stressors can be pleasant or unpleasant and stress can have positive effects—energizing a person, focusing attention, and stimulating behaviors of engagement and constructive adaptation—generally speaking it is the negative aspect of "distress" that merits our attention here.

Symptoms of stress may be physical (muscle tension, rapid heartbeat, dry mouth and throat, shallow breathing, headaches, gastric problems), cognitive (mental fatigue, inability to concentrate, poor judgment), affective (irritability, anxiety, mental fatigue, depression), or behavioral (impulsiveness, avoidance, withdrawal, loss of appetite, insomnia). Other researchers have emphasized the importance of the individual's appraisal of a potential stressor (a charging rhino thus eliciting a stronger reaction than a balky hypertext link); the degree to which the individual perceives that he or she can control the situation, personality differences, and social support mechanisms that affect individuals' reactions and adaptability; and the additive and cumulative effects of multiple stressors, including both negative and positive "life events."[3]

Compounding the effects of multiple stressors is the phenomenon known as the Zeigarnik effect, which confirms a common human experience: interrupted tasks tend to be remembered better than completed tasks, especially when the individual is highly involved in the task and when the interruption is unplanned.[4] This helps explain why staff and users of the bionic library, juggling a host of tasks, tend to carry around (and experience continuing stress from) their mental "to-do" lists, and why many find it difficult to derive much satisfaction from completed tasks.

Computers—or, more correctly, the ways in which people and organizations perceive, use, and relate to computers— are a potent source of stress, in the bionic library as elsewhere. Craig Brod, who introduced the term "technostress" in 1984, defined it as

> . . . a modern disease of adaptation caused by an inability to cope with the new computer technologies in a healthy manner. It manifests itself in two distinct and related ways: in the struggle to accept computer technology, and in the more specialized form of overidentification with computer technology. . . . The primary symptom of those who are ambivalent, reluctant, or fearful of computers is anxiety. This anxiety is expressed in many ways: irritability, head-aches, nightmares, resistance to learning about the com-puter, or outright rejection of the technology. Technoanxiety most commonly afflicts those who feel pres-sured—by employer, peers, or the general culture—to ac-cept and use computers.[5]

As Brod suggests, technostress takes several forms.[6] Physi-cal problems such as repetitive strain injuries, carpal tunnel syndrome, or back problems result from poor machine de-sign or ergonomics. Computer anxiety[7] comprises several problems, ranging from temporary confusion over how to use a system, to feelings of being rushed or dehumanized by the computer, to the distinct and more pervasive fear known as computerphobia or technophobia.[8]

At the other end of the attitudinal spectrum, those who are highly positive about and involved with computers also experience technostress. This effect can be quite subtle, as when people attempt to match their thinking and behavior to that of computer systems, especially when the interface de-sign does little to adapt the underlying functions of the ma-chine to human perceptions and behavior. Margaret Stieg's description of technostress underscores these effects:

> To use any technology successfully, the user is forced to conform to its patterns. . . . The computer has profoundly

altered our sense of time, a change with many aspects. It has made possible greater efficiency, therefore greater efficiency is now required. The computer requires immediate response. Many of us find the blinking cursor tyrannical and somewhat unnerving. . . . The acceleration of work the computer has brought inhibits reflection, which in turn inhibits understanding. All of these characteristics impart a greater sense of urgency to the worker, a compulsion not to waste time, a consciousness of stress.[9]

The same phenomenon is reflected in a recent handbook from a business consulting firm, intended to help corporate employees adjust to the fast-changing, computerized, global workplace: " . . . you need to operate with a strong sense of urgency. Accelerate in all aspects of your work, even if it means living with a few more ragged edges. . . . Sure, high quality is crucial, but it must come quickly. You can't sacrifice speed. Learn to fail fast, fix it, and race on."[10]

Any change in a person's life, whether positive or negative, can produce stress. Technostress is especially likely to occur when new technologies are introduced. Users of any computer system rely on their mental models to help them navigate among its various components and form assumptions about what will result from various actions.[11] When the technology changes, the old models no longer function; the more complex and less obvious the technology, the more difficult it is to form new ones. As Karl E. Weick points out in his analysis of this "sensemaking" process

New technologies . . . create unusual problems in sensemaking for managers and operators. For example, people now face the novel problem of how to recover from incomprehensible failures in . . . computer systems. To solve this problem, people must assume the role of failure managers who are heavily dependent on their mental models of what might have happened, although they can never be sure because so much is concealed. . . . Complex systems . . . make limited sense because so little is visible and so much is transient, and they make many different kinds of sense because the dense interactions that occur within them can be modeled in so many different ways.[12]

These general aspects of technostress affect both staff and users of the bionic library; but because these groups are in somewhat different situations, they are treated separately in the following discussion.

EFFECTS ON STAFF

By the nature of their work, librarians, like other members of the "helping professions," are subject to chronic stress (from multiple sources) in situations over which they have (or perceive that they have) little control. Several studies have documented this stress, and the related (though distinct and less common) phenomenon of burnout.[13] The effects of technostress on librarians have frequently been described in the literature.[14] The related problem of resistance to technological change in libraries has also been addressed.[15]

Although technostress affects all areas of the library, staff in public services (such as reference and interlibrary loan) are most directly impacted by the convergence of online catalogs, electronic search and delivery systems, and remote access. The type of stress affecting reference staff in the increasingly electronic library has been characterized as having four components: performance anxiety, information overload, role conflicts, and organizational factors.[16]

- *Performance anxiety*: the feeling that one cannot use the systems effectively or help others to do so; particularly difficult for those whose high standards and service ethic extend to perfectionism.
- *Information overload*: the sensation of being overwhelmed by the volume of new systems, databases, interfaces, and service initiatives. According to one recent estimate, reference staff in a university library deal with "a minimum of 30–50 different types of software for various on-line, CD-ROM, and word processing uses."[17]
- *Role conflicts*: uncertainty and confusion about one's

proper role—novice or expert, intermediary or teacher, reactive helper or proactive change agent.

- *Organizational factors*: the disparity between increasing demand (volume of work, rising expectations of users) and static or decreasing resources (insufficient staff, poor training, scarce or outdated equipment).

Common symptoms of technostress will vary among different staff members, but may include feelings of isolation and frustration; negative attitudes toward new computer-based sources and systems; indifference to users' computer-related needs (as in "It's not my job to fix that printer"); self-deprecating thoughts or statements about one's ability to cope; an apologetic attitude toward users; and a definition of self as "not a computer person."

Those most intensively involved with developing and managing the bionic library are under particular stress. They are required to combine creative, long-range, strategic thinking with intense analytical concentration on technical details—not a novel demand in library management, but certainly a taxing one. One librarian, working on a consortium project for electronic document delivery, recently commented:

As I observe [colleagues] losing energy, missing deadlines, forgetting assignments, and otherwise generally "melting down" from overwork and stress of all kinds, I'm beginning to wonder if we're seeing the beginning of a serious trend where significant numbers of middle- and upper-level library managers (if not those on the front lines, too) are just going to collapse from exhaustion.[18]

This description calls to mind the classic type A behavior pattern, associated with coronary heart disease and described as "an action-emotion complex that can be observed in any person who is aggressively involved in a chronic, incessant struggle to achieve more and more in less and less time, and if required to do so, against the opposing efforts of other things or other persons."[19]

EFFECTS ON USERS

Computerized library catalogs, periodical indexes, text/data systems, and Internet access are generally popular with students and faculty, especially with frequent users.[20] Yet, while technostress as such has not been formally studied among users of these systems (as it has in other populations), there is ample evidence that users often do not understand the systems or use them well. Many searches in online catalogs produce zero results or very large results. Users are often unable to reformulate their search strategies effectively, and most do not use the systems' built-in "help" features.[21]

Unsuccessful searches, of course, may result from several factors: conceptual mistakes in search formulation, typographical errors, or items not being in the database; but whatever the causes, the stress contributing to and resulting from such performance problems detracts from the success of the bionic library. When considering the user's situation, we should remember that, myths of the "ivory tower" notwithstanding, students and faculty tend to lead stressful lives.[22] Like the library staff, they bring a certain amount of baggage to the terminal. Unlike most staff, however, users have a convenient (if potentially self-damaging) means of stress reduction at their disposal: unless they are specifically required to use a certain system, they can simply walk away and opt to use other sources. The often-quoted Mooers' Law is relevant here: "An information retrieval system will tend not to be used whenever it is more painful and troublesome for a customer to have information than for him not to have it."[23]

Like the traditional print-based library, which demands literacy and familiarity with various cultural cues, the bionic library presents special difficulties—and extra stress—to users who are not accustomed to computers and online retrieval or who have specific needs that may not be met by standard user interfaces.[24] Any discussion of user-group characteristics should bear in mind the danger of drawing erroneous conclusions from narrowly focused studies, the problem of reinforcing negative images through stereotyping, the continuing spread and diffusion of computer knowledge, and above all the importance of individual differences.[25]

The research literature on gender and computer use discourages facile generalizations, but there is evidence that the stress and negative attitudes sometimes attributed to women as computer users may be more a matter of "computational reticence," a reaction to a traditionally male-dominated computer culture and to system designs that emphasize autonomy rather than connectedness, competition rather than communication.

In this sense, the networked nature of the bionic library appears to offer considerable promise.[26] Users from various cultures—particularly those with limited English-language skills or whose socioeconomic background has precluded contact with computers—naturally tend to respond to system cues in terms of their own preconceptions; system design and terminology should be carefully evaluated to reduce misunderstandings. Elderly users and those with disabilities may require special considerations in ergonomics and displays, but again this is an area where individual differences are paramount. One clearly disadvantaged group consists of new users, a sizable population on any campus and one that is replenished every year; relevant design strategies include providing a "novice mode" (discussed below) and choosing system terminology to match users' natural language. Those who design, manage, and teach electronic information systems should certainly be aware that users will be starting from many different points in their background knowledge and attitudes.

The individual using networked information systems from outside the library is often described in the literature as a "remote user," but for this discussion it is worth noting that from the user's point of view, he or she is central and the library is remote. Furthermore, for any individual, the "virtual library" means not only the local library's online system, but also other libraries' systems, and in fact the sum total of information resources to which one can connect in some meaningful way.[27] Users accessing a remote system from their office or home computers have the advantage of familiarity with their equipment, but may encounter problems if it is not compatible with the system being used. If they are new or infrequent users of the system, they may have special difficulties in understanding its structure and procedures. These users may also suffer from feelings of isolation as well as from the lack of information and feedback they could gain in a physical library through direct contact with other users or staff.[28]

Whether they are dialing in from home, connecting from a computer lab, or sitting at an OPAC terminal, people face a number of problems in using the complex of information systems that make up the bionic library. Most fundamental is the need to locate and identify the "library" itself. While it is generally easy to find the library building on a college or university campus, the corresponding electronic library may have several components (including a dial-up catalog/database system, a CD-ROM network, stand-alone page-image workstations, gopher and World Wide Web sites), each with a different point of contact and some not linked with the rest. In a sense, end-users in the 1990s are going through what library staff began to experience in the 1980s, adapting to one new system after another—and often to several at once.

When users do connect to one of these systems, they may have a hard time determining what it will do, or whether it is the best resource for the purpose, especially if the system is new or unfamiliar. Even in a well-organized, multidatabase system, users may not be aware of what file they are using; for example, 37 percent of students using a periodical index in one such system believed they were using the library catalog.[29]

The Internet offers further challenges. An academic librarian recently commented that

> Information overload and search anxiety are two common problems here. . . . The faculty feel overwhelmed by the information they have access to, and the disorganization of the Internet is a major factor for most of them not using it. They have learned to find information by browsing most of the time, but the Internet is too large to browse.[30]

A computer lab assistant in a large university library made a similar observation about student users: "The Internet just scares people to death. The Internet is so big and you get so lost."[31]

Once a user has settled on a particular information system, its interface may present further problems. Commands, error messages, and other terminology used in the system may not be understandable. Available commands and features may not be visible at a particular point. Depending on the system design, the user may feel—and may in fact be—unable to control the system properly.[32]

Irene Sever provides a useful metaphor when she portrays the experience of new users of electronic information systems as a form of culture shock:

> Today's library, and even more that of tomorrow, has many characteristics of an exotic, alien environment: its language is unfamiliar and specialized and evokes incorrect associations. The form taken by the equipment creates difficulties which must be overcome: screen versus printed page, . . . the need to press combinations of keys of baffling complexity instead of running a finger and an eye down an index page, the difficulty of mastering the order of functions necessary to run a simple "user-friendly" program. . . . An electronic library cannot be "learned" through instant coaching on which keys to press or even through the diligent perusal of a manual. What is necessary is to grow into an electronic library environment gradually through socialization as well as through education.[33]

Reading this passage, librarians experienced in reference or user education will recognize similarities to the situation of first-time or infrequent users in a physical library. In fact, while the specific problems may differ, the phenomenon of "library anxiety" is not fundamentally different in this new setting.[34]

IMPLICATIONS FOR SYSTEM DESIGN

As quoted above, Craig Brod defined technostress as "a modern disease of adaptation caused by an inability to cope with the new computer technologies in a healthy manner." The disease metaphor is useful, but it can be misleading. Computer technologies are not inherently healthy or right; users who have difficulty adapting to them are not inherently diseased or wrong. We can do much to help users adjust, but even more important is proper system design.[35]

Traditional mainframe-based information systems have generally been developed by large organizations: libraries, data processing centers, and commercial vendors. The designers have often been systems analysts who—in the best case— received feedback on user behavior from sources closer to the front lines, such as transaction logs, online user comments, customer groups, and usability labs. This "top-down" methodology has produced mixed results, the most successful systems coming from situations where user feedback was copious, frequent, and highly valued.

Recent developments in networking and client/server systems offer the potential for different kinds of products and development processes. The Gateway project at Ohio State University pioneered the concept of a library-developed front end tailored to students' research needs.[36] Moving beyond the limitations of any single interface, the Z39.50 standard permits the end-user to select from a variety of client software programs, much as one might choose a word processor, and use the program to access a variety of information servers. The various Internet tools, particularly the graphical browsers now available for use on the World Wide Web, allow public-service librarians—and even users themselves— to design and construct front-end access systems of various kinds. Web pages that combine instructional text and graphics with links to various information systems can offer flexible structures, helpful guidance, effective support, cultural cues, and communication mechanisms, making it easier for users to adapt to the new environment of the bionic library.[37]

On a larger scale, a consortium of federal agencies led by the National Science Foundation is currently supporting Digital Libraries Initiative projects at six universities, some of which aim to investigate usability as well as technical issues.[38] Whatever the interface, the same essential design principles apply—clarity and consistency of presentation; visibility and predictability of functions; "naturalness" of commands and actions; and keeping the user in control.[39] The designer has some basic tasks to perform in order to reduce stress for the user. The first is to develop and communicate the "system image" which the user will need to internalize in order to function effectively.[40]

The more accurate and memorable the user's mental model of the system, the less stress he or she will experience in staying oriented and carrying out various tasks. The primary tools for conveying this kind of information—"welcome" screens, menus, screen headers, logos, and other graphical cues—provide a consistent network of verbal and visual anchor points throughout the system, taking advantage of the user's powers of long-term memory and pattern recognition.

A basic decision at this point involves whether to give the user a choice of novice versus expert modes (the former offering a limited selection of options). This is one way to address the needs of the inexperienced user, but forcing people to choose between the two may actually increase stress, especially if the novice mode actually cannot access certain commands or functions. A "command-driven/menu-augmented" design offers more flexibility in that a basic set of options can be displayed to all users, with advanced commands or shortcuts available to any user and explained in the system's online and printed documentation.[41]

As suggested above, the electronic library presents users with many of the same cognitive problems as the traditional print-based library. Users must navigate through a different kind of space—defined in this case by screens, words, links, icons, and graphics rather than walls—but the "wayfinding" process is similar.[42] The natural transfer of imagery from the physical library into the electronic library is suggested by many users' continuing fondness for the term "electronic card catalog," and by the proliferation of commercial online systems based on metaphors such as a virtual desktop, home, or town. Thus architectural concepts (such as rooms, maps, and signposts) are also appropriate tools for library system designers, whether or not the final interface is presented as a "virtual building."[43]

An especially useful evaluation technique is to capture and study the comments of users, reflecting their awareness of and reactions to a system, much as designers will follow a naive user through a physical building, monitoring what the user is thinking and doing at various decision points. Once the design process moves into developing specific features, the principal stress-reducing task is to control complexity without "dumbing down" the system by hiding or omitting important functions.

The traditional admonition to "keep it simple" presents only one side of the equation; if carried too far, it leads to an impoverished result. During prototype testing of Microsoft's "Bob" operating-system interface, a novice user was shown some of the cartoon animals that serve as guides in the system. As the designer recalled, "This guy was very emotional about it—he grabbed my arm. He said, 'Save all the money on the manuals, just give me this duck to always be there and tell me what to do.'"[44] There may be a future for "social computing" interfaces in the bionic library,[45] but if a bird is in charge, perhaps it should at least be an owl.

As Donald Norman has pointed out, one of the prime features of any designed artifact is visibility: "Make things visible on the execution side of an action so that people know what is possible and how actions should be done; make things visible on the evaluation side so that people can tell the effects of their actions."[46] The designer walks a tightrope between overcomplexity and oversimplicity in developing displays of search results, hypertext links, or other information. Disorganized complexity is an obvious cause of stress, but the temptation to simplify and use low screen densities everywhere can lead to users missing important material or having to page through multiple (though perhaps elegant-looking) screens. Edward Tufte offers some useful guidance in this area:

> Confusion and clutter are failures of design, not attributes of information. And so the point is to find design strate-

gies that reveal detail and complexity—rather than to fault the data for an excess of complication. Or, worse, to fault viewers for a lack of understanding.[47]

User interfaces with high information resolution are . . . an appropriate match to human skills . . . [and] frequently optimal. If the task is contrast, comparison, or choice—as it so often is—then the more relevant information gracefully within eyespan, the better. Low-density displays, with screens scrolling scrolling scrolling, require users to rely on visual memory—a weak skill. . . . Low-information displays lead to breaking up of work into user-irritating micro-steps, with a consequent loss of coherence. . . . A common question asked by users of data-thin screens is "Where am I?"[48]

Tufte's recommended solutions include layering and separation of data. In fact, the complexity of library catalogs and database systems generally requires that available commands be presented in layers, with a command available to call up a display of advanced or seldom-used functions. Likewise, search results are often presented in a series of increasingly detailed levels. Tufte also recommends arranging data in small multiples, laid out so that the user can readily see patterns. The prevailing design of World Wide Web pages shows a historical evolution from lengthy text paragraphs sprinkled with links, to greater reliance on lists, arranged either vertically, or horizontally with graphic separators.

The verbal elements of presentation are also worth considering. While we have come a long way from barking at the user with messages such as "Invalid command code," designers should remember that users will experience less stress if the system speaks to them in a way that is, if not friendly, at least civil, and above all comprehensible.

User errors are a prime source of stress, whether these are simple typos or the result of search strategies and assumptions that do not match those of the system's designers. Forgiveness should be a prime design goal, achieved through such means as providing multiple access points to items, offering both browse and keyword search options, recognizing and fixing initial articles and other common errors, normalizing search input, accepting alternative command synonyms (including the NISO Common Command Language), and providing helpful prompts in case of zero results or large result sets. In 1994 the Research Libraries Group's Eureka system was enhanced with a package of changes collectively termed "Do what I mean"; these forgiveness features have reduced user errors by 80 percent.[49]

IMPLICATIONS FOR SYSTEM MANAGEMENT

Like the bionic library's designers, its managers can do much to reduce stress for users and staff. A prime goal in this area is coherence. As mentioned above, the electronic portion of a typical academic library presently resembles a loose aggregation of disparate elements rather than a tightly knit system. Whatever the manager can do to promote both the sense and the functional reality of a unified system—through judicious selection of resources, consolidation and linking of resource menus, and carefully presented publicity and instructions—will benefit both the students and faculty who use the system and the staff who explain and interpret it.

The greater control users feel over a system, the less stress they experience from it. This sense of control derives largely from the system design, but is also affected by how a system is managed. For example, incremental changes, announced both through advance publicity and at the point of use, are less likely to be disruptive than revolutionary changes made with no advance warning.

A closely related goal is to humanize the technology as much as possible. As John Naisbitt predicted in 1982, "The more high technology around us, the more the need for human touch."[50] The "high tech/high touch" approach takes advantage of users' natural tendency to relate to computers as if they were people. To this end, any text in a system—including banners, news screens, introductions, instructions, and error messages—should be written in a direct, positive, natural tone. Wherever feasible, managers should implement a "comment" or "mail to" function, offering users a chance to send feedback. Even if it is not possible to reply to every comment, posting a "frequently asked questions" file will give users a sense of dialogue with the machine, providing benefits that go beyond the information communicated.

Training, documentation, and online help are often cited as key elements in supporting users. These devices are certainly essential and require careful design, even though they may be infrequently used. There is some evidence that human help at in-library terminal locations improves user performance and increases satisfaction.[51] This is an expensive service to offer on a full-time basis, but some libraries have assigned reference desk staff to "float" through CD-ROM and OPAC areas during high-use periods, and some public libraries have begun using volunteer docents to provide such help.

Managers of the bionic library can also take various actions to reduce stress for staff members. The most obvious is to equip staff not only with computers and network connections, but also with the necessary skills and competencies to function in the new environment.[52] Roy Tennant points out that "Instruction and training are the cornerstone of any effort to retool library staff to meet the challenges and opportunities of electronic-based information."[53] Managers can further the success of training through selection of appropriate methods, sensitivity to the individual "starting points" and learning styles of staff, and provision of sheltered space and time for learning.[54]

Another important managerial task is to foster enthusiasm for the new information systems and a positive attitude toward change—something most effectively done by example. One of the best ways to overcome technostress is to learn, and one of the best ways to learn is to teach. The experience of library staff at the University of Texas at Austin, who volunteered to teach the Internet and other computer skills to several thousand users, suggests that aggressive involvement in such teaching can reduce the effects of stress and increase self-confidence as well as technical skills. The developers of this program have also contributed to stress reduction by fostering a culture in which both trainers and students are engaged in a joint learning experience, thus reducing the trainers' fear of system glitches or difficult questions.[55]

CONCLUSION

Technostress is part of the price we pay for living in a time of revolutionary and dramatic change. The bionic library embodies both print and electronics, with all the social and cultural structures that surround them: the old and the new ways of learning about the world and connecting with other people. This hybrid institution, full of new devices and continually "under construction," makes many demands on its users. We can learn much from the stress that people naturally experience in this situation. The success of the bionic library will be determined not only by economics and technology, but also by the extent to which its designers and managers can shape it as a tool for human use.

ENDNOTES

1. Harold Billings, "The Bionic Library," *Library Journal* 116 (October 15, 1991): 38.
2. Hans Selye, "The Stress Concept and Some of Its Implications," in *Human Stress and Cognition: An Information Processing Approach*, ed. Vernon Hamilton and David M. Warburton (Chichester, N.Y.: John Wiley & Sons, 1979), 11–32.
3. For an excellent review of stress theory and literature, see Gail Hackett and Susan Lonborg, "Models of Stress," in *Helping Students Manage Stress*, ed. Elizabeth M. Altmaier (San Francisco: Jossey-Bass, 1983), 3–21. For a more recent update, see Ronald M. Doctor and Jason N. Doctor, "Stress," in *Encyclopedia of Human Behavior*, ed. V. S. Ramachandran (San Diego: Academic Press, 1994), 4:311–323.
4. Reported by Bliuma Zeigarnik in 1927, this phenomenon is described in F. L. Denmark, "Zeigarnik Effect," in *Encyclopedia of Psychology*, 2nd ed., ed. Raymond J. Corsini (New York: John Wiley & Sons, 1994), 3:593.
5. Craig Brod, *Technostress: The Human Cost of the Computer Revolution* (Reading, Mass.: Addison-Wesley, 1984), 16.
6. John S. Craig, "Managing Computer-Related Anxiety and Stress Within Organizations," *Journal of Educational Tech-*

nology Systems 22 (1993–1994): 309–325; Amarjit S. Sethi, Denis H. J. Caro, and Randall S. Schuler, eds., *Strategic Management of Technostress in an Information Society* (Lewiston, N.Y.: C.J. Hogrefe, 1987). See also several studies by Richard A. Hudiburg and associates, including "Measuring Technostress: Computer-Related Stress," *Psychological Reports* 64 (1989): 767–772, and "Measuring Computer Users' Stress: The Computer Hassles Scale," *Psychological Reports* 73 (1993): 923–929.

7. Brett A. Cohen and Gordon W. Waugh, "Assessing Computer Anxiety," *Psychological Reports* 65 (1989): 735–738; Carol R. Glass and Luanne A. Knight, "Cognitive Factors in Computer Anxiety," *Cognitive Therapy and Research* 12 (1988): 351–366; Paula C. Morrow, Eric R. Prell, and James C. McElroy, "Attitudinal and Behavioral Correlates of Computer Anxiety," *Psychological Reports* 59 (1986): 1199–1204.

8. Mike Greenly, "Computerphobia: The Fear That Keeps People 'Off-Line,'" *The Futurist* 22 (January–February 1988): 14–18; Richard A. Hudiburg, "Relating Computer-Associated Stress to Computerphobia," *Psychological Reports* 67 (1990): 311–314.

9. Margaret F. Stieg, "Technology and the Concept of Reference, or, What Will Happen to the Milkman's Cow?" *Library Journal* 115 (April 15, 1990): 48.

10. Price Pritchett, *The Employee Handbook of New Work Habits for a Radically Changing World: 13 Ground Rules for Job Success in the Information Age* (Dallas: Pritchett & Associates, [1995]), 10.

11. Christine L. Borgman, "Mental Models: Ways of Looking at a System," *ASIS Bulletin* 9 (December 1982): 38–39.

12. Karl E. Weick, "Technology As Equivoque: Sensemaking in New Technologies," in *Technology and Organizations*, ed. Paul S. Goodman, Lee S. Sproull, and Associates (San Francisco: Jossey-Bass, 1990), 1, 2.

13. Karen A. Becker, "The Characteristics of Bibliographic Instruction in Relation to the Causes and Symptoms of Burnout," *RQ* 32 (Spring 1993): 346–357; Janette S. Caputo, *Stress and Burnout in Library Service* (Phoenix: Oryx Press, 1991); David S. Ferriero and Kathleen A. Powers, "Burnout at the Reference Desk," *RQ* 21 (Spring 1982): 274–279; Mary Haack,

John W. Jones, and Tina Roose, "Occupational Burnout Among Librarians," *Drexel Library Quarterly* 20 (Spring 1984): 46–72. For a critical review, see David P. Fisher, "Are Librarians Burning Out?" *Journal of Librarianship* 22 (October 1990): 216–235.

14. Julie Bichteler, "Technostress in Libraries: Causes, Effects, and Solutions," *The Electronic Library* 5 (October 1987): 282–287; Julie Bichteler, "Human Aspects of High Tech in Special Libraries," *Special Libraries* 77 (Summer 1986): 121–128; Sandra Champion, "Technostress: Technology's Toll," *School Library Journal* 35 (November 1988): 48–51; Katie Clark and Sally Kalin, "Technostressed Out? How to Cope in the Digital Age," *Library Journal* 121 (August 1996), 30–32; Linda S. Dobb, "Technostress: Surviving a Database Crash," *Reference Services Review* 18 (1990): 65–68; Kate D. Hickey et al., "Technostress in Libraries and Media Centers," *TechTrends* 37 (1992): 17–21; Richard Hudiburg, "Technostress" (paper presented at the annual meeting of the American Library Association, ACRL Instruction Section program, July 8, 1996); Virginia Moreland, "Technostress and Personality Type," *Online* 17 (July 1993): 59–62; MaryEllen Sievert et al., "Investigating Computer Anxiety in an Academic Library," *Information Technology and Libraries* 7 (September 1988): 243–252.

15. Sara F. Fine, "Technological Innovation, Diffusion, and Resistance: An Historical Perspective," *Journal of Library Administration* 7 (Spring 1986): 83–108; Sara F. Fine "Human Factors and Human Consequences: Opening Commentary" in *Information Technology: Critical Choices for Library Decision-Makers*, ed. Allen Kent and Thomas J. Galvin (New York: Marcel Dekker, 1982), 209–224; S. Michael Malinconico, "Hearing the Resistance," *Library Journal* 108 (January 15, 1983): 111–113; S. Michael Malinconico, "Listening to the Resistance," *Library Journal* 108 (February 15, 1983): 353–355; Wilson Luguire, "Attitudes Toward Automation/Innovation in Academic Libraries," *Journal of Academic Librarianship* 8 (January 1983): 344–351; Walter Giesbrecht and Roberta McCarthy, "Staff Resistance to Library CD-ROM Services," *CD-ROM Professional* 4 (May 1991): 34–38.

16. John Kupersmith, "Technostress and the Reference Librarian," *Reference Services Review* 20 (Summer 1992): 7–14, 50.

17. Kirsten Klinghammer, "Re: technostress," private e-mail message (March 31, 1995). Quoted by permission.

18. Julie Blume Nye, "Re: Virtual libraries -> technostress?" private e-mail message (March 31, 1995). Quoted by permission.

19. Meyer Friedman and Ray H. Rosenman, *Type A Behavior and Your Heart* (New York: Knopf, 1974), 84; quoted in Hackett and Lonborg, "Models of Stress," 9. This passage might not be cited here had the author not seen a colleague, involved in a high-profile database project, temporarily sidelined with chest pains.

20. Kenneth W. Berger and Richard W. Hines, "What Does the User Really Want? The Library User Survey Project at Duke University," *Journal of Academic Librarianship* 20 (November 1994): 306–309; Karen Markey, "Thus Spake the OPAC User," *Information Technology and Libraries* 2 (December 1983): 381–387. See also Rachel Applegate, "Models of User Satisfaction: Understanding False Positives," *RQ* 32 (Summer 1993): 525–539.

21. Christine L. Borgman, "Why Are Online Catalogs Hard to Use? Lessons Learned from Information-Retrieval Studies," *Journal of the American Society for Information Science* 37 (1986): 387–400; Larry Millsap and Terry Ellen Ferl, "Search Patterns of Remote Users: An Analysis of OPAC Transaction Logs," *Information Technology and Libraries* 12 (September 1993): 321–343; Patricia M. Wallace, "How Do Patrons Search the Online Catalog When No One's Looking? Transaction Log Analysis and Implications for Bibliographic Instruction and System Design," *RQ* 33 (Winter 1993): 239–252.

22. Glenn P. Gray and Leon H. Rottmann, "Perceptions of Stress in Undergraduate College Students," *Journal of College and University Student Housing* 18 (Winter 1988): 14–20; Dona M. Kagan and Vada Fasan, "Stress and the Instructional Environment," *College Teaching* 36 (Spring 1988): 75–81; George V. Richard and Thomas S. Krieshok, "Occupational Stress, Strain, and Coping in University Faculty," *Journal of Vocational Behavior* 34 (1989): 117–132; Robert E. Seiler and Della A. Pearson, "Dysfunctional Stress Among University Faculty," *Educational Research Quarterly* 9 (1984–1985): 15–26.

23. Calvin N. Mooers, "Editorial: Mooers' Law; or, Why Some Retrieval Systems Are Used and Others Not," *American Documentation* 11 (July 1960): ii. Mooers' article actually concerns the pain and trouble of possessing and working with information; however, his law as stated seems to apply as well to the difficulties of using the retrieval systems themselves.

24. A good starting point for exploring this area is the section on "Accommodation of Human Diversity" in Ben Shneiderman, *Designing the User Interface: Strategies for Effective Human-Computer Interaction*, 2nd ed. (Reading, Mass.: Addison-Wesley, 1992), 21–31.

25. Christine L. Borgman, "All Users of Information Retrieval Systems Are Not Created Equal: An Exploration into Individual Differences," *Information Processing and Management* 25 (1989): 237–251; Brenda Dervin, "Users As Research Inventions: How Research Categories Perpetuate Inequities," *Journal of Communication* 39 (Summer 1989): 216–232.

26. Sherry Turkle, "Computational Reticence: Why Women Fear the Intimate Machine," in *Technology and Women's Voices: Keeping in Touch*, ed. Cheris Kramarae (New York: Routledge, 1988), 41–61. See also Robin H. Kay, "An Examination of Gender Differences in Computer Attitudes, Aptitude, and Use" (paper presented at the Annual Conference of the American Educational Research Association, San Francisco, April 20–24, 1992), ED 346848. For Internet resources on this topic, see Mary Lynn Rice-Lively, "Guide to Women in Technology" (http://fiat.gslis.utexas.edu/~marylynn/wit.html) and Ellen Spertus, "Women and Computer Science," (http://www.ai.mit.edu/people/ellens/gender.html).

27. As an example, 18 percent of the items gathered in preparation for this chapter were obtained directly from electronic sources: WWW and gopher sites, periodical index systems with e-mail and fax delivery of articles, and e-mail messages including a survey of PACS-L listserv subscribers. Of the print items obtained from four different libraries, approximately 80 percent were identified and located using online catalogs and computerized indexes; the rest were found through browsing.

28. Sally W. Kalin, "Support Services for Remote Users of Online Public Access Catalogs," *RQ* 31 (1991): 197–213; Karen

Weilhorski, "Teaching Remote Users How to Use Electronic Information Resources." *Public-Access Computer Systems Review* 5 (1994): 5–20.

29. Data gathered by the author from users on library terminals at the University of Texas at Austin. Remote users, having to select databases from menus, would likely be more aware of selecting a particular database. Screen designs were subsequently modified to provide more prominent indication of the database being used.

30. Margaret F. Riley, "Re: Virtual libraries -> technostress?", private e-mail message (March 31, 1995). Quoted by permission.

31. Mary Lynn Rice-Lively, "Trip to Bountiful: Personal Snapshots of the Campus Computing Center" (paper submitted for graduate course at the University of Texas at Austin, June 9, 1994), 20.

32. For a review of the extensive literature on such problems, see Martha M. Yee, "System Design and Cataloging Meet the User: User Interfaces to Online Public Access Catalogs," *Journal of the American Society for Information Science* 42 (1991): 78–98.

33. Irene Sever, "Electronic Information Retrieval as Culture Shock: An Anthropological Exploration," *RQ* 33 (Spring 1994): 336–341.

34. Constance A. Mellon, "Library Anxiety: A Grounded Theory and Its Development," *College and Research Libraries* 47 (March 1986): 160–165.

35. Rob Kling and Margaret Elliott, "Digital Library Design for Usability," in *Digital Libraries '94: Proceedings of the First Annual Conference on the Theory and Practice of Digital Libraries* (College Station, Tex.: June 19–21, 1994), http://www.cdsl.tamu.edu/DL94/paper/kling.html; Shneiderman, *Designing the User Interface*; Robert Waite, "Making Information Easy to Use," *ASIS Bulletin* 9 (December 1982): 34–37.

36. Philip J. Smith and Virginia Tiefel, "The Information Gateway: Designing a Front-End Interface to Enhance Library Instruction," *Reference Services Review* 20 (Winter 1992): 37–48.

37. As of this writing, a useful collection of pointers to "Innovative Internet Applications in Libraries" is being main-

tained by Ken Middleton at the Todd Library, Middle Tennessee State University (http://frank.mtsu.edu/~kmiddlet/libweb/innovate.html). The "Electronic Classroom" of the Science and Engineering Library, University of California, San Diego (http://sehplib.ucsd.edu/electclass/classroom.html) offers an exemplary set of course-specific home pages, many developed through partnerships between librarians and teaching faculty.

38. To access these projects via the World Wide Web, go to http://www.grainger.uiuc.edu/dli/national.htm.

39. Anyone involved in designing a system should read Donald A. Norman, *The Psychology of Everyday Things* (New York: Basic Books, 1988) and Donald A. Norman, *Things That Make Us Smart: Defending Human Attributes in the Age of the Machine* (Reading, Mass.: Addison-Wesley, 1993). For a useful discussion of library catalog design principles and procedures, see Walt Crawford, *The Online Catalog Book: Essays and Examples* (New York: G. K. Hall, 1992), 49–82.

40. Norman, *The Psychology of Everyday Things*, 189–191.

41. For a specific instance, see John Kupersmith, "UTCAT: Applying Design Principles to an Online Catalog," in Crawford, *The Online Catalog Book*, 507–520.

42. Roger M. Downs, "Mazes, Minds, and Maps," in *Sign Systems for Libraries: Solving the Wayfinding Problem*, ed. Dorothy Pollet and Peter C. Haskell (New York: Bowker, 1979), 17–32. For relevant discussions of navigation in hypertext systems, see Shneiderman, *Designing the User Interface*, 403–418; and Ben Ide, "Hypertext and Hypermedia: The Effect on Libraries, Patrons, and Information Organization" (undergraduate departmental honors thesis, School of Library Science and Instructional Technology, Southern Connecticut State University, April 1992), http://acad.bryant.edu/~bide/thesis.html.

43. For a discussion of these parallels, see Kristina Hooper, "Architectural Design: An Analogy," in *User-Centered System Design: New Perspectives on Human-Computer Interaction*, ed. Donald A. Norman and Stephen W. Draper (Hillsdale, N.J.: Lawrence Erlbaum Associates, 1986), 9–23; John Kupersmith, "YOU ARE HERE, But Where Is That? Architectural Design Metaphors in the Electronic Library," in *Finding Common*

Ground: Creating a Library of the Future without Diminishing the Library of the Past (proceedings of a conference in Cambridge, Mass., March 30–31, 1996) (New York: Neal-Schuman, 1998).

44. Don Clark, "How a Woman's Passion and Persistence Made Bob," *Wall Street Journal*, 10 January 1995, B1.

45. For a serious discussion, see Mark S. Ackerman, "Providing Social Interaction in the Digital Library," in *Digital Libraries '94*, http://www.cdsl.tamu.edu/DL94/position/ackerman.html.

46. Norman, *The Psychology of Everyday Things*, 197–198.

47. Edward Tufte, *Envisioning Information* (Cheshire, Conn.: Graphics Press, 1990): 53.

48. ———, *Visual Design of the User Interface* (Armonk, N.Y.: IBM Corp., 1989).

49. "RLIN Forum at ALA Midwinter 1995," *RLIN Focus* (April 1995): 1.

50. John Naisbitt, *Megatrends: Ten New Directions Transforming Our Lives* (New York: Warner Books, 1982), 53.

51. Jennifer Mendelsohn, "Human Help at OPAC Terminals Is User Friendly: A Preliminary Study," *RQ* 34 (Winter 1994): 173–190.

52. Cecilia D. Stafford and William M. Serban, "Core Competencies: Recruiting, Training, and Evaluating in the Automated Reference Environment," *Journal of Library Administration* 13 (1990): 81–97.

53. Roy Tennant, "The Virtual Library Foundation: Staff Training and Support," *Information Technology and Libraries* 14 (March 1995): 46.

54. Stuart Glogoff, "The Staff Creativity Lab: Promoting Creativity in the Automated Library," *Journal of Academic Librarianship* 20 (March 1994): 19–21. For a review of staff support methods and other organizational strategies, see Kupersmith, "Technostress and the Reference Librarian," 12–14.

55. John Kupersmith, "Teaching, Learning, and Technostress," in *The Upside of Downsizing: Using Library Instruction to Cope*, ed. Cheryl LaGuardia et al. (New York: Neal-Schuman, 1995), 171–182.

PART II:

INFORMATION'S DOMAIN

3

Leadership Teams: Making Meaning from Puzzle Pieces

Susan Lee

Just as the food pyramid is being established in our minds as good for the human constitution, the hierarchical pyramid is being debunked as "baaaaaad" for institutions. The old-style administrative pyramid is being replaced wholesale by new theories in management. Although there are a wide variety of practices that define and distinguish these various theories, the main constant among them is (drumroll please, although you know the word that's coming, don't you?) TEAMWORK. If a unified library management mantra exists, this is it. But for all the happy talk that goes on about teamwork, are we really convinced as yet of teamwork's true virtue? Susan Lee makes a logical and compelling argument for it in this essay on leadership teams.—CML

Research libraries are exceptionally complex systems that interact with even more complex environments. And the increasingly dynamic environment of higher education is demanding that research libraries adopt new management practices, new organizational structures, and new leadership models. Tomorrow's research library model will be composed of networks, clusters, cross-functional teams, modules, matrices, almost anything but the traditional functional-based pyramid.

LATERAL INTEGRATION

Our research libraries are made up of parts, each of which engages in different internal activities and responds to different parts of the university and the external environment. The staff within these parts fill different roles, have different experiences, and view different aspects of the library, the campus, and the environment. Our organizations are fragmented into functional specialties with "walls" that separate different functions into independent and often warring fiefdoms. In a large research library, no one person, not even the director, can see it all, much less understand all the ways in which its components are connected internally and externally.

Today our research libraries must be capable of making conscious trade-offs. The necessary systematic solutions to complex, multifaceted choices can be developed only through lateral integrative processes. To do this, forums must be created where people with diverse organizational perspectives develop solutions to complex problems and opportunities. In response to these pressures for the integration and coordination of work between groups, a range of integrating mechanisms are being applied.

Galbraith and Kazanjian[1] have discussed a continuum of integrating mechanisms that can be employed when organizations need to make trade-offs, solve problems, and make adjustments to work on the basis of information from knowledge that resides in different parts of the organization. Traditionally our research libraries have relied on standard procedures, shared goals and objectives, and organizational processes such as long- and short-term planning. In addition, such informal approaches as the establishment of rich interpersonal networks have been common. These approaches have created a strong base for cooperation while involving minimal investment.

In today's complex and dynamic situations, the need for integrative devices increases dramatically.[2] To facilitate lateral integration, a range of new structures and processes is being tried and can be expected to characterize our research libraries increasingly in the future. These approaches to connect units laterally include self-directed teams, task teams and councils, special project management roles, matrix reporting, shared information systems, goal setting, and the use of overlaid teams and cross-functional teams.

In today's environment, with its uncertainty and dynamic conditions, complex interdependence calls for more formal approaches to ongoing adjustment between individuals and groups. In many research libraries, the formal responsibility for integration has been given to cross-functional teams. More recently teams have gained influence as they have been given resource control and decision-making authority.

Research has demonstrated that in highly complex, dynamic situations, a wide range of integrative approaches are likely to be in place.[3] If used effectively these mechanisms enable adequate integration and also result in balanced influence of the various viewpoints required to excel simultaneously in several interdependent areas when the strategic importance of these focuses changes through time.

Effective collaboration involves being well informed about how your particular function and processes affect the entire organization—even those parts of the organization not directly in the cause-and-effect chain. Each part of the organization has a role to fulfill, and this role nurtures some specific outcome. Each part must understand how it fits into the broad purposes of the whole and must make ongoing adjustments to its behavior to ensure that the whole can perform at the highest possible level. This requires a high degree of upward, downward, and lateral information sharing.

Effective collaboration requires additional costs of time within the organization to arrive at joint decisions and to make difficult trade-offs. The movement toward lateral integration requires a belief that "process" hours are productive, and that they will lay the foundation for coordinated effort. Managers must be willing to look across and beyond their departments to new, more powerful integrative processes. In our research libraries (with their years of commitment to traditional, functionally based organization) this is no easy task. It will require leaving the comfort zone of our functional-based authority and expertise.

THE ROLE OF MANAGEMENT

The role of management in this new research library environment is being significantly altered. The new manager supports the work of the team, sees that the teams are trained, facilitates communications, and provides access to the unique expertise of the larger organization. The new managerial role is one of strategic support, expert advice, and orchestration of change initiatives. In today's research library, successful change through cross-functional teamwork is often the real source of potential added value.

In many research libraries today cross-functional teams report to a higher level team which exists to integrate functions at a more strategic level. The more compelling the need for integration of the operations in the organization, the greater the need for a hierarchy of teams that deal with increasingly aggregated levels of the organizational system. Ironically, lateral integration requires vertical integration through a hierarchy of teams. Knowledge of the bigger picture, required for the lateral resolution of issues, can to some extent be built into the lower levels of the organization, but complex trade-offs are often strategic in nature and require higher-level teams.

INTEGRATING PROCESSES AND SHARED PURPOSE

The effectiveness of such integrative structures as teams is closely tied to the existence of integrating processes.[4] For example, strategic planning processes are needed to provide a framework for the work of the team. A shared mission, strategy, and values provide guidance and direction for decision making and conflict resolution. To support work toward a shared purpose the strategic direction must cascade throughout the organization to work units and teams at all levels. This new emphasis on lateral integration must be supported by top management's ability to ensure a common direction and context for operational decisions.

Through these integrating processes, energy is focused on the definition and achievement of purposes and goals. Shared values, vision, mission, and goals support unifying behaviors. Organizational purpose is sharpened, encouraging the parts to align and work together toward common purpose. Through collaboration, people focus on achieving accepted goals, and work together to plan and implement their shared vision. Departments openly share information, exchange quality products and services, and cooperate and collaborate rather than compete with each other.

EXECUTIVE LEADERSHIP AND MODELING OF LATERAL INTEGRATION

In addition to periodic, library-wide strategic planning processes, day-to-day executive level teamwork is essential. Executive leadership and modeling of lateral integration at the top of the organization is key to promoting a teamwork culture that ensures that the library achieves balance among its multiple focuses. We have reached a time when most traditional approaches to leading simply do not work anymore. The call is for new approaches and new thinking about leaders and leading. The new perspective on leadership is about shared leadership, cooperation, and multiple perspectives.

Because decision making at the top organizational levels is complex, the right decision is rarely obvious. At the executive level, knowledge about cause and effect is not usually possible and information relevant to the decision is often equivocal. Library leaders regularly face situations of great ambiguity and incomplete information. Conditions such as these mitigate against rational individual decision making. Today's issues are complex, demanding multiple perspectives and an intelligence beyond the limits of a single individual. The prevalent belief, based on findings in business organizations, suggests that "organizational success, regardless of whether it is defined as the ability to innovate, achieve adaptability in adverse circumstances, or get an edge on productivity, is more likely to be achieved when leaders embrace a teamwork approach." [5]

FACILITATING LEADERSHIP

The ideal leader of today is not a solo hero who makes all the right decisions and tells others how to carry them out. Rather, the ideal leader is someone who knows how to find and bring together diverse minds—minds that reflect variety in their points of view, in their thinking processes, and in their questioning and problem-solving strategies; minds that differ in their unique capacities as well as in their unique limitations. The ideal leader is skilled at pulling a group of thinkers together and facilitating their collective "mindwork." What we can get through teams is the ability of a group of people to think together in more expansive and creative ways than any one person can alone.

When the leadership process is built around an individual, management's ability to deal with various issues is limited by the time, energy, expertise, and interest of that individual. This limitation is particularly problematic during periods of change when different issues demand competencies that a single individual may not possess. Different types of strategic changes make different managerial demands and call for different personal characteristics. Given the limitations of the individual leader, the challenge is to broaden the range of individuals who can perform the critical leadership functions during periods of significant organizational change. The group of individuals who report directly to the individual leader— the executive or senior team—is the first logical place to look for opportunities to extend and institutionalize leadership. Development of an effective, visible, and dynamic senior team can be a major step in getting around the problems and limitations of the individual leader.[6]

Today our research libraries face a degree of complexity that requires intelligence beyond that of any individual. To solve problems in complex systems we must learn to tap the collective knowledge of groups. Promoting collective thinking and communication is the key challenge of the team leader. To begin to think together, the team members, who are usually specialists in their field, need to learn how to talk across specialties. If the team is to learn how to think about difficult issues, the team leader must facilitate movement away from defending parts and toward fostering interconnected wholeness.

THE STUDY OF LEADERSHIP TEAMS

As part of the Institutional Leadership Project of the National Center for Postsecondary Governance and Finance, researchers examined the nature of presidential executive teams, their organization, functions, and internal dynamics.[7] In addition to learning how the presidents and the persons whom they had designated worked together as a team, data were collected on how faculty perceived their administrative leaders, including their president, individual team members, and the leadership team collectively. The intent of the study was to explore models of teamwork in higher education; how presidents and their team work together; how team members perceive the quality of their working relationships; how presidents select, shape, and maintain particularly effective teams; and how teams address conflict and diversity of orientation among the team members.

The findings of this study are valuable to research library leaders concerned with building effective leadership teams and promoting teamwork. In thinking about the experiences of other people in other teams we can gain insight into those aspects of our own team life that we should actively preserve and affirm, and those that we should change. I have long held the belief that the role of the library director is akin to that of the president of the university and that the research on what makes for a successful college/university presidency is directly relevant to research library leadership.

One point is clear from the research: the team is part and parcel of good leadership. As teamwork becomes a clearer, more understandable part of institutional life, the chance that leaders will give the quality of their teamwork the attention it deserves is enhanced. Amid the unpredictable contingencies and seemingly insurmountable complexities of organizational life, persons in leadership positions must develop teams that act and think as effectively as possible.

To make the shift to team-based leadership, leaders
(whether directors, associates, department heads, committee
chairs, or others) need to put aside the long-standing belief
that leadership is a force for marshaling commonality and
consensus to the point of excluding unique points of view
and unique definitions of reality. Rather than insisting on only
talking about views that people share, effective leaders search
actively to see issues from multiple perspectives. Moreover,
to conceive of leadership as a collective and interactive act, it
is necessary to build a view of leadership that counters the
traditional emphasis on individualism, hierarchical relationships, and bureaucratic rationality.[8]

COGNITIVE COMPLEXITY

In Bensimon's research effective presidential leadership was
characterized by cognitive complexity.[9] Cognitive complexity is the degree of complexity of a person's cognitive processes. The amount of available cognitive power is represented
by the size or scale of the world that an individual is able to
construct, pattern, live with, and work in. The number and
range of variables that individuals are able to use in the construction of their world is a measure of their cognitive skills.

Related research has found that presidents may increase
their cognitive complexity by being frequently presented with
evidence of the existence of multiple dimensions.[10] Presidents
may produce such evidence by consulting broadly enough to
permit the emergence of multiple views, remaining open to
evidence that disconfirms their own predilections, and actively
seeking information about campus functioning. The use of
administrative teams whose members see the organization
from different perspectives and who fulfill different cognitive functions can help a president avoid simple thinking.

HOW LEADERS USE THEIR TEAMS

Effective presidents typically deploy complex strategy in getting things done, drawing on a large repertoire of strategies
for addressing changing circumstances. With complexity

comes understanding and appreciation of subtleties. Effective leaders can use their teams to maximize their cognitive complexity. Teams can help to enlarge leaders' understandings of what others see. As our environment becomes more complex, leaders must become equally complex if they are to sense changes and make appropriate adaptations.

Many executives lack a conceptual map of the functions teams can fulfill, however, and they tend not to utilize their teams as fully as they might. One of Bensimon's major findings is that presidents who are effective team builders think in complicated ways about their team's work.[11] He identifies three major functions: utilitarian, expressive, and cognitive. The following discussion summarizes these findings.

Viewed as a utilitarian tool, the simple executive team keeps the institution running and gets necessary jobs done. It is purposive and task-oriented, gathering information, coordinating and planning, and making decisions; but its repertoire of responses is tied to the person in charge, giving it limited capacity to discern the complexities of organizational life. Dominated by the team leader, simple teams have limited ability to respond to change in meaningful ways.

More highly developed teams can also fulfill an expressive function providing mutual support and counsel to the group leader. Teams that develop beyond politically expedient relationships have a sense of internal connectedness that provides support and a setting within which collaborative teamwork may occur. Likewise, the extent to which teams can fulfill the role of counselor depends heavily on whether the leader-team relationship is based more on intimacy and collegiality than on purely official ties.

In more advanced cognitively functioning teams, the members are collectively involved in perceiving, analyzing, learning, and thinking. They enlarge the intellectual span of individual team members, viewing problems from multiple perspectives; questioning, challenging, and arguing; and acting as a monitoring and feedback system. They view the institution as a complex system in which the team is the sense-maker. For the team to be effective there has to be some tolerance for disorder. Teams that are truly effective (that think out loud, that challenge each other, and that argue among themselves) frequently consider new, unfamiliar, or unclear courses of action.

Leaders trying to encourage team development at this level need to bear in mind that creative problem-solving is more likely to emerge from unstructured talks, which may appear chaotic and wasteful to those who are impatient to get to the point, than from carefully ordered, formal agendas. The team dialogues most conducive to course adjustment are more likely to take place in informal settings that allow the conversation to take the group in unexpected directions and toward new or different understandings. Such unstructured discussions can be encouraged by pausing to focus on thinking and talking about what the team members are hearing and seeing; on pondering what lies beneath the information that comes to the table.

Many times over the span of my career I have seen the individual in the team leader position unknowingly undermine real teamwork. Tight control of the agenda; negative nonverbal gestures (facial gestures that indicate disapproval, shuffling of papers); attention to other matters such as messages, phone calls, and papers all subvert the team. Members feel silenced and rebuffed and begin to restrain themselves. They begin to think twice before saying something and shift their focus to trying to figure out what the leader wants. Self-censorship, fear of saying the wrong thing, a hesitancy to voice one's thoughts all severely limit the team. Without a sense of connectedness, both the expressive and cognitive functions of the team are blocked.

In spite of the rewards of collaboration, many leaders remain set in the old ways. They are open to an exchange of ideas but do not share the final decision making. Most seem unaware that they have deprived themselves and their organization of the benefits of creative and complex thinking and real teamwork. The external signs are there. The team members go through the expected motions, go to meetings, give progress reports, and show loyalty to the team leader; but they do not come together, do not think in complex ways and usually do not generate new creative ideas.

TEAM COLLABORATION

A collaborative work mode enables an executive team to look at a specific issue as a whole rather than in a segmented fashion. The team's collaborative approach makes it possible for team members to think beyond the boundaries of their specializations. Rather then being bounded by the limits of their "territories," they focus on what they can do collectively about problems that belong to all. Karl Weick says that when people use the plural pronoun, collective sense-making is under way.[12]

Collaboration calls for a new conception of human relations in what Zuboff calls "posthierarchical" designs.[13] In terms of research library leadership, it requires reconceptualizing power as a means including rethinking the roles of the team leader and team members. Bringing the issue of team collaboration to the table is only the first step. Much more difficult is building a culture of collaboration. On the part of the team leader this requires lessening status differences and an authentic desire to share power. Zuboff's conception of posthierarchical relationships views power as regenerative; the more power you share the more power is generated. This does not imply that differentials of knowledge, responsibility, and power no longer exist. Rather they can no longer be assumed. Instead they shift and flow and develop in relation to the situation, the task, the actors at hand.

Cognitively oriented teams are in a position to shape, alter, and otherwise fashion the team builder's and other team members' understanding of a given situation, as well as the team's potential responses to that situation. It is important to note that this approach differs from the conventional belief that the team builder should shape the views of those that work with him or her. In teams that think together, the utilitarian, expressive, and cognitive functions inform each other. What results is a team engaged simultaneously in active reflection and in reflective action.

TEAM THINKING

Different people make sense of the same reality in different ways and a complete interpretation of what is really happening is likely to combine facets of multiple frames rather than adopt one view to the exclusion of others. Team thinking assumes that individuals see the world differently, that they process information differently, that they make sense of life in organizations differently. It also requires team members to develop their own unique thinking capacities and to exercise them openly, actively, and freely. In addition, team thinking requires that the members be open to the different thinking processes of other members of the team, and tolerant of different thinking approaches and different ways of making sense.

The aim of real teamwork is to exceed the natural limitations of the human mind. To do this involves fostering connectedness, interaction, and collaboration. When leadership is shared in the team, the leader has multiple ways of sensing environmental change, checking for problems, and monitoring performance. Shared leadership is more likely to provide a leader with more complex ways of thinking and problem solving. The use of executive teams whose members see the organization from different perspectives helps leaders continually to challenge their experience and their conclusions. They regularly consult with team members who see the organization from different perspectives.

As environmental complexity increases, the usefulness of shared leadership increases as well. Today's leadership is not a reductionist activity, where we learn to analyze and take problems apart. In the emerging age, effective leadership of our research libraries is a holistic and integrated venture where we make meaning from puzzle pieces. The decisions and dilemmas of leadership emphasize what the institution should do when faced with uncertainty. Given the challenges, frustrations, ambiguity, and even chaos leaders face, a team, by providing mutual support and counsel, fills an important role. An effective team permits the leader and the team members to retain their equilibrium even as they are buffeted by a panoply of events.

THE LEADERSHIP TEAM AS A LEARNING SYSTEM

For a senior management team to benefit from its involvement in leading change, it must become an effective system for learning about the organization and its environment. The challenge is to bond the team together while avoiding insularity. In addition to shaping and managing the internal group process of the team itself, it is essential to work hard to keep the team an open system receptive to outside ideas and information. This can be accomplished by creating a constant stream of events that expose the members of the team to new ideas—speakers or visitors brought in to meet with the team, visits by the team to other organizations, frequent contact with faculty and students, and planned "deep contact" in the organization (informal personal contact such as breakfasts, focus groups, and visits to work groups).

REFLECTION IN ACTION

The cognitively complex executive is a flexible thinker, making decisions on the run, decisions that are based on (and revised because of) ever-changing information. If he or she makes a decision today, it might be somewhat revised tomorrow because new information inputs arrived and are available for modified strategies and goals. Such an organizational decision maker exercises the option to consider a wider variety of implications, actively considering a number of contingencies and their implications. He or she is likely to reopen or modify decisions making shifts and changes in strategies.

Such leaders have developed the capacity for acting and reflecting and for designing and redesigning action as they perform it. These leaders practice what Donald Schon describes as reflection in action.[14] They make adjustments in what they are doing while they are doing it. Drawing on Schon's work, I would describe the process roughly as follows:

- We try something and immediately reflect on what we did.
- We continue doing what seems to work and stop doing what doesn't.

- As we experiment, we constantly reflect on what works and what doesn't.
- We see mistakes as merely steps toward learning rather than as failure.

The key is to start doing and then to reflect on the results and fine-tune as the situation plays out.

Fundamental to building leadership capacity are well-developed skills for continuous learning. In today's world, successful leaders learn their way through situations where the challenges are enormous and where most of the rules and recipes of the past no longer apply. In this environment, the greatest capacity leaders can develop is the capacity to learn and then immediately apply those lessons. Learning and acting on learning are practically simultaneous, different from the past, when we had the luxury to learn and reflect and then at some later time to apply the results.

The changing environment demands a new adaptive organization and a new adaptive approach to leadership. It requires that we stay comfortable with uncertainty, making it up as we go along, not because we lack expertise or planning skills but because we are ready to give up predictability for potential.[15] This disequilibrium can be unnerving and requires new resiliency rather than stability. Reflection in action is a process of constantly creating the world, evoking it, not discovering it. Successful leaders in such an environment are distinguished by their capacity to respond with great flexibility to change through their skilled use of a fully evolved, cognitively complex executive team.

ENDNOTES

1. J. R. Galbraith and R. Kazanjian, *Strategy Implementation: The Role of Structure and Process*, 2nd ed. (St. Paul, Minn.: West, 1986).

2. P. Lawrence and J. Lorsch, *Organization and Environment* (Boston: Harvard Business School, Division of Research, 1967).

3. Galbraith and Kazanjian, *Strategy Implementation*; Lawrence and Lorsch, *Organization and Environment*.

4. D. A. Nadler, M. S. Gerstein, and R. B. Shaw, *Organizational Architecture: Designs for Changing Organizations* (San Francisco: Jossey-Bass, 1992).

5. E. M. Bensimon, "How College Presidents Use Their Administrative Groups: 'Real' and 'Illusory' Teams" *Journal for Higher Education Management* 7 (1991): 35–51.

6. D. A. Nadler, R. B. Shaw, and A. E. Walton, *Discontinuous Change: Leading Organizational Transformation* (San Francisco: Jossey-Bass, 1994).

7. E. M. Bensimon and A. Neumann, *Redesigning Collegiate Leadership: Teams and Teamwork in Higher Education*. Baltimore: The Johns Hopkins University Press, 1993.

8. J. Blackmore, "Educational Leadership: A Feminist Critique and Reconstruction," in *Critical Perspectives on Educational Leadership*, ed. J. Smyth (London: Falmer Press, 1989), 93–129.

9. E. M. Bensimon, "The Meaning of Good Presidential Leadership: A Frame Analysis." *Review of Higher Education* 12 (1989): 107–123.

10. S. Streufert and R. W. Swezey, *Complexity, Managers, and Organizations* (Orlando, Fla.: Academic Press, 1986).

11. Bensimon, "How College Presidents Use Their Administrative Groups," 1991.

12. K. E. Weick, *The Social Psychology of Organizing*, 2nd ed. (Reading, Mass.:Addison-Wesley, 1979).

13. S. Zuboff, *In the Age of the Smart Machine* (New York: Basic Books, 1988).

14. D. Schon, *The Reflective Practitioner* (New York: Basic Books, 1983).

15. Margaret J. Wheatly, *Leadership and the New Science: Learning about Organization from an Orderly Universe* (San Francisco: Berrett-Koehler Publishers, 1992).

4

Designing Scenarios to Design Effective Buildings

James Rettig

Dire predictions about the demise of the physical library have been surfacing in the library literature for years, but for the immediate and foreseeable future, these predictions have about as much chance of survival as the proverbial snowball cast down into the nether regions. I'm of the belief that these dire prognostications are really just wishful thinking on the parts of those who have a slight under-standing of the problems attendant on building new libraries: they would have it all go away rather than try to deal with the reality of making a new library building work. Fortunately (and in contrast to the craven naysayers), in this essay Jim Rettig bravely airs the problems and suggests practical strategies for improving library buildings of the future.—CML

A SCENE (AND A METAPHOR)
EVERYONE CAN RELATE TO

A memorable, emblematic, metaphorical scene occurs about a third of the way into the film version of Kazuo Ishiguro's *Remains of the Day*. The elder Mr. Stevens (played by Peter

Vaughan), recently hired, on his son's recommendation, as an assistant butler to Lord Darlington, trips on a paving stone at the edge of a patio and takes a cropper, sending the silver tray and tea service he is carrying clattering across the stones. In another scene soon after, his son (Anthony Hopkins), the head butler at Darlington Hall, visits him in his room where he lies abed recuperating from the fall. The scene brims with the adult son's uneasiness as he takes on the parental role, a role the proud elder Stevens is loathe to surrender to his son:

Son: I've, uhm, I've come to talk to you about something.

Father: Well talk, then; I haven't got all morning.

Son: I'll come straight to the point.

Father: Do and be done with it. Some of us has got work to be getting on with!

Son: Yes. There's to be a very important international conference in this house next week. People of great stature will be his Lordship's guests. We must all put our best foot forward. And because of Father's recent accident, it has been suggested that you no longer wait at table.

Father: I've waited at table every day for the last fifty-four years!

Son: It has also been decided that you should no longer carry heavy trays. Now, here's a revised list of your duties.

Father: Well I fell because of these paving stones! They're crooked! Why don't you get them put right before someone else does the same thing?

Son: Will you read the revised list of your duties, Father?

Father: Get those stones put right! You don't want all those gentlemen of stature trippin' up and breakin' their necks, do you?

Son: No, indeed I don't.[1]

In the next scene Miss Kenton, head housekeeper at Darlington Hall (Emma Thompson), summons the younger

Stevens to a second-floor window of the great house. They look down together and see the older Stevens testing the perimeter of the patio with his toe, feeling for a point of safe passage across the stones' raised edges. He then pantomimes the action of carrying a large tray past its edge and across its breadth.

Hazards to Research in Libraries

Although his lifetime of hard work (he is 75) and his feeble condition (he dies within days) contributed to the elder Stevens's spill, he undoubtedly would have enjoyed safe passage to the patio had its stones been even—in other words, if he had not encountered an architectural hazard. Many users of college and university libraries can surely empathize with Stevens's plight when they reflect on the ways in which architectural hazards have tripped them up in their research. They probably also agree with his suggested solution to the problem: eliminate the hazard rather than force library users to change their behavior to avoid the hazard. The design, layout, and allocation of space in academic libraries does not threaten personal safety; modern building codes see to that. Yet undoubtedly every building includes architectural features that inadvertently interfere with users' success in using those libraries. Indeed, a group of experienced librarians could no doubt play a lengthy game of one-upmanship in recounting architectural features that pose hazards to users of the libraries they have worked in as students, researchers, or staff members.

For example, one university library building was designed to have its main entrance on the second floor; hence its main service points were designed for and placed on that floor. The students and faculty at that institution voted unequivocally with their feet, however, and made the first floor the library's main entrance. As a result, during busy hours, patrons entering the front door had to worm their way through crowds awaiting service at the very busy reserve desk, situated just a few feet inside the front door on the first floor. Alternatively, they could avoid the crowd by ascending one of two narrow staircases, situated in a small foyer, to the second floor. Once there, however, these stairs terminated and patrons could not identify any clearly visible way to reach the library's third or fourth floors. (Significant renovation of this building has ameliorated some of these problems.)

Another university library tucked its reference desk behind a spacious lobby and a fleet of card catalog cabinets. Until its catalog is fully converted to an online catalog and the cabinets are removed, users of this library who seek reference service will continue to need the persistence and determination of Odysseus. Another university library is designed in multiple stack towers with very limited passage among them. A user following citation chains, especially in an interdisciplinary field, must descend the elevator in one tower to reach a lower connecting floor and then ascend the elevator in another tower (and so on) to track down successive items in that collection! Another university library exiles its reference books dealing with the Third World and international relations to a beautiful wooden gazebo-like structure in its lobby. This structure was erected in deference to the wishes of a major donor, not to the library, but to the parent institution. (This is a rather raw example of the maxim "Form follows funding.")[2]

Libraries in which a cacophony of handmade, word processor–produced, and faded professionally designed signs (the last most likely being relics of opening day) greet patrons defy numbering. This variety of signs can remind one of the blight of roadside billboards before highway beautification efforts took hold. Examples of buildings in which users complain about inadequate interior lighting are legion. All of these examples constitute design flaws that can and often do impede the research process.

Why do institutions dedicated to service allow their buildings to work against the institutional mission? Since each library building is the product of a unique set of circumstances and competing forces, the answer to that question is unique for each flawed facility. Typical explanations are readily available, however. Sometimes a major donor's or the university president's ideas for the library building differ from the librarians' ideas and must be accommodated for obvious, compelling, political or fiscal reasons. Sometimes an architect's commitment to design concepts conflicts with the librarians' ideas about functionality. Other times the fire or building code collides with the librarians' wishes, as, for example, in the case of one university library's addition that had to be partitioned from the original building since sprinklers were installed only in the addition (and, therefore, the state fire marshal declared them two separate buildings that had to be separated by a wall). And sometimes the librarians' concepts of how space should be designed and how different spaces should relate to one another fit the time during which the building is designed far better than they fit the time during which the building is later occupied and used as a service instrument.

There is yet another possible—and, if valid, absolutely insidious—explanation of why library buildings, even on day one, harbor architectural hazards that can sink users' efforts to navigate the information seaways. That explanation is librarians' loyalty to a narrow paradigm of the library, a paradigm that has come under intense questioning in recent years: the paradigm of the library as collection, a parading in which library services are treated as auxiliary activities designed to facilitate use of the local collection rather than as an integral part of the library's overall purpose and program.

A sampling of guides written for librarians planning building projects demonstrates the power of this paradigm to shape thinking about building purpose and building planning. These books note the importance of service provision in the overall plan, but not with the vigor one would expect in an era in which customer satisfaction has become a major measure of the success of any enterprise. For example, one public library director allows that in developing a design, "user needs should probably be given the highest priority."[3] A checklist of design considerations takes a very traditional, collection-centered approach but allows for users' needs, especially those addressed by the Americans with Disabilities Act.[4] Yet the checklist does not display a concern for creating a design built around users' behaviors and their information-seeking and information-handling needs. Finally, the standard guide to academic library facility planning opens with a list of the purposes any academic library building serves. It places "accommodation of readers and other clientele who need immediate or frequent access to collections and services" fourth in a list of ten, behind three purposes related to the collection and bibliographic access to its contents.[5]

The Need for User-Centered Design

One need meditate only momentarily on Ranganathan's mystical and eternal Five Laws of Library Science ("Books are for use. Every reader his book. Every book its reader. Save the time of the reader. A library is a growing organism.")[6] to understand that effective building design needs to be more user-centered than collection-driven. This will be especially true in the future. In the past the collection's imperatives for space, combined with the available limited and largely linear access paths to the contents of that collection, dictated a collection-driven design in which service considerations played a secondary role. Today, however, information technology necessitates a new approach. The long-standing linear model of library research, often promoted in basic bibliographic instruction classes, has been shattered by the varied possibilities offered by established and emerging technologies. Always an oversimplification of the research process, the model whereby students were advised to begin by reading an encyclopedia article on their topic, then progress to relevant periodical indexes to identify articles and to appropriate Library of Congress subject headings to identify books nevertheless gave those students a life raft they could cling to in the ocean of information available to them in a university library. Only when they sought information on a topic that straddled disciplines or that was too recent to be included in printed information sources (other than not-yet-or-never-indexed newspapers) were they cast adrift from this comforting but ill-fitting, one-size-fits-all, linear search strategy.

In an era of OPACs, remote access to OPACs (even from remote corners of the world), online access to periodical indexes via the Internet, CD-ROM databases, and the ability to hopscotch freely among information sources linked together through the World Wide Web, some question the need for library buildings and collections in the future. Starry-eyed futurists such as Negroponte imply that all a researcher will need in the future will be a computer, a telecommunications line, and an account that provides access to the Internet.[7] False prophets such as Negroponte will never see their visions realized. Indeed, the apparent irony is that, even though more varied means of access to information call for a more user-centered approach to library facility design, use of libraries' collections of books and printed journals is increasing as a result of the ease and speed with which people can identify materials. Crawford and Gorman have cogently argued the case of enduring roles for print in the 1990s and beyond.[8] Yet they are not reactionaries and they, more so than the much higher-profile Stoll (whose arguments regarding the limitations of digital information are streaked with sentimentality),[9] see and welcome a role for all varieties of electronic media.

The first challenge that increased access to bibliographic information poses to users of this information is to judge the value and relevance of the item represented by its surrogate record. This is not a new challenge; any patron examining a card catalog record faced the same challenge. The challenge has been magnified, though, by the ease with which library users can obtain access to great numbers of such records. Furthermore, users can access these records from innumerable sites outside the library facility. Increasingly, librarians must come to consider nearly all users of bibliographic systems as remote users; whether a user accesses a library catalog from the building next to the library or from another continent, each user has only the bibliographic record—and, in the case of some commercially produced databases, an abstract—by which to judge the value of the item represented. This is an issue that needs to be addressed in the next revision of the Anglo-American Cataloging Rules; the description of items must be much fuller and must focus less on the physical artifact and instead must focus more on its intellectual content. This will allow potential users, whether next door or a continent away, to make better-informed judgments about whether to retrieve the item described (or about whether to have it delivered to them).

In an era during which the scale of the challenges facing librarians and library users was less monumental and less complex than today, Melvil Dewey wrote that

> It is a great undertaking to so arrange and administer a collection of 100,000 volumes that to any man it will be possible, within a few moments, to give from that collection not only the book or pamphlet, but the article hidden away in some volume of transactions, or in some periodical, which to him, then and there, is the thing he most needs.[10]

It is a greater undertaking today in larger open-stacks collections and greater still in a world in which remote sources available though licensing agreements or free for the taking on the World Wide Web proliferate more rapidly than rabbits. Finding tools and behavioral patterns in library use are more varied and more complex today.

DESIGN IMPLICATIONS OF BEHAVIORAL CHANGES

In today's world, the ways in which students and faculty seek and gather information are changing. Library facilities need to be redesigned (or, in those rare cases, designed from scratch) to accommodate these changes in behavior. The facility will continue to be important since the collection of printed and other locally owned materials will continue to be important. (Gorman and Crawford successfully disabuse dreamers of the notion that all of that print, audio, and video material now in library collections will eventually be digitized and thereby will free users of any need to use a central facility to consult these materials in their original formats.)[11] The facility will become more of a workshop and less of a warehouse. Using scanners, optical character recognition transcribing technologies, and digital audio and video input, students and faculty will be able to draw on a variety of media (including those hundreds of thousands of printed volumes—old, new, and yet-to-be-published—in every university library) and integrate information from these media into a new whole. Just as hypertext documents allow a user to approach a text's contents from many directions, library users will take a "hyperuse" approach to the library's collection and remote resources, eclectically using print, sound, video, and still images and integrating these into new presentations. In their selection of materials for use, the medium will matter less than the content.

Type-of-use patterns evident now will likely persist. For example, undergraduates will continue to engage in a process of analysis, synthesis, and presentation of existing knowledge. Graduate students (to a certain extent) and faculty (to a much greater extent) will engage in this same process but also transcend it; they will follow hyperlinks among information sources and the surrogate records that describe them. They will use these intellectual jumps as stimuli for developing new theories and for seeking evidence that supports or refutes those theories. Because the investment in the equipment necessary to do all of this is likely to cost too much for a university to equip every faculty office, and because many (and probably most) of the materials drawn on and sampled during the scholarly process will reside, for the convenience of all members of the user community, in the library, the library as place will persist in importance.

The implications, especially for building design, of users' behaviors when drawing upon all of these forms of information and integrating them are not at all clear. Only recently have some of the old verities of library design fallen in the face of technological change. Whereas once the catalog department and the card catalog that its staff nurtured and maintained in an intense symbiotic relationship necessitated their close proximity, online catalogs have since freed catalogers and database maintenance workers from that need even as the relationship has continued. An emphasis on collections and security for their contents has made circulation desks the most prominent feature users see when entering most academic libraries.

THE NEED TO REEXAMINE OLD
DESIGN ASSUMPTIONS

In a library of 100,000 volumes in which successful retrieval of the one item needed at a particular time was the measure of success, the proximity of the card catalog and the circulation counter to the entrance surely made sense. Access to materials, both bibliographic and physical, were primary concerns. In an era when options for access to information—both that held locally and that available electronically from other sites—abound, however, neither the catalog of local holdings nor the service point at which users can borrow locally owned materials need the same prominence. The time-honored assumptions, perhaps no longer valid, that gave these service points preeminence need to be questioned. Perhaps the future can be gleaned from the experiments at Brandeis, Johns Hopkins, and other universities, whereby all-purpose reference desks have been transformed into filtering points supplemented by referral to or appointments with reference librarians who work in an in-depth, extended, consultative mode with individual patrons.[12] These experiments focus on helping each user find the best path to the information needed for a particular purpose.

As information access tools proliferate and change rapidly over time, space allocations and patterns once appropriate in an era during which the card catalog and printed periodical indexes remained stable for decades and provided the primary bibliographic access to local collections (an era during which access to remote resources was at best awkward and limited), now fall short of serving library users' changing needs and behavior. Some users will be familiar with multiple access tools and will know when to use one rather than another. Many users will need counsel about how best to approach the combined (and ever-evolving) universe of local and remote resources available to them in a particular situation. It may be, therefore, that the most prominent feature users see once they enter a university library's doors is a customer service center at which they can receive guidance, help in selecting among access options, or referral to specialists.

As media and access tools change, user behavior changes. For example, the advent of end-user searching of CD-ROM periodical indexes has resulted in a dramatic reduction in the number of mediated online searches and the almost absolute abandonment by library users of printed periodical indexes. As user behavior changes, design principles and concepts for library facilities need to change so that facilities are designed to serve users' needs. Two tools, one old, the other not yet fully refined, offer opportunities to improve library design and make it more responsive to user needs and working preferences.

ADDITIONAL DESIGN TOOLS

The old tool is market research. Librarians and library architects need to know more about how library users actually seek, select, and use information sources. University librarians have been using various sorts of user surveys for years; only recently have they gone a step further and enlisted the services of professional market research firms to refine their investigations of user behavior and preferences.[13] Before redesigning a library facility or designing a new one, they would do well to use these tools. They should even take the market research process a step further. The Intuit company, producer of the Quicken personal finance software and popular tax preparation software, sends company employees into the homes and offices of users of their software products to watch how users interact with the programs' features and options. This allows them to refine their products to serve users better. Microsoft has used similar practices in debugging and improving its products before releasing them in the marketplace. OPACs and CD-ROMs have allowed librarians to peer over users' shoulders and see how they use these systems, but librarians (as well as, to their shame, the producers of these systems) have yet to use in a systematic way the information thus gathered about user behavior and interaction with these systems. The refined, methodical practices of the Usability Lab at OCLC, the lab in which OCLC tests how representative users interact with new OCLC online products, may serve as a model for such market research.

The other, newer tool is virtual reality computer-assisted design. It is becoming possible for architects to simulate three-dimensional space and structures. By using this tool, not only with librarians engaged in some phase of a building planning project, but also with a variety of users of that library, costly mistakes can probably be avoided and likely hazards to the research process can be identified and eliminated before they are built.

O Flexibility, Flexibility! Wherefore Art Thou Flexibility?

Even after thoroughly tapping into these additional tools, library design still faces one monumental challenge. Flexibility is the Holy Grail of library design, especially in a building intended to accommodate a campus's library needs for 25 years, the period the standard guide to academic library building planning recommends as a target.[14] It is almost certain that no library has both achieved this much-desired flexibility initially and retained it for 25 years. Book stacks encroach on study areas to accommodate growing collections; unsightly network cabling snakes across walls to provide needed telecommunications connections; service and other public areas are pressed into use as staff work areas; partitions snatch away grand ceremonial spaces for offices; holes are bored into service desks to accommodate power supplies for new technologies; additional electrical outlets and their connecting conduits run across floors and along baseboards to accommodate OPAC and CD-ROM stations; study rooms are converted into microcomputer labs; and on and on and on as building after building, each designed to be flexible, undergoes makeshift revision after makeshift revision to meet the demands of new modes of library use.

A desire for flexibility underlies every library program statement; some, such as the one written before construction of the Regenstein Library at the University of Chicago, explicitly state this value's importance. Indeed, the University of Chicago's program addressed it with judicious realism in a section headed "Flexibility."

It is not contradictory to assert that the success of a large, research library building will be critically related to an accurate analysis of functions and a skillful translation of these into efficiently planned and related space and equipment, while at the same time one asserts, with equal conviction, that changes in library functions and requirements are absolutely inevitable, and the library must be able to adapt to them over a long period of time. The new library building reflects the dual nature of this problem; that is, it must be well planned to perform its tasks as these are now understood, and it must have very great capability for easy and economical change in space use and relationships in the future. The building must achieve these objectives at reasonable cost.

"Total" flexibility is in some ways a chimera and, in a building of this size, such complete flexibility in the use of space may be prohibitive in cost and, in terms of probable functions, not absolutely essential. Nevertheless, a substantial degree of flexibility is a firm requirement, and can, I believe, be provided at reasonable costs.[15]

Librarians have been heavily involved in library building design issues for a century and more. Why, then, have they not been able to achieve long-term flexibility in building design? A partial explanation is, of course, the compromises mentioned earlier: compromises with architects' ideas, donors' demands, or senior administrators' visions. But a deeper explanation lies in the traditional practices and procedures whereby major building projects are planned. Brand would say that part of the problem lies in too much concern for "its tasks as these are now understood" and a single, linear vision of how those tasks will change in the future.

LIMITATIONS OF PROGRAMMING AS A PLANNING TOOL

In his proposal for a new way of looking at buildings and for a new discipline that would focus on the study of buildings and the way they adapt to and interact with human needs over time, Brand states a self-evident truism, one so obvious it is easily overlooked unless stated explicitly:

All buildings are predictions. All predictions are wrong.[16]

Little wonder, then, that every library building fails the long-term flexibility test. Brand finds fault with the planning process as it has become refined and institutionalized. The foundation of the planning process—programming—fails to provide sufficient flexibility for an unpredictable future.

It's not that future considerations are left out of programming. Often they dominate the process. But it is narrow, wishful futures that are considered. "We'll wire the whole building with fiberoptic cable so we'll be ahead of the game when broadband technology comes on line." (Then office technology veers toward wireless instead.) "We only have funds for the core building now, but we'll leave the north wall windowless and made out of Dryvit instead of brick so it will be easy to add the north wing later." (The wing is never built, and the peeling, windowless wall depresses generations of occupants and passersby.)[17]

Definitions of programming available in guides written for librarians validate Brand's criticism of the process's limitations. One says that

> A program is the client's statement of design requirements, and the designer's instrument for meeting those requirements. In the process of examining functional requirements and space relationships, the program is used by the client in deciding the feasibility of the project, determining if facility needs have been adequately addressed, and for making project and budget authorization decisions. The program is used by the designer as a guide to the design criteria which must be fulfilled, as a source of data for preparing design solutions, and as a reference for making and evaluating design decisions.[18]

Another more simply states, "A building program statement is 'a practical description of the library's functional needs, based on projected use and service goals.'"[19] And finally, the program "should provide, if not the exact size of each area, an indication of the required size in terms of readers, staff, and collections to be housed and the desired spatial relationships among the different areas."[20]

SCENARIO PLANNING

As an alternative to programming, Brand recommends "scenario planning."

> Like programming, scenario planning is a future-oriented process of analysis and decision. Unlike programming, it reaches into the deeper future—typically five to twenty years—and instead of converging on a single path, its whole essence is divergence.[21]

In proposing use of this approach, Brand explains that

> scenario planning has been evolving quietly for thirty years, first in a military context, later by corporations forced to think ten years ahead by a business environment which had become so turbulent that traditional forecasting was useless. The product of skilled scenario work is not a plan but a strategy. Where a plan is based on prediction, a strategy is designed to encompass unforeseeably changing conditions. A good strategy ensures that, no matter what happens, you always have maneuvering room.[22]

This flexibility is the strength and advantage of the scenario planning process. Brand also explains, in sufficient detail so that others can apply it, how it works:

> Whoever is going to lead the scenario exercise begins by interviewing the major players in the organization or the project at hand, to pick up their vocabulary, the major issues ("What keeps you up at night?"), and the consensus expectations about the future. Then the policy-making people and a few of their advisors are gathered for a two-day session. The first day begins with identifying the focal issue or impending decision that makes the scenario exercise necessary. Then the group explores the "driving forces" that will shape the future environment. In business, driving forces often include changes in technology, regulation, the competition, and the customers. For a building, driving forces might include changes in technology,

in the neighborhood, in the economy, and in tenant use. The group ranks these driving forces in terms of importance and uncertainty, placing the most important and most uncertain highest, because it is the important uncertainties that will drive the scenarios apart. At the same time the group should be identifying "predetermined elements"—reliable certainties such as the aging of baby boomers—which will be in all the scenarios.

Now, working with the crucial uncertainties, the group identifies scenario logics: basic plot lines. The goal is to develop scenarios that are both plausible and surprising— shocking, in fact. One artful way to do that is to identify and spell out the "official future"—the future everyone thinks he or she is supposed to expect. Make it one scenario. Then start thinking the unthinkable. Let people top each other in imagining terrible and delightful things that might happen, exacerbated by the crucial uncertainties. Typically these scenarios soon acquire a frightening plausibility that makes a mockery of the "official future."

Sleep on that. Next day the group revisits the preliminary scenarios, adjusts them (often radically), and then begins to flesh them out into detailed, vivid stories. There should be two to five scenarios, no more. The probability of one or another happening is not useful to explore, except for including one or more "wild-card" scenarios considered quite unlikely but horrifying if they were to occur.

Now the group goes back to the focusing issue or decision to devise a strategy that will accommodate all the scenarios. The thing to avoid is a "bet-the-company" strategy that wins in only one scenario and loses in all the others.

As the new strategy emerges, it changes how the scenarios would play out, so the group needs to cycle through the process a few times to get a set of scenarios and a strategy that make sense with each other. The final task is to identify some leading indicators that will be monitored to see which scenario (if any) is actually occurring in life.[23]

Brand suggests that two suitable times to use this process are at the beginning of building planning when a vision for the project is emerging and/or after some preliminary programming has been done and can be tested against scenarios for the future.

Scenario planning has the potential to be a powerful tool, if not for achieving the long-sought-after goal of long-term flexibility in library building design, at least for bringing librarians and architects closer to fulfilling their ambitious fantasy of flexibility. Any increased success will benefit their institutions. Thus far scenario planning possesses untested potential for library buildings, a potential that library and architectural associations and individual librarians and architects engaged in planning new or renovated academic library facilities should put to the test as rigorously as possible. To optimize its value, however, it should be combined with such other tools as market research, user behavior studies, computer-assisted design, virtual reality, and the well-developed tradition of building programming. When the stakes are as high as they are in an eight-figure building project budget, every promising and proven planning tool and strategy ought to be employed and synchronized to enhance opportunities for success.

Scenario planning is not unknown to the library world. Most scenarios developed for libraries, however, have focused primarily, like traditional library planning, on information materials and media and only secondarily on how users will seek, identify, and use information sources and the libraries that facilitate their access to those sources. These scenarios play an indispensable role in library building planning; however, they do not address a broad enough range of questions and possibilities to optimize, let alone assure, long-range flexibility and adaptability of the resultant building.

ONE LIBRARY SCENARIO

Were one to bring together a group of library planners to apply Brand's method for scenario planning, the group would probably identify the following (or at least many of the following, perhaps with some variations in particulars) consensus expectations about the future of information media.

Increasingly, information—text, sound, still images, and video—will be available in digitized form. This information will be available to users through computer networks. This mode of access will be available around the clock and from any place in the world at which a user has appropriate equipment, software, and telecommunications capabilities—and authorization.

There will be a cost for access to most information available in this way. Depending on an array of circumstances (such as the user's affiliation with an institution, contractual arrangements, licensing agreements, ability to pay) either an institution with which the user is affiliated will foot the bill or the individual will have to pay for access to and use of the information. Various complex factors (based on such criteria as user status, amount of information retrieved, and value placed on the information by its producer or vendor) will determine its cost.

Digitized information will be made available by a variety of competing providers, some in the private for-profit sector and others (for example, universities, scholarly societies, and professional associations) in the not-for-profit sector. Because information will be provided by a variety of organizations, the command languages, protocols, and online interfaces through which users interact with this information will lack standardization. This lack of standardization will sometimes challenge users' patience.

Additional consensus expectations are also likely. Printed collections will remain important for their retrospective and historical information since demand for most of this information will not be great enough to justify the cost of digitizing it. Publishers will continue to produce printed material, but information in this format will increasingly be limited to popular and ephemeral matters. Because of their economy as an information storage medium, scholarly books will continue to be published in print, but they will gradually fade in significance in the sciences and social sciences. Printed books will be most significant in the humanities.

Librarians will play a more visible and more vigorous role in organizing information in electronic form and they will provide a wide array of interpretive, guidance, and instructional services to users of such information. They will serve as consultants to and collaborators with systems developers as they create new information systems and refine existing systems. Librarians will also customize local access to electronic information to fit the needs of that community's members.

The "driving force" that will shape the future's environment will be technological change that results in changes in the way in which information is distributed and obtained. The cost of obtaining information will rise and may become iterative, whereby an individual or an institution pays for the same piece of information each time it is obtained or used. Shrinking subscriber bases and markets for printed publications will result in fewer materials published in this form; as these bases and markets shrink, the unit cost of these publications will rise. The interacting phenomena of shrinking markets and rising costs will feed each other.

Advances in technology will change jobs throughout society and necessitate updating knowledge and skills. This need will increase demand for continuing education courses (both credit courses and short, targeted skills courses) among students well beyond the traditional college student age.

The decline of print as an information medium ranks high on the uncertainty scale; technological change ranks equally high in importance. Demographic projections for enrollment, faculty size, average age of students, and percentage of revenue derived from tuition ought to be considered "predetermined elements." These will, of course, be highly institution-specific and will, consequently, differ a good deal among institutions.

The "official" scenario, based on the crucial uncertainties, is that libraries will continue to engage in a mix of print and electronic media but that the balance will shift more and more each year in favor of electronic information. Another possible (although perhaps not shocking) scenario based on the crucial uncertainties is that information technology will become both so ubiquitous and so user-friendly that it will eliminate the need for information seekers to visit the library to obtain any of this information on demand. Yet another possible scenario is that digital information will fully supplant print in libraries as a medium for new information and that the only role printed information will play will be retrospective. As a result, library buildings will not need to increase in size although their allocations of space and the functions carried out in various spaces may need to change. In yet another scenario there may be widespread disenchantment with the high costs of digital information and the difficulty in identifying the existence of relevant information in digital form, leading to a strong resurgence in the use of printed information sources and the dependable (if imperfect) methods of identifying them through library catalogs and other familiar tools. In this scenario, the need for additional book stacks will continue to accelerate; demand for reprographic equipment will rise; and users will continue to come to the library to use materials on site.

The above is but one librarian's rudimentary illustration of how scenario planning can be applied to building design. This sample application focuses on information media, however, not on the ways in which users make use of information sources and their contents. A similar (and more extensive) process must be applied to the ways in which users will interact with information. The driving forces may be the same as those that will shape information media, but the scenarios that flow from analyzing these forces may differ considerably. Will students and faculty use library resources as individuals or as members of collaborative teams? Will there be differences in behavior and habits among disciplines? How much use will take place in the library facility and how much will come from outside the facility? Answers to these questions have implications for design. For example, the answer to the last question will have implications for the number of workstations, the amount and distribution of electrical outlets, the type of equipment, and the amount of study space that will be needed. It will also have implications for the number of telefacsimile devices and the size of the shipping and receiving area needed to support an on-campus document delivery service as well as interlibrary resource-sharing programs. The much broader question of just how library users will interact with the library's local and remote resources and the facility itself deserves a collective effort throughout academic librarianship to use scenario planning and other tools to tease out plausible answers. The scenarios that emerge, when tested and applied at the local level, will help shape a library facility that minimizes, and perhaps even eliminates, hazards to its user community's research processes.

BUILDING PLANNING AS
COMPREHENSIVE REVIEW

Building planning provides a library staff with opportunities to look at more than building needs. Because building program writing often results in plans that calcify organizational structures in brick, mortar, Sheetrock-clad walls, mill-worked counters, and reinforced concrete, it behooves a library's administration to conduct a review of the library's strategic plan and its organizational structure in conjunction with the building planning processes. As the library staff and others involved in planning examine the scenarios outlining the ways library users will interact with information in the future, they should ask questions about what sort of organizational structure and personnel allocations, as well as what sort of physical structure, will optimize users' success in those interactions.

Building planning also provides a good opportunity to review the strategic plan to judge whether the plan's goals and strategies are realistic in the worlds spun by the scenarios. Modification of these goals and strategies may also have implications for the organizational structure. And, of course, all of these plans must take local issues into account, such as foreseeable or predictable changes in academic policies, program offerings, teaching methods, and curricular emphases that could affect the library's role and the needs and behavior of its users. Like any issue academic library administrators face today, building planning and the concentric rings of planning issues that surround it are not for the faint of heart.

Because the ways in which the members of a university community seek, identify, and use information sources change with increasing rapidity and because the traditional processes for planning academic library buildings have proved inadequate for incorporating long-term flexibility, the premises and processes of building planning need to be rethought. Perhaps the combination of market research, computer-aided design techniques, virtual reality, and scenario planning is not the answer or falls short of being a complete answer. But the traditional approach has not provided a good enough answer, so new approaches must be explored. Those new approaches must include scenarios not just about how information media and their distribution may change, but also about how user behavior and preferences may change.

ENDNOTES

1. *Remains of the Day*, prod. Mike Nichols and John Calley (a Merchant Ivory production), dir. James Ivory, 134 min., Columbia Tristar Home Video, 1994, videocassette.

2. Stewart Brand, *How Buildings Learn: What Happens After They're Built* (New York: Viking, 1994), 5.

3. William W. Sannwald, "Functional Requirements and Space Relationships," in *Libraries for the Future: Planning Buildings that Work*, ed. Ron G. Martin (Chicago: American Library Association, 1992), 60.

4. William W. Sannwald and Robert S. Smith, *Checklist of Library Building Design Considerations* (Chicago: Library Administration and Management Association, 1988).

5. Keyes D. Metcalf, *Planning Academic and Research Library Buildings*, 2nd ed. By Philip D. Leighton and David C. Weber (Chicago: American Library Association, 1986), 1–2.

6. S. R. Ranganathan, *The Five Laws of Library Science*, 2nd ed. (Bombay: Asia Publishing House, 1963).

7. Nicholas Negroponte, *Being Digital* (New York: Alfred A. Knopf, 1995).

8. Walt Crawford and Michael Gorman, *Future Libraries: Dreams, Madness, and Reality* (Chicago: American Library Association, 1995), 13–35.

9. Clifford Stoll, *Silicon Snake Oil: Second Thoughts on the Information Highway* (New York: Doubleday, 1995).

10. Melvil Dewey, "The Relation of the Colleges to the Modern Library Movement" in *User Instruction in Academic Libraries: A Century of Selected Readings*, ed. Larry Hardesty, John P. Schmidt, and John Mark Tucker (Metuchen, N.J.: Scarecrow Press, 1986), 51. First published in Proceedings of the Second Annual Convention of the College Association of the Middle States and Maryland, 78–83. (Philadelphia: Globe Printing, 1891).

11. Crawford and Gorman, *Future Libraries*, 86–103.

12. Virginia Massey-Burzio, "Reference Encounters of a Different Kind: A Symposium," *Journal of Academic Librarianship* 18 (November 1992): 276–286.

13. Kenneth W. Berger and Richard W. Hines, "What Does the User Really Want? The Library User Survey Project at Duke University," *Journal of Academic Librarianship* 20 (November 1994): 306–309.

14. Metcalf, *Planning Academic and Research Library Buildings*, 11.

15. Ibid., 533.

16. Brand, *How Buildings Learn*, 178.

17. Ibid., 181.

18. Sannwald, "Functional Requirements and Space Relationships," 60.

19. Anders Dahlgren, "Outline of the Building Planning Process," in *Libraries for the Future: Planning Buildings that Work* ed. Ron G. Martin (Chicago: American Library Association, 1992), 16.

20. Metcalf, *Planning Academic and Research Library Buildings*, 75.

21. Brand, *How Buildings Learn*, 181.

22. Ibid., 178.

23. Ibid., 182–183.

5

Human Resource Management for the New Personnel

An Interview with Hazel Stamps

Just as library buildings are undergoing transformations, so, too, are library staffing needs being redefined. This area embraces some of the most delicate and complex issues facing academic libraries: what kind of work will be done in academic libraries in the future, what qualities are needed in library staff, and how can such staff be identified, created, or retooled? It takes intelligent planning, time, money, and concerted effort to prepare a staff rooted in the traditions and practices of the past for the systems and practices they will encounter in an increasingly complex research environment. In this interview Hazel Stamps outlines a number of concerns important to both administrators and front-line librarians and gives a practitioner's perspective on what it will mean to manage library human resources effectively in future.—CML

The Harvard College Library consists of 11 separate libraries serving the Faculty of Arts and Sciences at Harvard. The College Library employs a permanent staff of approximately 500 individuals in the various libraries; about two-thirds of these are clerical and administrative support staff and the remaining one-third are professional staff, librarians, and other officers of the university. The part-time workforce consists of students who routinely work from 15 to 20 hours a week as well as "casuals," a term used to describe nonstudent, part-time workers in nonbenefited positions. There are approximately 900 student and casual workers in the College Library in addition to the 500 permanent staff. This interview was conducted by the editor in 1996.

CL: Could you talk about your own work history and what it is you do?

HS: I celebrated my 34th anniversary at Harvard this year. More than ten of those years have been in Personnel. I began in a library assistant position, as a staff assistant. Then after I spent more than 15 years working my way up in various administrative positions, I was made Personnel Officer. I remember going home and saying to my mom, "I've just been promoted; I'm a Personnel Officer!"

    She said, "That's fine honey, but what do you do?"
    I said, "I'm the Personnel Officer."
    She said, "Yeah, I know, but what does that mean?"
    And that's your question: what is it that you actually do? First, I should say we're in the process of changing the name of this office from Personnel to the Human Resources Office.

CL: Is this a significant change, or just a semantical one?

HS: Oh, it's a significant change in that it recognizes the larger scope of what we do in this office in the 1990s. Personnel never really described fully what we do in terms of the organization and its future direction: defining jobs, recruiting, staffing, training, developing resource potential . . . I think it's safe to say that this is a trend in libraries, developing and managing human resources rather than simply recruiting and administering personnel.

CL: Could you describe the differences between "Personnel" functions and "Human Resources" functions in more detail? I'm not sure I see the distinctions.

HS: Some of it's perception: people have seen Personnel more as the paper-processing administrative function. The recruiting and hiring and the paper processing to get someone on staff . . . for many years Personnel functions were viewed as these mechanistic functions alone. This is where you go to get a piece of paper, that is where you go to process a piece of paper. And our office will indeed continue to carry out these administrative functions. But we are much more than that, and changing the department's name is a step towards demonstrating that within the organization. Human Resources is concerned with all aspects of our staff's life.

CL: For instance . . . ?

HS: Take recruiting. Our personnel office has been actively involved in the recruitment and selection of staff for the library for a long time. But contrary to some perceptions, we are not the last link in the recruiting chain. Supervisors don't just come to us and say, "Well, I've hired someone. Can you put them on the payroll?"

        We're involved in the recruiting process early on: we help design and develop positions before they're posted. We're in partnership with the managers within the organization to help determine just what the future of the organization is going to be, to help form the face of the organization.

CL: And for the—for want of a better term—paper-pushing aspects of human resource management, you're responsible for all that.

HS: That's right. We have a centralized human resource operation within the College Library. All departments regularly hire students and casuals to work in their areas. Their hire isn't complete and official until the paperwork has passed through and been signed off in Human Resources.

CL: The numbers you deal with—500 permanent staff and 900 student and casual workers—are enormous. Can we talk, for a bit, about downsizing? Obviously, it's been a trend in many libraries over the past five years or so, and from the looks of things in academe it promises to continue. Do you see that happening here?

HS: Academic institutions and libraries within those institutions are not immune to the issues affecting corporate America. We have already had to decrease our numbers, although thus far we have been able to do it through attrition. For a number of reasons, not least of which is the significant position the College Library and libraries in general hold in the University, we have not had to downsize according to the more generally accepted interpretations of the term, with large-scale reductions. We scrutinize every position that comes open now very carefully, making case-by-case decisions on whether or not a position needs to be refilled and, if so, at what level, and we have done some shifting of positions from some staff areas into others.

CL: Where do you see the trend for staffing heading in libraries? Is there a staffing revolution in progress?

HS: Well, yes. We have made concerted efforts to increase the number of positions and resources in the public services area. Traditionally in libraries the technical services areas have been the most heavily staffed, and that trend is changing. Certainly it is here at Harvard.

Technology, for the most part, has made it possible to process, catalog, and file more materials with decreased numbers of staff. There has been a corresponding increase, however, in the need to service collections and explain and teach access through the technology; thus the increases in public services staff, especially public services staff who can access and translate electronic resources for our patrons. This transition has not come about without some pain and some impact on those staff remaining in technical services.

It's been an interesting time for all of us, trying to find ways to do new and different things with the staff that we have. We are not growing, yet the tasks we have to carry out are. Trying to maintain high levels of activity while at the same time reducing staffing creates some pressure within the organization.

CL: Can you give us an example of how your office has "retooled" staff?

HS: I can give you a recent example that I think typifies the kind of "retooling" we may be doing for the foreseeable future. It's related to what I just described as the movement from technical services into public services arena, and the evolution of public services into positions providing increasing support for electronic resources.

We had someone in one library in technical services who had highly developed skills in working with electronic reference sources. This individual also had a strong interest in public services, and was curious to try their hand at public service, so we worked out an arrangement in which they contributed five to ten hours a week in reference. They've been very good at it, there are no problems, and they're very interested in pursuing their knowledge of electronic resources. Of course they made themselves a little more accessible in order to make the transition from tech services to public services.

This individual completed an MLS degree during this process, and, with excellent in-house experience combined with work in electronic resources, this person was an ideal, and indeed, the successful, candidate for a newly created position in that library.

That's an example of how you may identify an individual and develop their skills and interest for the mutual benefit of the individual and the organization. It could have backfired on us because of the risk that comes into play when an individual's personal interest develops and grows to such an extent that the organization may or may not be able to accommodate it. In this case it ended up an ideal match. There are two potential downsides to this: one, that of the individual's interest driving the hiring process rather than the organization's need; two, that of the individual not being able to be accommodated by the organization and needing to move on to satisfy their personal interests.

We cannot be all things to all people always. The development of the individual and the development of the organization are both processes that must be carefully managed. Development is not something that just happens. Fortunately in this case it was a perfect match of interests and needs on both sides. It doesn't always work out that way, but I strongly believe you still need to encourage the individual to develop their skills for their best interests. Even if they eventually have to move out of the organization to pursue their goals, fostering an atmosphere of collaborative development is much to be preferred over stunting people in their professional growth. No one wins in that scenario.

CL: What happens when a staff member outgrows a position and there is not an appropriate place to move to within the organization?

HS: That involves managing the other side of staff's career development. You asked earlier about downsizing. Well, Harvard University and the Harvard Library have been very stable areas of employment for many years. At one time, you were hired, you did a wonderful job, you advanced in your career and you retired 40 years later. That's no longer the case. As in corporate America, as in everywhere else you can name, the idea of having one job in one organization for life is no longer realistic. We need to begin focusing more attention on the career development of our staff and helping them prepare to transition elsewhere.

Actually, Harvard may be credited with having fostered the trend of preparation, development, and growth. When I think back to when I first came to the Personnel office and began to become acquainted with some of the names of librarians both here and nation-wide, it wasn't long before I realized that Harvard had been a training ground for many librarians who had been successful in their careers here and then had moved on and up. I don't know if this happens insti-tutionally elsewhere, but a number of librarians came here relatively early in their careers, developed their skills, grew, and moved on. A number of them went on to become directors of major research libraries.

Harvard has provided a training ground for many, given them the preparation to segue elsewhere, and then, in many cases, has attracted them back to Harvard. But there have also been large numbers of people who have remained at Harvard from beginning to end, and have grown in their careers here. This pat-tern will probably not continue into the new millen-nium, as the major research libraries continue to raid one another for the best and the brightest.

CL: Can you talk some more about that?

HS: The personnel raiding? You have a position that you're seeking to fill and early on in the conversation, as soon as you have a good idea of what the position consists of, the conversation turns to who everybody knows elsewhere and can we get them to come here.

CL: Among the research libraries, at least among the people in your area, is there a cooperative friendliness where people acknowledge that yes, somebody does need to move on, that your opportunity offers their person something they can't, so the human relations officers will then help the "raiding" process rather than hinder it? Or do people tend to try to hang on to that cadre of good people and have it become a kind of struggle?

HS: There is competition, absolutely. I am aware of any number of academic institutions that have similar po-sitions open and there is pretty much an identical can-didate pool. We're all trying to attract that one obvi-ous person for the job—the cream that has risen to the top. We all want that first person, we all want the best and brightest for our institutions. There's a lot of competition amongst us.

CL: There are a number of ways that you can compete for people, of course. Salary is only one part of the package that you can use to attract somebody. What are some of the hiring incentives being used at Harvard, and what are the kinds of attractions that people are looking for nationwide?

HS: You're absolutely right: salary is only one piece of the total benefits picture, and it's not always the deciding factor for someone accepting a job. Harvard's benefit structure, its total compensation package, is unrivaled, I have to say. We may not offer our benefits exactly the same way as other institutions—there's always a debate and discussion about faculty status versus nonfaculty status, about TIAA and our retirement package and how Harvard's retirement package compares to others. That certainly doesn't seem to have affected negatively our ability to recruit.

We're very much aware that we have a lot to offer librarians in terms of opportunity and resource. We make use of that in raiding. But more and more we're finding that candidates are interested in making spousal and partner arrangements part of their decision-making process. There is a definite trend in individuals asking about what resources the university may have for significant others. They're willing to uproot and relocate, but a spouse or partner needs to consider their career. Are there resources available at the university—is there a job?

CL: I know that there was a period of time when universities used to cut deals to get a good candidate. They would go out and find a job for someone's spouse or partner. Do you see that continuing, or is it, given economic and downsizing issues, going to become a thing of the past?

HS: In the academic community it continues as an accepted way of life. In terms of faculty recruitment, there are any number of instances when a faculty member has been recruited and Harvard will accommodate them by finding a position for a spouse. But everyone's looking for ways in which they can provide that extra inducement without setting precedents so that it becomes a standard part of your recruitment package.

I have had a number of candidates discuss with me opportunities for their spouses. Our position is that we will provide as much assistance as we can in terms of opening doors, making introductions, helping someone become aware of what the possibilities are, of vacant positions. The Boston metropolitan area has a large number of universities and libraries. We will help, but we make no promises.

CL: I want to shift gears now because we've been talking about the specifics of one institution, and I'd like to get the benefit of your personnel experience applied to broader issues. Let's talk about the ideal candidate for the year 2000.

Can you give a list of words describing the qualities that come to mind as ideal for a librarian coming in—the things that make you say, "We *want* this person!" What are the blue flags in a resume that say "this is great," and what are the red flags that say "trouble" or "no thank you!"

HS: After reviewing the education, background, experience, et cetera, the first thing I look for is evidence of flexibility. Flexibility is the main blue flag that pops into my head. I also look for evidence of service to the academic institution, service to the library community, service to the profession. We're looking for people who show signs of being able to make themselves valuable to the institution. When I review a resume, I ask myself how this candidate will bring added value to the organization.

As far as red flags go, I look askance at an application that assumes I'll know what they mean without them telling me. I pick up on gaps in employment, changes in jobs that don't appear to be progressive in terms of advancement for the person. Has someone jumped around a lot or do they appear stable? If they have moved around, have the jobs been progressively responsible or not?

I also look to see if the individual is doing the job on the home front: how are they spending their time? You look at a résumé and see a long list of accomplishments, committee work, elected positions in associations, research, et cetera, and it makes me wonder if they're doing the job at home. You want a nice balance, where the person is actively involved with the job in the library as well as in the wider profession.

CL: Is there anything specific that puts you off about a résumé?

HS: One thing I don't find attractive at all is the "accomplishments" type résumé. A résumé that's constructed around areas of accomplishment, listing management skills without any indication of where those skills were acquired or where they were practiced, where there's no institution or association listed—that kind of résumé is meaningless to me. It's very difficult to analyze that and get any sense of what a candidate may or may not be able to do, what they are or are not familiar with. Sometimes with this type of résumé you have to go to the second or third page just to see that they're indicating previous employment and where they've worked. There's something that isn't quite forthcoming there. Frankly that's the type of résumé I put aside because that résumé's making me work more for the same information that another candidate gives me freely. The key is to make it easy for me, in reading the résumé, to get a sense of what the candidate's about. Making it a guessing game does not rate highly.

We've talked about our staff size: with that large a staff, we're almost always looking at applications, and if you are looking for two or three or four positions at a time, you can have several hundred people apply and you want something to leap out at you so that you can make your piles of yes, no, and maybes quickly but confidently.

CL: You've said that "flexibility" is a blue flag for you in terms of intangibles on a résumé. What does that translate into for you in terms of the work?

HS: I think that evidence of flexibility means to me that a person has the potential, background, ability, and experience successfully to become a member of an effective team.

CL: Do you have an agenda or a position on team building in Personnel?

HS: When I think of team players, I think of individuals who have the capacity to work across traditional boundaries and barriers and be able to do that successfully. It takes very strong interpersonal skills. If you see that an individual has put down on their résumé that they have had some formal training in contract negotiation, team building, whatever you want to call it, it gives you a little more of a clue that this person is attuned to the necessity of working well with others, and will probably be receptive to the idea of teamwork.

The nature of library work is certainly changing: no one works by themselves in a back room anymore. You have to be able to work successfully with your colleagues. So I'd be interested in a résumé that had some evidence of team-building qualities, and not only for a position that has explicit management and supervisory responsibilities.

CL: I recently had a conversation with a colleague at another institution about her annual evaluation. In it her supervisor talked about this individual's ability to be a team member and help build teams at work, and referred to this quality in terms of leadership abilities. My colleague said it sounded to her like they were talking about someone else. She found it unusual that her supervisor described her as a leader. My interpretation was that her leadership qualities came not from being in a position of control or authority, but from the highly effective role she played within the organization and within her work groups. My colleague is not a leader in any swaggering or heroic sense, but she gets things done—both on her own and assisting the rest of the group in completing their common tasks.

HS: Exactly. We don't always use the words "leader" and "leadership" as well as we could. Leadership is a quality. We're looking for people that demonstrate leadership by identifying and initiating projects and carrying them through. To me it isn't necessary that that person has the formal title that automatically says he or she's the leader of the project. I've been a member of committees in which the chair of the committee is not necessarily the real leader of that committee. Other members of the committee stepped up, and along with the chair in a collaborative effort led the project. So to me leadership is a quality; it's not inherent in a position.

CL: Let's go on to a related issue: mentoring. It seems to have become such a loaded term. When I talk about mentoring, some people throw up their arms and say, "Don't talk to me about mentoring, I can't stand any more of it!" Others say, "Oh, I wish we had it." What are your thoughts about it?

HS: The way to go with mentoring is for the institution to foster and encourage it, but not require or force it. As with all other interpersonal relationships, it's difficult to put two people together—the mentor and the "mentee"—without a real relationship already existing. The most successful professional relationships I've witnessed have been in cases where people gravitated towards each other. Something like: "What do you want to be when you grow up?" "I want to be like him, I want to be like her, this is my ideal."

When you talk about formal mentoring, as soon as you want to formalize something, that is when the individual begins to think of it as an intrusion, an invasion on their time, rather than it being a natural association—occasional lunches with the person, pulling someone aside as you leave a meeting and saying "You know that was a nice presentation." All those things are mentoring.

One of the first institutes I attended as a personnel officer was sponsored by ARL [Association of Research Libraries]. They gave a buddy workshop in which they matched us up with somebody who had shared the same experiences professionally with whom you could remain in contact after the institute. This was many years ago, and to this day I remain in contact with my ARL buddy. We call each other up and swap stories and consult each other. That is a formal mentoring program that actually succeeded. I can't remember how we were paired up, but we did take it seriously and we kept in touch. It's a two-way street: we consult each other. So I guess that contradicts some of the negative things I just said about formal mentoring.

CL: Was it initially a two-way street or did one of you have more experience?

HS: We were both bumbling at the same time. It was like kids holding hands in kindergarten. We were both scared, so let's hold on together. So that's a buddy system, not necessarily a mentoring system where one has more experience in an area and is going to share that and guide you through. We were guiding each other, so that's the difference between a buddy system and a mentoring system.

CL: That goes along with what I've read about internship
        programs. Having more than one person at a time in
        an internship program usually enhances the situation
        for all those involved.

HS: I absolutely agree with that. It's not easy being the only
        one. To have someone else or others who are going
        through the same experience that you're going through
        helps tremendously.

        I think you need mentors at all different levels. It
        isn't just one mentor, it isn't just one person. It's a vari-
        ety of people with different experiences within the or-
        ganization that they can share with you. Nobody sees
        that organization in exactly the same way, but hearing
        others' perspectives usually is good for anyone new
        to the organization.

CL: What are some of the specific skills you suggest people
        develop to prepare for a library career in the new li-
        brary? I asked this question a little differently earlier,
        and your immediate response was "flexibility." It's my
        guess that if asked that question ten years ago, your
        answer would have been the same, and ten years from
        now it could easily be the same.

HS: That's one constant—libraries change, and we need
        people who are flexible enough to change with them.

CL: Just as there are trends within libraries, there are trends
        in library schools for preparing future librarians. How
        would you differentiate between what's important and
        not so important in library education and preparing
        oneself to enter the profession?

HS: The interpersonal skills are most important. They en-
        able you to add value to any institution with which
        you become affiliated. These are not the skills that are
        easily acquired. You develop some of them over time;
        some of them are innate.

        Transitory skills, the latest fashion in programming
        or coding, we may need "right now." But a two-day
        workshop can give you a good basis for these, whereas

neither library school nor an employer can give you the attitudinal skills that fit you for librarianship. That's your lookout.

CL: So what's the bottom-line kind of advice you'd give somebody to prepare themselves to be a successful hire here or at a similar academic library?

HS: Get a well-rounded liberal education and pay a little more attention to Psychology 101. A lot of what you'll be doing as a librarian well past the year 2000 involves human relations, human interaction. Yes, we're headed towards a time when some people are going to be working at home—telecommuting—but what they'll really be doing is telecommunicating, and that will demand even better communication skills than in-person communication requires. We are going to have to be able to apply some psychology to the world at work. I'd recommend every aspiring librarian read Douglas McGregor's *The Human Side of Enterprise*[1]; it's a classic in the psychology of work. Unfortunately, it's the side of our work that typically receives the least attention.

The ability to work with others effectively is a critical measure of someone's success in the organization. As human resource managers, it's our goal to communicate this throughout the organization, and to support our middle managers and supervisory staff in getting this message across.

CL: Thank you very much.

ENDNOTE

1. Douglas McGregor, *The Human Side of Enterprise* (New York: McGraw-Hill, 1985).

6

Computer Ergonomics for Library Staff and Users

John Vasi

Ergonomic problems are part of the price we pay to use technology. No matter how well-organized or well-designed a library is, if large numbers of staff are ailing or on surgical leave from carpal tunnel syndrome, materials won't be selected, acquired, processed, or served. In short, the library won't function properly. To prevent this snafu, here is John Vasi's prescription for how we can work—and feel—better in the recreated academic library.—CML

The impact of computer technology on academic libraries is evident in all major public service areas and technical operations. Library employees, as well as library users, are dependent on computer technology to gain access to even the most basic library functions. The simplest tasks, from locating a book in the stacks to circulating it at the loan desk, are no longer handled without interacting with a computer. The more difficult tasks, which were not even possible with any manual system, are now accomplished on computer without a second thought. This rapid changeover to computer technology and our nearly complete dependence on it has often occurred without much prior thought to the physical demands that intensive or long-term use of computers imposes on users. Similarly, the need to provide computer hardware in the library's public and staff areas has often resulted in installations without sufficient thought to building and furniture requirements. But library users and particularly library staff (who work at computers for hours at a time) need to have computer installations that are comfortable, functional, and healthful.

This chapter highlights some of the basic ergonomic considerations for the use of computers in libraries. The term ergonomics generally refers to the proper and, more importantly, healthful use of computers. Although the original use of this word (in the 1950s) had broader implications and addressed the efficiency or productivity of the worker in his environment, today's connotation of ergonomics has focused more on the health of the worker in his environment.

Furniture and computer-related equipment are the focus of this discussion because the potential problems they cause can be easily addressed. Recommendations are included for integrating computer hardware installations safely and comfortably into library public space. Building-related issues, such as improper lighting, may involve greater expense and professional assistance, and they are not considered here.

Computer terminals ("dumb terminals") are a major component of most library computer systems, but they are being replaced at an ever-increasing rate by personal computers (PCs) which provide greater power and functionality. Most libraries use computers as well as computer terminals in a variety of locations. Both types of hardware present similar ergonomic problems and requirements for users, and the distinction between computers and terminals is not meaningful in the discussion that follows.

Computer users in libraries face the same problems as anyone else whose activities require significant use of computer equipment. However, library patrons and library staff must be considered separately when discussing ergonomics because the short-term use by most library patrons and the continuous use by some library staff give rise to different ergonomic concerns.

LIBRARY COMPUTER USE BY PATRONS

Some librarians may be fortunate to work in buildings constructed recently enough that building design, furnishings, and equipment have been planned to accommodate computers and terminals efficiently and properly. A wide range of specifically designed computer furniture and peripheral equipment is available today for outfitting public areas of libraries. Most architects and interior designers today are familiar enough with building and furnishing requirements to integrate computer workstations into public areas without problem. Many library managers, however, will be faced with installing computer equipment in public areas that were not originally designed for computer use. Former card catalog areas, reading rooms, and areas adjacent to book stacks are now all prime candidates for computer installations. Putting the computers or terminals where they provide the greatest benefit often requires installations very close to entryways, elevators, or high-traffic areas. A comfortable and efficient computer installation in a public area of a library needs to take into account the requirements and comfort of the library user.

Most public use of computers will be for relatively short periods of time. While some users will spend a significant amount of time in front of a computer monitor reviewing results or modifying search instructions, actual inputting (keyboarding) will probably not be intensive or of long duration. Addressing health concerns important to long-term computer users is not really an issue when selecting equipment for public users, but planning a good computer installation must take into account a number of other factors that facilitate comfortable and efficient use in the library's public areas.

If new furniture is being ordered, purchase typing-height computer tables rather than traditional desk-height tables. Generally, typing height is approximately 27 inches, and desk height is approximately 29 inches. For most users, the lower height is ergonomically "correct," resulting in a horizontal position between the elbow and the wrist. Traditional desk height (or reading-table height) will require most users to raise their wrists and hands above the height of their elbows, making the position less comfortable and natural. A wrist position that is not level with the user's elbows (that is, the "neutral" position)[1] is thought to be a frequent cause of hand and wrist injuries for some computer users. Even for public installations where ergonomic concerns are not paramount, the average user will be more comfortable with the lowered table height.

In most public areas, patrons using computers will need to take notes, write down call numbers, or refer to other material. Provide a worksurface large enough to accommodate at least note-taking. Even better is a surface large enough for users to set down books, purses, or other items. Most tables designed for computers come in three-foot, four-foot, and five-foot lengths. A four-foot-long table is a good choice for most sit-down installations in a public area. It is surprising how many library computer installations do not provide even a minimum table surface surrounding the computer for convenient note-taking or other work.

Some computer workstations are designed at the 29-inch height of a reading table, but they have a dropped keyboard shelf to provide a comfortable typing height. This design seems to be a transitional form between a reading table and a computer workstation, with the dropped-shelf worksurface designed to provide the correct typing height while keeping the computer monitor closer to eye-level. The dropped keyboard shelf chops up the table surface if it is placed in the center, making either side of limited use. Some manufacturers offer left- or right-hand offsets for the dropped shelf, but this limitation forces consideration of handedness. Offset shelves should have no place in a public area where use by all patrons is the goal. For the relatively short-term public use, eye-level height for the monitor will not really be an important consideration, but if it were, raising the monitor a few inches can be easily managed without resorting to the less-usable surface created by the dropped keyboard. The simplest solution of lower-height, flat tables of sufficient size will comfortably accommodate the majority of users.

Libraries might also want to consider different types of

furniture to accommodate special needs. In a public area with a number of computers or terminals, consider placing different types of terminal tables for different types of use. Standing-height workstations are ideal for quick retrieval of basic information, and a library might well consider placing them in areas where brief searches are expected. Someone needing only to find a call number does not need to sit down to do so. Also consider a standing-height workstation that is only three feet wide, to discourage long sessions or copious note-taking. These installations might be profitably used in book stack areas where only a single terminal is provided. Providing tall chairs or stools at standing-height workstations is a difficult decision. On one hand, providing chairs defeats the purpose of moving users in and out quickly because some users will find the tall tables with chairs equally or more comfortable than traditional table-height workstations. If all the low tables with chairs are in use, however, there may well be complaints from users who have to stand for extended use of the computers. Consider a variety of table heights and sizes to match the type of use expected for a particular area of the library. Not only can the librarian encourage different use patterns by varying furniture types, but the library may well look more attractive and inviting than one with standardized rows of identical furniture.

Before selecting furniture, check with a knowledgeable source about ADA (Americans with Disabilities Act) requirements for your library. You will probably want to provide some 29-inch-high tables to accommodate wheelchair users in a number of public areas.

Perhaps this is a good opportunity to consider how computer terminals in public areas are used. The greater functionality of computers over manual files or indexes creates some interesting trade-offs. There are still users who need to look up a quick call number, but the ability to refine searches easily with the computer leads to generally longer sessions by computer users. You may note that many libraries do not have enough public catalog terminals during busy times, even though those same libraries never had crowding around the card catalog. Despite the ease of finding information on the computer, sessions will be longer as users manipulate information and tailor searches to higher degrees of specificity. The majority of computer workstations in public areas should accommodate users comfortably for these longer sessions.

Chairs provided at public computer workstations need not be special or expensive. While secretarial chairs with wheels and without arms provide some flexibility for the general computer user, they are not essential in public areas. In the absence of lengthy or intensive keyboarding sessions in library public computer installations, perfect ergonomics are not a concern. Even if a library did provide special seating with adjustable ergonomic features, such as pneumatic seat-height adjustment or movable back support, public users would not be interested in finding the adjustments or learning how to use them. Traditional library side chairs (without arms) are actually a good choice for computer areas. Providing chairs with wheels greatly increases the chances that the chairs will be moved away from the areas for which they were intended. Metal glides on the chair legs or another feature appropriate for your floor covering will provide for easy adjustment of chairs at computer workstations—just as easily as library users adjust chair positions when sitting at reading tables. The same advice holds true for any tall chairs or stools provided for standing-height tables. In those instances, wheels and the high center of gravity of the tall stools constitute a definite hazard and should not be considered.

In our library, we did purchase wheeled secretarial chairs for a public computer and terminal installation. We now have a regular procedure of retrieving those chairs periodically from other areas of the building because they are so easily moved. The fewer specialized chairs that your library provides for computer or ergonomic considerations, the more the computer installations will blend in with traditional operations. As in other considerations, the short-term use by the library user lessens the need for a different or special type of chair.

In areas where multiple computers or terminals are located, consider lowering the light levels slightly if possible. Computer screens provide their own illumination, and the reduced lighting may eliminate some possible glare on the screens—depending on the juxtaposition of lights (or windows) and monitors. Many computer users are more comfortable with lower ambient light levels. In addition, libraries often have high light levels (sufficient for prolonged reading) in all areas including lobbies, terminal areas, and stacks. Having lowered light levels in a computer area creates an interesting change and gives the area some definition. The lowered light levels can be achieved with lower wattage bulbs or by merely removing some existing bulbs. (With fluorescent lighting fixtures, check with your building maintenance staff or electrician to determine the best way to remove bulbs without causing potential problems for light fixture ballasts.)

Many librarians will not have the luxury of designing a new space, but will be retrofitting an existing area with computer connections and terminals. The most difficult problem will probably be getting power and telecommunications connections to an area that was not originally designed for those connections. How to achieve this efficiently and in a cost-effective manner could probably fill a chapter (or book) by itself, but there are some basic considerations that will make a public computer installation more attractive and functional.

CABLES/CONNECTIONS

Providing connections along a wall is the easiest alternative because power sources probably exist already and can be expanded to accommodate PC and terminal requirements. Power requirements for computer hardware are usually handled easily with standard wiring. Consider increasing the number of electrical connections with multioutlet surge protectors which may solve several problems simultaneously. They increase the number of outlets available and provide some degree of electrical surge protection for your equipment (depending on the quality of the surge protectors you provide). Check with an electrician for what's appropriate for your installation.

More often than not, a library may not have the luxury of placing all the computer hardware along walls. This will be particularly true in public areas with large open spaces that are being converted for computer use. It is very important to create a safe and clean computer area that has electrical cords and communications cables safely covered or enclosed in an appropriate manner. The connection from a telecommunications or power source along a wall to a location more than a few feet away from the wall should be done in a professional way—with permanent floor molding or conduit for the cabling to pass through. Power poles from the ceiling to the floor are another option.

Makeshift arrangements with rubber cord covers, self-adhesive cable clips, or multioutlet extension strips will cause several types of problems. Since the public installation will get hard use, any of these nonpermanent arrangements will begin to fail. Rubber cord covers along the floor will get kicked out of place, self-adhesive clips used to guide cabling will come loose, and exposed cords or cables will suffer wear and tear. We have used self-adhesive plastic conduit (a popular brand is Panduit) effectively in many applications, but not for public areas. Temporary cable-handling arrangements also cause problems for library custodial personnel who need to clean around them.

The best option is to get the power outlet and the telecommunications jack installed as close as possible to the computer location, using permanent conduit or floor molding to make the connection cables impervious to users' feet, books, handbags, or chairs. The connections should be safe from inadvertent damage by users, and they should also be out of the way so that users don't need to work around them. In addition to designing around these concerns for users, local electrical or other code considerations may define what is acceptable for your installation. Get informed advice on these matters as soon as possible in your planning. This is an area where trying to economize is not a good idea. Unfortunately, getting power and telecommunications unobtrusively to where it's required is often an afterthought. In reality, it may be one of the more expensive components of a public computer installation and should be considered early on in the location and design of public terminal areas.

STAFF WORK AREAS

An entirely different set of ergonomic concerns needs to be addressed when considering computer use in staff work areas. Most computer users who spend significant amounts of time in front of a workstation will experience some level of discomfort, ranging from eyestrain, muscle stiffness, and neckaches all the way to truly debilitating conditions, such as the well-reported carpal tunnel syndrome (CTS). This inflammation of the nerve running through the wrist causes considerable pain and requires rest or sometimes corrective surgery for those afflicted.

CTS or repetitive motion injuries may arise from a specific situation or may be caused by a combination of several factors. During long sessions of computer use, poor posture, distance from the computer, keyboard height, wrist angles, and other similar factors can cause CTS or other injuries. As workers are tied more and more to keyboarding functions, the possibility of computer-related injuries increases. It is the repetition of physical actions, the lack of change in position, and the long duration of computer sessions that causes physical problems. In a recent study, Winstead found that ergonomic problems were high on a list of staff concerns at an academic library, with specific problems cited such as eyestrain, backaches, headaches, and general physical stress from lack of movement. The study, initially done in 1987 and repeated in 1993, showed no evidence of wrist or CTS problems in 1987 but did show complaints for these injuries in 1993. The study also showed that library staff believed they could work for two hours at a computer without a break in 1987, but only for one hour without a break in 1993.[2]

Although the recommendations listed below may be effective at improving the ergonomics at staff workstations, they will not be a substitute for an effective and affirmative program by library managers to design employee work schedules and duties to reduce the possibility of ergonomic injuries. Just as there will be employees who are unaffected by continuous computer operations, there will be others whose tolerance is not nearly so great. Those employees may experience minor problems or even disabling injuries despite any efforts to provide ergonomically designed work areas. Managers should be alert to the potential for problems before they arise and should avoid situations that have proven to cause ergonomic problems.

Continuous inputting at a computer workstation is one of the main causes of computer-related injuries. Work schedules should be varied for employees responsible for a high volume of keyboarding. Reduce total time at the keyboard or provide alternate duties. Assign some non-keyboarding activities to break up the computer time; enforce break times or periods of rest from computer work; reassign duties among employees to level the keyboarding load; use part-time or student help for repetitive keyboarding activities. Varied work schedules and changes of activity will be essential for some employees to avoid physical problems. Many campuses and government agencies today have access to professional advice through their personnel offices on proper ergonomic practices and conditions. Take advantage of such outside expertise to formulate a program which addresses the prevention of ergonomic injuries.

In addition to managing employee work routines to avoid ergonomic injuries, it is important to provide a proper physical environment for employees whose jobs require a significant amount of computer use. Well-designed equipment, proper lighting, and the adoption of good ergonomic work practices will reduce the frequency of many common injuries. However, there are no universal answers and there are no foolproof ergonomic designs to prevent the onset of physical problems and injuries that derive from long and unvaried keyboarding activities. Many library supervisors are already familiar with the recommendations below, but this brief list should serve as a starting point.

Chairs: Many people consider the chair to be the single most important ergonomic item for the employee. The Winstead study found that 74 percent of respondents blamed their chairs for physical problems they were experiencing.[3] There is, however, no single chair that will be suited for all employees. The key, as in other ergonomic choices, is the ability for the employee to be comfortable at his or her workstation. Being comfortable, though, encompasses a number of factors, including the ability to change positions. Several features should be included on a good chair for computer users, but two general attributes stand out. The chair must be a good fit for the individual using it, and the chair must be easily adjusted. Even with a wide range of adjustments, one or two chair designs will not be comfortable for all users. Good chairs come in many different styles, fabrics, designs, and sizes. The ideal situation is to allow computer users to try a range of chairs and select the one that feels comfortable. Any good chair today will have most of these desired adjustment features: easily adjustable backrest, lumbar support, pneumatic height adjustment, short arms to allow the employee to rest occasionally during keyboarding sessions, seat angle adjustment, and a stable base with wheels appropriate to the floor surface. Most furniture manufacturers or suppliers will have a line of ergonomic chairs with a wide selection and varying prices.

Managers should consider allowing individual employees to select their own chairs. This will assure a high degree of comfort for the employees, and it will also give them a stake in the process—a realization that the library understands individual needs and is concerned about the health and comfort of individual employees. Yes, the chairs will cost more than standard secretarial chairs, and the process of individual selection is more of an effort than a decision from the administration to purchase 20 identical chairs. However, good chairs should be considered a cost of doing business in the highly computerized environment of libraries. In our library, we have for the past several years purchased a number of chairs each year for those employees with the highest level of computer inputting work. We cannot afford to provide new chairs for everyone at once, but ten or 15 chairs a year makes a good dent in the overall need after a few years. To a person, the employees consider their self-selected chairs one of the most important components of their workplace.

Computer worksurfaces: As with public workstations, consider a flat, typing-height worksurface for employees. Any dropped keyboard shelf reduces flexibility and utility for the worksurface. Think seriously about redesigning employee work areas around computer workstations—not around that existing desk which is now of limited functional value. Almost all employees will require a worksurface large enough to accommodate copy, reading materials, and other items required for their job. Raising the monitor to eye-level is easily accomplished in a variety of ways, and should not determine the worksurface height. Some taller employees may require a higher, table-height (29 inches) workstation to accommodate their individual needs. Computer tables are available in the standard heights described above or with legs that can be adjusted up or down in one-inch increments.

In furnishing work areas, the location and connectivity requirements of the computer hardware are essential, but so too is consideration of the type of work that needs to be done by the employee. Most computer work in libraries requires the user to consult many sources while using the computer itself: notes, files, books, copy, cards, and so on. In a random look at computer workstations, you will probably find insufficient worksurface areas available for the activities required. For example, a right-handed person who needs to make notes while using the computer may well have the mouse in the only spot convenient to write. Printers, paper supply, and other materials are often on the same worksurface as the computer. In some instances, this may be the best (or only) alternative, but in other cases, the worksurface might be better designed to facilitate the specific tasks being done. Consider larger or L-shaped computer worksurfaces as appropriate for the majority of workspaces. As with chairs, individual needs and requirements, rather than standardized equipment, should define the furniture when appropriate.

Only a few years ago, a majority of computer workstations in library staff areas (particularly in technical services) were shared, reducing the desirability for individualized equipment and furniture. Most computer workstations are now used solely by one employee, and the ergonomic fit of that work area to the employee and the specific job activities should take precedence over concerns of standardization.

Peripheral equipment: In accommodating individual needs, there is also a wide range of peripheral equipment to address valid ergonomic needs. Copy holders, for example, provide relief for cluttered worksurfaces. They also address a common ergonomic problem, eliminating the need for continual head and neck movements by placing copy at eye-level. Providing wrist rests for those employees who can benefit from them is essential. As with chairs, there is no universal wrist rest that employees will choose. Provide a few for users to try for several days before making a decision.

Give employees the opportunity to select those items that customize the workstation and provide a comfortable physical environment. Foot rests sometimes help from an ergonomic point of view; sometimes they are merely a comfortable change of position—which may preclude a health problem in the future. There is often an indistinct line between a comfortable workplace and a healthful one. Employees who feel good about their workplace and are comfortable with the equipment they need to do their job will be less likely to suffer the range of ergonomic injuries that may afflict unhappy or uncomfortable employees. As with many other illnesses, there is a psychological component. Giving employees some degree of decision-making and control over their computer work area will be cost-efficient when productivity and sick time is considered. There is not consensus on the efficacy of individual workstation components (such as wrist rests, ergonomic chairs, and copy holders) in reducing or eliminating employee injuries, but the overall effect of self-selected improvements for an individual's workstation will be positive. Consider this: the price tag on absences for CTS injuries will be thousands of dollars for medical costs, in addition to a typical four-to-six-week recuperation period of lost work time.[4]

Ergonomics was not an issue for the previous generation of workers—particularly library workers. As the science of ergonomics progresses and as information on good design of work areas becomes more readily available, library managers can take a leading role in providing comfortable and safe work environments. Proper design of computer areas can no longer be considered an added expense, but rather one of the requirements for a healthful and productive workplace. In a profession dominated by the use of computers, the provision of ergonomically correct equipment and an appropriate environment for public and staff work activities cannot be merely an afterthought. It must be consciously considered and designed, and funds must be budgeted to meet ergonomic needs.

On a pragmatic level, providing for these needs promotes effective use of our resources by library users. It also prevents disabilities, injuries, and unhappiness among employees. On a more visionary level, library managers should recognize their role in the computerized environment of today and tomorrow. Providing for the effective and healthful use of computer tools is an enlightened approach that library managers should embrace and promote—not one we are forced to accept to remedy the consequences of improper planning and inappropriate equipment.

ENDNOTES

1. For a very detailed and sometimes technical discussion of wrist injury and related problems, see Allen Hedge, *Beneficial Effects of a Preset Tiltdown Keyboard System on Posture and Comfort in Offices* (Ithaca, N.Y.: Cornell University, 1995).

2. Elizabeth B. Winstead, "Staff Reaction to Automation," *Computers in Libraries* 14 (April, 1994): 18.

3. Ibid., 18.

4. Robert D. Chadbourne, "Ergonomics and the Electronic Workplace," *Wilson Library Bulletin* 69 (January 1995): 24.

PART III:

IN/FINITE
RESOURCES

7

New Collections for Old

Stella Bentley

Would that we had world enough, and time . . . but as the poet notes, we don't. At least we don't have world enough to acquire all that our users need or want. Academic library budgets shrink at great rates annually—if not in actual figures then in proportion to the burgeoning amounts of published materials available. Although all-electronic collections beckon seductively, they are not yet (and may never be) a far-reaching reality. Our new academic library collections will actually be our old collections . . . plus a whole lot more. We're going to encounter new and challenging problems in creating the amalgamated print/electronic library of the future, as Stella Bentley describes in this essay.—CML

THE NEW COLLECTIONS' CONTEXT

Collection managers are operating in an entirely different context from that of just a few years ago. Downsizing and budgetary reductions in the 1990s have forced many librarians to take on new collection development roles. A number of factors facing the academy as a whole have converged to reshape the nature of collection management and development work. These factors include the rapid development and availability of new technologies and digital information, access versus ownership issues, increased user expectations, decreased budgets, and changes in the scholarly communication processes.

SCHOLARLY COMMUNICATION

Several issues fall under the umbrella heading of scholarly communication. First, there are the escalating twin problems of the costs for materials and the amount of materials growing at faster rates than our budgets. The current crisis in scholarly communication—the increasing inability of research libraries to acquire the materials needed to support research in their institutions—will continue. There is every indication that the steep increases in the extent and costs of information that we have seen in the past few years will continue, especially with the proliferating mergers and conglomerations of publishing into a few profit-seeking and profit-maximizing entities and the continued instability of the value of the dollar.

This ongoing trend means that libraries will spend more and more each year to acquire less and less of the year's scholarly production. Research libraries acquire a smaller percentage of the available published literature each year—over the past eight years, ARL (Association of Research Librarians) libraries spent 93 percent more for 4 percent fewer serials and spent 17 percent more for 22 percent fewer monographs.[1]

As a result, there is a growing concern among librarians, administrators, and scholars that research libraries can no longer acquire the very information that the research universities have paid their faculty to produce. Consequently, some are acknowledging that changes need to take place in the role of the university and the library in the research, production of knowledge, and copyright processes. They believe that the library, in its role as manager of knowledge, should take a more active role in the scholarly communication process. The new role might include such activities as distributing digitized information, taking on a more direct role in communicating and preserving new information through discipline-oriented invisible colleges, and maintaining electronic texts.

The second area that must be addressed is the changing

nature of scholarly communication as we move into a digital world. We must manage the transition to a digital future and build the infrastructure to handle digitized information. With the growth of the Internet and the advent of the World Wide Web, the ability to share information with others almost instantaneously, and the easy delivery of information to an individual's workstation, wherever it might be located, there will definitely be changes in the scholarly communication process. The changes will be dramatic in some areas, and much slower, if at all, in others. There is little doubt that print will continue to predominate in many disciplines for some time for a variety of reasons:

- Affordability—Print is affordable for most individuals. It does not require any additional hardware or software to access.
- Ease of use/convenience—It is easy and convenient to carry around and use almost anywhere and any time.
- Familiarity—It is familiar to all; the traditional scholarly process has developed around its production and review.
- Reluctance to change—Many scholars, especially those who have been in academe for some time, are very comfortable with the print environment; it is what they know, and they have no interest at this stage of their careers in changing their methods of using information.

Therefore, libraries will certainly continue to acquire sizable portions of their collections in print form for the foreseeable future. At the same time, there is an increasing need to acquire more materials in electronic form. A significant amount of the materials budget is now spent on electronic formats, especially abstracting and indexing tools, but more and more on full-text materials as well (many research libraries currently spend from 4 to 6 percent of the materials budget on electronic formats).[2]

The basic criteria and collection development policies applied to print collections can be used to determine what to organize and catalog on the Internet, with some additional considerations concerning such issues as archiving and access.[3] The time frame for a shift from a predominance of print to electronic formats is ripe for speculation—estimates range anywhere from ten years to never. It is the advent of some of these tools and the availability of electronic formats or the ability to convert materials easily to electronic formats that makes it possible to look at access as a viable option to ownership for some materials.

ACCESS AND OWNERSHIP ISSUES

Access versus ownership will cease to be such a large issue in time, since it is clear that we cannot own everything that our users need. Ownership of materials, the who-owns-what and where-it-is-located issues, will continue to be relevant considerations for those who deliver information to those who need it, but it will be increasingly less relevant to users—provided that access is efficient, appropriate, timely, and essentially transparent to them.

As our purchasing power continues to erode, it is inevitable that access will play a larger and larger role in what we do. Because of technology, we are able to provide greater access to information located almost anywhere in the world: the access tools are much more readily available to our users, often from their own workstations. From my desk, I now have access to a wide variety of bibliographic databases, hundreds of full-text journals, library catalogs from all over the world, the databases of the major library utilities, and the World Wide Web. With little effort, I can easily identify materials (and their locations) that only a few years ago might have taken days or even weeks to verify.

As a result of the increased capability for access, libraries have been implementing policies, services, and reallocated budgets to meet the users' information needs and to cope with the rising demands for materials. Libraries are developing and implementing policies and services that emphasize access and document delivery. Some libraries have even adopted a "just-in-time" philosophy of providing access to information and documents versus the "just-in-case" approach to building collections.

USER EXPECTATIONS

A further impact on collection development in the 1990s is the change and growth that has taken place in user expectations. Rapid bibliographic access has engendered an accompanying desire for rapid document delivery; libraries are responding to these demands with an increased emphasis on service, especially in terms of rapid delivery of documents to the user. An increasingly larger proportion of current, commercially published materials is accessible in ways that make remote access an acceptable alternative to local ownership. In addition, the development and wide availability of electronic indexing and abstracting tools, and even some full-text information, makes it easier than ever before for users to know what is available "somewhere."

We must continue to work on the development of tools that integrate access to traditional and electronic resources for our users while we work to design programs that serve the scholarly information needs of the academic research community into the 21st century. With the increased ease of access comes an expectation that the actual delivery of materials should also be much quicker and timelier, and that other materials should be equally accessible in an easy manner. In the academic environment, there are growing expectations that access to the resources that individuals want will be easy and efficient; that there will be fully searchable online scholarly literature; that complete information will be available online (and that graphics, tables, equations, and color will be present); and that there will be extensive navigational tools.

We should continually assess users' needs to obtain an appropriate balance between innovative delivery technologies and traditional print resources. While we must continue to satisfy demand for the traditional resources, we must also increase the proportion of electronic resources we provide to meet the increased demand for them. To monitor and address user expectations, and to insure that the systems we create will meet their expectations and needs, we need to collect better information about their needs and expectations. We must continue and expand the ongoing dialogue with our users about their current needs and their future plans. We should develop more formal user surveys, which will help us understand current information-seeking behaviors better so we can adapt our systems where necessary.

COLLABORATIVE COLLECTION DEVELOPMENT

The real question for us at this point is whether there really is the possibility for collaborative collection development on a scale any larger than what we see now. Yes, any number of statewide or regional projects are operating at various levels of scope and participation. Yes, one can point to some national efforts as demonstrating that at some minimal level we can work in a collaborative mode. Yes, we all understand that none of us can build comprehensive collections, and not many of us can be comprehensive in even a few well-defined areas anymore. Yes, at a certain level we believe that collaboration is the only way we will be able to have a comprehensive collection that is available when there is a need for some very specific materials.

The reality is, however, that the level of collaboration has not changed appreciably during the past ten years, even as many of us have had to cope with tremendously reduced purchasing power. (My materials' allocation at University of California, Santa Barbara in 1997 purchased about half what it did in 1991; due to budget problems in California, the allocation remained essentially unchanged, while we all know what happened to prices in that time.) Even those collaborative programs that are operating successfully do not entail great expenditures compared to the extraordinary funds spent on library materials in this country each year.

In the University of California system, for example, the collection development officers of the nine campuses jointly funded a number of shared purchases in 1996, but the amount that we spent was less than 0.5 percent of the total collectively spent on materials in 1997. For very nominal sums, again just a fraction of a percent of total expenditures, some members of the Center for Research Libraries joined together to purchase some materials that we wanted available but for which the center did not have the resources.

Why have collections librarians not been able to cooperate more than we have? There are a number of reasons, most of which are political and pragmatic. Our primary clientele expects that the majority of materials that they require will be available in their library. Most do not see any reason for us to cancel a journal they want in order to keep another that they do not want, but that fulfills a cooperative commitment. As more of us become so squeezed by the current economic situation that we are no longer able to buy even what is narrowly considered the general core materials essential to support basic teaching and research, it is no longer financially possible nor politically feasible for us to assume any primary collecting responsibilities.

Whither collaborative collection development? We will continue to pay lip service to cooperation, and we will continue to cooperate at the rather modest levels we do now, but I doubt that its future is any brighter than its past.

STAFFING FOR COLLECTION DEVELOPMENT

From its growth periods in the 1960s and 1970s, collection development staffing has undergone a number of changes in the 1990s, particularly in terms of the number of full-time bibliographers. A major impact of the "reengineering" many of us have had to do is consolidation of units and positions. The recent ARL/OMS (Office of Management Studies) SPEC Kit on the organization of collection development reports that "a decentralized staff, composed, in part or wholly, by librarians having responsibilities in collection development as well as other areas . . . is the most frequent pattern." [4]

Not only is collection development one of several assignments held by most academic librarians in the recreated library, but often the individual is now responsible for a number of subject areas. Unfortunately, good collection development takes much more time when resources are scarce—it takes more time and is a much harder decision when the funding is so limited in contrast to the available materials. As a result, most bibliographers today are feeling very stretched by their multiple collections assignments, the difficulty in

making collections decisions, the seemingly unending necessity to cancel subscriptions, and the demands of their other
responsibilities in the library.

The increasingly interdisciplinary nature of much research
poses another challenge for bibliographers. With the collections work divided among a number of individuals, each responsible for specific areas or subjects, it is too easy for interdisciplinary works to fall between the cracks of the guidelines for each collection. Many of us have sought to restruc-
ture the organization of collection management and development within our libraries to address this change, and enable
our bibliographers to work together more easily to identify
and purchase such materials. A team-based approach has
worked well in those situations where many individuals are
responsible for collection development. By working together
as a team, and having some collections funding provided for
the team as well as for specific subjects, the bibliographers
are able to identify the materials that were falling through the
cracks and not being acquired.

Will we ever return to a period of more individuals involved in collection development? It is certainly likely, although not inevitable. As we select more and more from the
Internet, while continuing to select in the more traditional
formats, the amount of time needed to develop collections
will increase steadily if not dramatically. More time and resources may be needed to be dedicated to collections work,
especially as we try to bring order to the vast materials out
there—identifying items to add to our catalogs, providing the
links and access points so our users can readily identify materials they would like to see from the millions of bytes of
stuff that is on the Net. The role of the collection manager as a
subject specialist who uses his/her expertise to select materials and to guide users to relevant materials will be enhanced,
moreover, as we bring order to the chaos of the Internet.

CRITICAL ISSUES

There are a number of critical issues that collection management and development professionals must face with the in-

creased availability of remotely available electronic resources. Some of these issues are out of our hands, and many others are changing rapidly even as we discuss them, but we at least need to be aware of them as we plan our information future. Issues that must be dealt with include

- achieving a balanced approach among electronic resources, traditional materials, and preservation needs;
- using the same criteria for selection of resources, regardless of format;
- determining what must be acquired and housed or delivered locally versus what might better be provided through the Internet;
- making the choices regarding how to deliver electronic information (digitized page-images or marked-up text);
- determining what navigational tools we will develop or use to point to information on the Internet;
- establishing reliable distribution mechanisms for networked information;
- working out fair and appropriate means of handling copyright concerns;
- working cooperatively to ensure information integrity and archival preservation;
- assessing users' needs and interests continuously to strike the correct balance between innovative delivery technologies and traditional print resource delivery methods; and
- integrating access to traditional and electronic resources.

THE SHIFTING COLLECTION
DEVELOPMENT PARADIGM

Libraries have always been in the information business, and the role of collection management and development in the academic research library has been traditionally to acquire information appropriate for the research and teaching needs of academe. While few if any libraries actually collected exhaustively in all appropriate areas, until quite recently many were able to build research-level collections in most disciplines located in their university, and even to build exhaustive collections in a few more narrowly defined areas.

With the declining support for higher education that hit most U.S. colleges and universities during the late 1980s and early 1990s, coupled with the continued increase in the prices of research materials and the continued growth of materials available in all formats, the collection development paradigm has undergone a transformation. Under the old paradigm, research collections were print-based collections, and they were built to be as self-sufficient as possible; interlibrary loan (ILL) was available for those esoteric materials that not everyone could be expected to own, but ILL was definitely not a predominant means of supplying access (indeed, many students, particularly undergraduates, were not even permitted to use interlibrary loan).

With the decline in purchasing power that has beset academic research libraries over the past few years, and the forecasts and predictions for continued diminishing ability to build research-level collections, major shifts have taken place in the collection development paradigm. While the paradigm certainly still emphasizes ownership (and the vast majority of funding still goes for ownership), providing access to information is increasingly accepted as a necessary alternative to ownership.

Two factors are at work here: we can provide access more readily than ever before because of the technology, and we can no longer afford to provide ownership at the levels possible even a few years ago. The new paradigm emphasizes both ownership and access rather than ownership versus access. The essential elements of the new paradigm are that

- Research libraries will continue to acquire materials for the foreseeable future.
- Access should be viewed as a complement to and enhancement of local collections.
- Libraries must know much more about their primary users' information needs in order to purchase the core materials needed on-site.
- Collection development policies should be oriented to-

ward what is needed as a core collection for local needs and what will be acquired for a comprehensive collection as part of collaborative agreements to ensure that access to comprehensive research collections is maintained.

• Delivery mechanisms must be enhanced so that access equals ownership and is as transparent to the user as possible.

Another important change in the paradigm of collection development is a movement away from the view that the library is the collector and repository of information (waiting for a user to come to it), and toward instead the notion that librarians must become active managers of knowledge, more proactively involved in the process of both acquiring and delivering information to the users. If this change takes place, the role of the recreated academic library in scholarly communication will have changed dramatically.

ENDNOTES

1. Anthony Cummings et al., *University Libraries and Scholarly Communications: A Study Prepared for the Andrew W. Mellon Foundation* (Washington, D.C.: Association of Research Libraries, 1992), 46.

2. Based on the 1995 University of California Libraries' self-study in collection development.

3. Cheryl LaGuardia and Stella Bentley, "Electronic Databases: Will Old Collection Development Policies Still Work?" *Online* 16 (July 1992): 60–63.

4. Gordon Rowley, comp., *Organization of Collection Development*, ARL SPEC Kit 207 (Washington D.C.: Association of Research Libraries, 1995), 10.

ADDITIONAL RESOURCES

Atkinson, Ross. "The Acquisitions Librarian As Change Agent in the Transition to the Electronic Library." *Library Resources and Technical Services* 36 (January 1992):11–15.

————. "Networks, Hypertext, and Academic Information Services: Some Longer-Range Implications." *College and Research Libraries* 54 (May 1993): 199–216.

————. "Old Forms, New Forms: The Challenge of Collection Development." *College and Research Libraries* 50 (September 1989): 507–520.

Dougherty, Richard M., and Carol Hughes. *Preferred Library Futures II: Charting the Paths.* Mountain View, Calif.: Research Libraries Group, 1993.

Johnson, Peggy, and Bonnie MacEwan, eds. *Collection Management and Development: Issues in an Electronic Era.* Chicago: American Library Association, 1994.

Martin, Harry S., III, and Curtis L. Kendrick. "A User-Centered View of Document Delivery and Interlibrary Loan," *Library Administration and Management* 8 (Fall 1994): 223–227.

Rutstein, Joel S., Anna L. DeMiller, and Elizabeth A. Fuseler, "Ownership versus Access: Shifting Perspectives for Libraries." In *Advances in Librarianship,* ed. Irene P. Godden, 33–60. San Diego: Academic Press, 1993.

Scholars and Research Libraries in the 21st Century. ACLS Occasional Paper 14. New York: American Council of Learned Societies, 1990.

8

Access Is Everything

Mary Cahill

The degree of current library specialization is such that there are segments of library work about which many of us would never vouchsafe to utter an opinion (at least openly)—for example, public services librarians tend to leave technical service issues to tech services librarians. There is too much to be deeply knowledgeable about for any one of us to think we know better about the minute details of others' spheres of influence in academic libraries. With one exception: interlibrary loan. Staff and patrons alike have strong opinions about ILL. If we consider just a few of the questions that can be posed about the process ("should it be done?" "who for?" "to what extent?" "for a price?" "instead of buying materials?" "as a general acquisitions policy?") the reason for these opinions becomes clear—ILL affects so many different aspects of a library organization and its services. As a former ILL librarian I know intimately what a hotbed of controversy this work can be, so I find Mary Cahill's essay especially thought-provoking.—CML

IN THE BEGINNING . . .

Interlibrary loan (ILL) has a long history of providing scholars, researchers, students, and citizens access to library materials not available in their local libraries. Delivered items were usually books or copies of journal articles. This resource-sharing activity was most often carried on among reciprocating libraries under various local, national, and international codes or rules designed to govern interlibrary loan practices. The first formal ILL Code dates back to 1917,[1] but an examination of recent code revisions articulates fundamental shifts in the purpose of interlibrary loan services.

The National Interlibrary Loan Code of 1980 defined interlibrary loan as an adjunct to, but not a substitute for, collection development in individual libraries.[2] The 1993 revision defines interlibrary loan as a "national resources sharing system" where borrowing is an "integral element of collection development for all libraries, not an ancillary option" and is no longer restricted only to items needed for "research and serious study."[3]

Seasoned interlibrary loan/access-services librarians may well note the code revision with some irony: as some libraries decide to access more materials with "just-in-time" collection development attitudes, it is important to remember that these materials ultimately must be retrieved from the "just-in-case" collections of other libraries or purchased from commercial suppliers.

"Interlibrary loan started out as an occasional privilege, but is rapidly becoming a necessity and even a right." Richard DeGennaro drew this conclusion in 1980 about the ways in which the automation technologies of that time were increasing demands for resource sharing. Current assessments of resource sharing indicate that access to information not available in local collections has become one of the most essential services libraries offer their users.

In 1992, interlibrary loan activity in the United States was estimated to have reached 27 million loans, with academic libraries accounting for 7.2 million, public libraries 13.2 million, and federal and special libraries 6.6 million. By the year 2000 the number of loans is predicted to reach 33 million.[4]

The traditional vision of the library in a "mediating" role providing access to information may be challenged in the very near future. Global information technologies and communication networks like the Internet will provide electronic publishers, information system providers, and authors alike the ability to take information products directly to people in their homes and offices.[5]

TIGHT BUDGET TIMES

A study of research libraries carried out by the Andrew W. Mellon Foundation in 1992 found that for the previous 12 years there had been a decrease in the proportion of institutional funding available for college, university, and research libraries.[6] While the libraries' shares of institutional budgets had shown a steady increase during the period from the mid-1960s to the early 1970s, by 1980 it had leveled off, and funding percentages began declining alarmingly from that point. By 1990 the average library budget share had shrunk to 1966 levels.

Budget proportions for salaries decreased while proportions for technology increased. In that period, materials budgets remained at about the same level. Brook and Powell calculated that from 1990 to 1994 academic libraries had experienced price increases for periodicals of over 52 percent with academic serials prices exceeding the increases for journals of all other library types.[7] A survey designed to assess the impact of serials price increases on small- and medium-sized public college libraries found that 95 percent of respondents were experiencing problems with escalating periodical costs and most of that group were reducing their periodical expenditures by canceling subscriptions.[8]

The prices of serials have seriously affected libraries since the 1970s but the greatest—and most damaging—increases have occurred during the last decade. In 1994 Perrault studied the effects on library collections of diverting funds from monographs to serials and cautioned that the success of future resource sharing was being jeopardized.[9]

In the period from 1985 to 1989 U.S. members of the Association of Research Libraries (ARL) showed a 28 percent decline in the total number of monographs purchased with many fewer unique and foreign language titles being collected by the libraries. By 1993 research libraries were spending 16 percent more to buy 23 percent fewer monographs than they purchased in 1986.[10]

In a 1995 article, Carrigan speculates that the growing gap between the number of materials published and what libraries are able to purchase will mean that even research university libraries will be unable to continue in the traditional "just-in-case" collection model where material is acquired and warehoused for future use.[11] Add to this fiscal incongruity the perception that students and faculty are growing increasingly dissatisfied with local collections once they gain access to electronic databases and it is apparent that the issue of access is a volatile, highly pressurized topic for discussion in and about libraries.

MEASURING THE COSTS

Identifying costs and effectiveness measures for access services has become increasingly essential in this era of no budget growth and decreased funds. Cost studies provide libraries with suggestions for developing methodology for local cost analysis as well as providing benchmark data to compare their operational costs for borrowing and lending.

In 1989 Dickson and Boucher developed a methodology for estimating the costs of interlibrary lending.[12] The authors cautioned that the derived costs were estimates and not absolute costs. Yet aggregate data gathered according to this methodology from a number of libraries could yield credible estimated cost information for those setting reimbursement fees.

More recently a methodology was developed to assist libraries in the Research Libraries Group (RLG) to execute a broad study of their interlibrary loan costs. Seventy-six U.S. and Canadian private and public research libraries collected information on their 1991 borrowing and lending operations for the ARL/RLG Interlibrary Loan Cost Study. Costs included staff, networks and communications, materials delivery, photocopy supplies, equipment and software, and direct and indirect charges for borrowing. Subscription, per search, telecommunications, and document delivery charges for use of fee-based search and retrieval services such as CARL, UnCover, CitaDel, and FirstSearch were also eligible for inclusion in the calculation of unit costs. Interlibrary loan activity for both documents (returnables) and photocopies (disposables or nonreturnables) was derived. Performance measures in terms of fill rates and turnaround time was not studied—cost alone was at issue.

The average (mean) cost to lend was calculated at $10.93 (low $6.29, median $9.18, and high $17.49). The average cost to borrow was $18.62 (low $9.84, median $17.55, and high $30.27). Costs for borrowing are typically higher, as borrowing materials is a more complex process than loaning and requires greater amounts of professional (more expensive) staff time. Of the $29.55 average cost for a filled ILL transaction (borrowing and lending), $22.62 or 77 percent was personnel costs. In a report of the cost study, Roche proposed that libraries decide, based on analysis of cost data collected from their own interlibrary loan activities, how they could best obtain items.[13] A reworked cost study designed for small- to medium-sized academic libraries could provide undergraduate libraries with a more accurate tool to compare costs.

COMPARING ACCESS TO OWNERSHIP

When tallying costs of serial subscriptions, libraries have not always included some of the hidden (yet substantial) costs of those subscriptions, such as processing, space, and binding fees for journals. Even though interlibrary loan access costs are high, various studies have demonstrated that it can, in many cases, be cheaper to buy individual journal articles and essays rather than pay outright for subscriptions. Signs point to this continuing to be the case even in the emerging online publishing world, where journals are published electronically and libraries pay for "site license" access to a title.

This market for individual, "unbundled" articles may grow, especially when the demand from the professional and business community for scientific, technical, and business literature cannot be met by library subscriptions.[14] But before canceling subscriptions and relying on "acquisition on demand" for journal literature, responsible librarians will study usage patterns, compile estimates of costs for providing document delivery of articles, and anticipate differences in user needs for information.

THE COLUMBIA STUDY

During the spring of 1991 Columbia University Library carried out an information needs study for access versus ownership. A survey team used estimated borrowing costs derived during Columbia's participation in the ARL cost study and compared costs for ownership versus the costs to access all titles requested through interlibrary loan.[15] The "fully-loaded" costs (which included costs for acquisition and processing) to own books and journals were compared with what it would cost to borrow or use document delivery. Between January 1991 and September 1992 the study analyzed over 1,500 interlibrary loan and commercial document delivery requests processed from library users in the biology, physics, and electrical engineering departments. Eighty-five percent of the requests were for periodical articles. Most books and periodical titles were requested only once during the study.

The study found that if a monograph was used only once the costs for owning it far exceeded the costs for accessing it through interlibrary loan. The study also confirmed that for periodicals it was less expensive to access an article on demand than to subscribe to the journal. However, when ten or more articles were requested from an individual title the costs were almost equal. In some cases, depending on the cost of the journal subscription and the number of times it was requested, it would have been less expensive to subscribe to the journal than to use point-of-access methods.

A collection analysis of all requested titles determined that 80 percent of the periodical titles and 40 percent of the monographs were appropriate for the collection. The study concluded that titles should be selected for access on demand over ownership on a title-by-title basis, weighing potential use, cost of subscription, and charges for access through document delivery. The importance to researchers of browsing new periodical issues was also noted as a nonmeasurable, yet significant aspect of access versus ownership.

THE UNIVERSITY AT ALBANY'S COST STUDY

In preparation for a major periodical cancellation project, librarians at the University at Albany (N.Y.) conducted a similar cost comparison study, but investigated ownership versus access of low-use periodical titles using data from local use studies and access costs derived from the ARL guide.[16] Specifically the authors studied whether the cancellation of a low-use journal costing less than $100 per year would be cost effective.

The study concluded that it was more cost effective to borrow or obtain articles on demand from low-use titles rather than to own them. Titles that were low use and low cost were also cheaper to access through interlibrary loan or document delivery, as long as the frequency of use stayed below five requests per year.

This particular study yielded data that refuted the common notion that because the sciences depend more on periodicals for their scholarly communication, journals in scientific fields would be more heavily used. Data revealed that, considering the size of the user population at the institution, science periodicals at the University at Albany were not particularly heavily used. The study also found that a majority of faculty were content with the typical three- to seven-day turnaround time for article delivery.

Access to various online current awareness databases was supported by the university to address faculty needs to browse the tables of contents of latest issues of periodicals in their subject disciplines. The authors did note, however, that outsourcing all journal use at Albany would have cost the institution almost twice as much as the cost of current subscriptions.

LIBRARY COOPERATION AND RESOURCE SHARING

Interlibrary loan is principally a resource sharing activity carried on between reciprocating libraries. Libraries like Iowa State University's rarely needed to pay fees because they participate in a number of resource sharing consortia. But there are costs for resource sharing. Dannelly contends that many administrators mistakenly view resource sharing as a means of providing access to information while saving money on library expenses. Yet "It is not free and it does not absolve the local institution from supporting its own programs from an appropriately developed collection."[17]

Dougherty also cautions that "financially strapped administrators" may see cooperation as a way to save money or justify budget reductions.[18] Interlibrary resource sharing arrangements have usually been a part of successful cooperative collection development programs. In the networked environment users may benefit more from cooperative efforts as libraries share costs for expensive resources in new electronic formats.[19]

Kingma has developed an economic model to analyze the cost efficiency of journal subscriptions and commercial and consortium document delivery which includes determining the monetary value of information delivery or "value to patrons."[20] Logan studied attitudes and cooperative behavior of personnel in six libraries.[21] While local politics and administrative problems were mentioned as barriers to cooperative behavior, funding was the "largest single perceived barrier" to interlibrary cooperation.

The OhioLINK consortium is an example of an attempt to "Create a virtual, statewide library system."[22] Based on a model of fundamental ("even radical") cooperation, OhioLINK provides a union catalog of holdings for all participating libraries, patron-initiated requests for book and periodical articles, a commercial index, abstract and full-text databases, and the Internet. Regional storage facilities hold materials accessible through the system and a statewide courier system promises delivery within 48 hours.

While each institution must absorb the local costs of resource sharing, central funding from the state pays all automation costs for the system. OhioLINK libraries have also agreed not to duplicate in local collections any of the electronic resources available from OhioLINK. Future developments include an image database, customized current awareness services, automated links to document supply services from article databases and the development of a scholar's workstation.

USING AND EVALUATING COMMERCIAL
DOCUMENT DELIVERY AND INTERLIBRARY LOAN

In an article titled "Striking a Balance: Document Delivery in the Nineties" Pamela Bluh discusses the efforts libraries are making to address reduced budgets and still improve and increase services.[23] She cautions that in canceling subscriptions and adding document delivery services librarians not overlook the need to provide better access to bibliographic and holdings information for the many subscriptions and materials we are still collecting locally. Bluh recommends user-friendly interfaces such as a current awareness service based on the library's own collection, which like many local collections may be underused.

Considering the overall cost models for ILL borrowing derived by the ARL/RLG cost study, Roche advises that potential borrowers consider acquiring recent journal articles from fee-based services.[24] This practice would allow libraries holding older, more specialized collections to respond more quickly in filling requests for these items.

USER INFORMATION-SEEKING
BEHAVIOR AND ACCESS

In her discussion of "social marketing" philosophies in libraries, Johnson points out that asking librarians to study customer needs, wants, and perceptions often can "provoke a vague sense of unease," as the request seems to disregard the librarian's professional judgment.[25] Library service has generally been built not on what customers want but what professional librarians have been trained to determine as their users' needs. Even using the word "customer" in reference to library users has caused more than one professional information provider to bristle.

Many enterprises consider "customer satisfaction" an important effectiveness measure of their service. Libraries have looked to everything from acquisition statistics to use statistics as output measurements of effectiveness. Johnson believes that libraries dealing with decentralized collections and new technologies may need to increase their focus on customers, especially in designing appropriate technical interfaces, managing local and remote collections, working with consultants, and generally getting involved with aspects of library and community development.

THE ART (AND IMPORTANCE) OF BROWSING

King and Griffith researched the economics of electronic publishing and distribution of scholarly articles and the behavior of readers of scholarly articles.[26] According to their findings, professionals identify journals they will read most often by browsing personal subscriptions, routed issues, or the current periodical section of the library. Seminal articles are identified first by referrals from colleagues, then from citations found in other articles studied, and then from automated bibliographic tools, and, finally, by online and printed indexes. Identified articles are obtained by personal subscription, library copy, interlibrary borrowing, document delivery colleagues, and from the author.

The source chosen for retrieval depends on the journal price, membership in a professional society, available funds to buy journals, number of times a journal is read, distance from the library, age of the article needed and the purpose for reading the article. Scholars will use the library to read those journals they consult infrequently, especially if the price of the journal is high—as long as the time and distance to the library is not too great.

FUTURE ACCESS ARTS

The Problems: Defined by ARL

In 1992 the ARL Committee on Access to Information Resources released the White Paper "Maximizing Access, Minimizing Cost: A First Step toward the Information Access Future."[27] This paper, which focused on the future of library access and delivery services, offered a scathing critique of current interlibrary loan practices.

Among the many problems the study found were "a system clogged with badly prepared or improperly handled requests," "lack of data on cost-effectiveness," and an accounting system that involved too much paper work. Delivery systems which varied from fourth-class mail to immediate transmission via Internet or fax delivery made it difficult to gauge meaningful delivery times. In light of dwindling materials budgets and staff support, "resource sharing" and cooperative collection development were "imperative" for all libraries. Effective resource sharing was dependent on effective interlibrary loan operations.

The report called for reengineering to include new systems for automatic billing, load leveling, more end-user initiation of requests, and increased use of the Internet for the transmission of articles. In essence, the report called for an interlibrary loan system designed to support resource sharing in the emerging new library environment.

An ongoing project to address the challenge of the ARL report is known as the North American Interlibrary Loan and Document Delivery (NAILDD) Project.[28] It is based on the premise that, as academic and research libraries depend more and more on each other to meet the information requirements of their local users, interlibrary loan and document delivery services will "emerge as key success factors in measuring overall library performance." The goal of the project is to promote developments that will improve the delivery of library materials to users at costs that are sustainable for libraries.

Some Solutions

Arizona State University

A study of user behavior in a nonmediated document delivery environment was conducted during a 1994 pilot project at Arizona State University (ASU). The purpose of the project was to provide alternative access to journals not owned in the ASU library.

Faculty were introduced to a selection of end-user online resources which they could use to search for relevant journal article citations. They could then order copies of articles they

selected for fax or Internet delivery using the document ordering mechanisms available on the service they were using.
No limits were set on price or number of articles that could be
ordered; the library paid all charges using funds from the
library's materials budget and a serials cancellation project.

About 150 faculty members participated. Preliminary results showed, however, that faculty used the commercial services mostly for convenience, and that 76.5 percent of the articles ordered through the service were actually held in the
library. ASU subsequently added a campus document delivery service for ASU-held titles, and restricted access to these
titles from the commercial services.

The University of Arizona

Brin and Cochran reported on the task force approach used
by the University of Arizona Library in recommending policy
and services for access.[29] The library was faced with inadequate funding for renewal and acquisition of new resources
and decided to "explore new avenues for providing information resources in the coming decade." A task force composed
of all levels of staff in the library was charged to study access
and ownership issues. Focus groups made up of graduate students and faculty from across disciplines discussed topics
ranging from "how users did research" to "identifying essential resources."

The report's recommendations supported implementation
of an integrated library system which would interface with
other information networks and include access to journal article databases, Internet-accessible online catalogs, and a commercial document delivery database. As a result of the focus
group activity, all ILL costs (except rush delivery) are now
fully subsidized by the library. A major development was the
conversion of the Materials Acquisition Budget (which allowed only capital purchases) into the Information Access
Budget, which now allows for the purchase of such services
as online searching and document delivery.

The University of Tennessee at Knoxville

Heck and Baker discuss the development and implementation of the Scholar's Workstation Project at the University of
Tennessee at Knoxville.[30] The project developed a library-sup-
ported Scholar's Workstation to provide timely access to information at remote nonlibrary sites. The project would install microcomputer workstations configured for access to the
library's OPAC, citation databases, electronic journals, interactive ILL forms, and various other Internet services; publi-
cize availability of the new workstations and train users to
become self-sufficient in searching, accessing, and managing
online information resources; and provide document delivery via the electronic ILL request form, provide campus delivery of library information access model (which could serve
as a vehicle for the introduction of new resources), distribute
model reference assistance (that is, outside a centralized library building), and provide training in the use of electronic
library resources.

CONCLUSION

Technological advances are creating a new library: some call
it a virtual library, others a digital library. Neither is an accurate depiction of what that new library will be, since it must,
inevitably, contain and provide patron access to a multitude
of formats for some time to come. But in exploring the question "What are digital libraries?" Levy and Marshall provide
a neat definition of a "document," especially for our future
use. A document is "all enduring communicative records, including paper materials, electronic files, videotapes, and audiotapes."[31] Our continuing challenge will be to provide access to the documents of the future in the new library.

ENDNOTES

1. Mary E. Jackson, "Library to Library: Revising the National ILL Code: An Overview," *Wilson Library Bulletin* 67 (February 1993): 75–76.

2. Virginia Boucher, *Interlibrary Loan Practices Handbook* (Chicago: American Library Association, 1984).

3. "National Interlibrary Loan Code for the United States, 1993," *RQ* 33 (Summer 1993): 477–479.

4. OCLC's Resource Sharing Strategy, 1994, [Online] at http://www.oclc/org/oclc/man/7959rs.htm

5. Christopher Anderson, "The Accidental Superhighway: A Survey of the Internet," *Economist* 336 (1995): 1–18.

6. Anthony M. Cummings, et al., *University Libraries and Scholarly Communication: Study Prepared for the Andrew W. Mellon Foundation* (Washington, DC: Association of Research Libraries, 1992).

7. Dixon F. Brooke and Allen Powell, "EBSCO 1995 Serial Price Projections," *Serials Review* 20, no. 3 (1994): 85–94.

8. Stuart L. Frazer, "Impact of Periodical Cost Escalation on Small and Medium Sized Academic Libraries: A Survey," *Journal of Academic Librarianship* 18 (September 1992): 159–162.

9. Anna H. Perrault, "The Shrinking National Collection: A Study of the Effects of the Diversion of Duns from Monographs to Serials on the Monograph Collections of Research Libraries," *Library Acquisitions: Practice and Theory* 18, no. 1 (1994): 3–22.

10. Kenden Stubbs, *1992–93 ARL Statistics* (Washington, D.C.: Association of Research Libraries, 1994).

11. Dennis P. Carrigan, "From Just-in-Case to Just-in-Time: Limits to the Alternative Library Service Model," *Journal of Scholarly Publishing* 26 (April 1995): 173–182.

12. Stephen P. Dickson and Virginia Boucher, "A Methodology for Determining Costs of Interlibrary Lending," in *Research Access Through New Technology*, ed. Mary E. Jackson (New York: AMS Press, 1989), 137–159.

13. Marilyn M. Roche, *ARL/RLG Interlibrary Loan Cost Study* (Washington D.C.: Association of Research Libraries, 1993).

14. Miriam A. Drake, "Buying Articles in the Future," *Serials Review* 18, no. 1–2 (1992): 75–77.

15. A.W. Ferguson and K. Kehoe, "Access versus Ownership: What Is More Cost-Effective in the Sciences?" *Journal of Library Administration* 19, no. 2 (1993): 89–99.

16. Eleanor A. Gossen and Suzanne Irving, "Ownership versus Access and Low-Use Periodical Titles," *Library Resources and Technical Services* 39 (January 1994): 43–52.

17. Gay N. Dannally, "Resource Sharing in the Electronic Era: Potentials and Paradoxes," *Library Trends* 43 (Spring 1995): 661–678.

18. Richard M. Dougherty, "A Conceptual Framework for Organizing Resource Sharing and Shared Collection Development Programs," *Journal of Academic Librarianship* 14 (November 1988): 470–496.

19. Patricia Puck Dominquez and Luke Swindler, "Cooperative Collection Development at the Research Triangle University Libraries: A Model for the Nation," *College and Research Libraries* 54 (November 1993): 470–496.

20. Bruce R. Kingma, "Access to Journal Articles: A Model of the Cost Efficiency of Document Delivery and Library Consortia," in *ASIS 1994 Proceedings of the 57th ASIS Annual Meeting* (Medford, N.J.: Learned Information, 1994), 8–16.

21. Elizabeth Logan, "What Price Cooperation: Economics and Interlibrary Cooperation" in *ASIS 1994 Proceedings of the 57th ASIS Annual Meeting* (Medford, N.J.: Learned Information, 1994), 17–25.

22. David Kohl, "OhioLINK: A Vision of the 21st Century," *Library Hi Tech* 12, no. 3 (1994): 29–34.

23. Pamela Bluh, "Striking a Balance: Document Delivery in the Nineties," *Law Library Journal* 85 (1993): 599–608.

24. Roche, *ARL/RLG Interlibrary Loan Cost Study*.

25. Diane Tobin Johnson, "Focus on the Library Customer: Revelation, Revolution, or Redundancy?" *Library Trends* 43, (winter 1995): 318–325.

26. King and Griffith. 1994.

27. Association of Research Libraries, Committee on Access to Information Resources, "Maximizing Access, Minimizing Cost: A First Step toward the Information Access Future," (Washington, D.C.: Association of Research Libraries, 1993).

28. Mary E. Jackson, "Library to Library: NAILLD Project," Wilson Library Bulletin 68 (November 1993): 66–68.

29. Beth Brin and Elissa Cochran, "Access and Ownership in the Academic Environment: One Library's Progress Report," *Journal of Academic Librarianship* 20 (March 1994): 207–212.

30. Jeff Heck and Gayle Baker, "The Scholar's Workstation Project at the University of Tennessee," *Library Hi Tech* 13, no. 3 (1995): 55–66.

31. David M. Levy and Catherine C. Marshall, "Going Digital: A Look at Assumptions Underlying Digital Libraries," *Communications of the ACM* [Association for Computing Machinery], 38, no. 4 (1995): 77–83.

9

The Evolution of Technical Services to Serve the Digital Academic Library

Liz Lane and Barbara Stewart

Here is a compelling summary of accomplishment and a tantalizing outline of possibilities. Liz Lane and Barbara Stewart's description of technical services' progress from the old library into the new sounds much more revolutionary than evolutionary: the changes wrought by computerization on technical services have transformed these library operations from a "stable," predictable environment into a hotbed of constant change and seemingly endless prospects for greater efficiency, access, and service. The message Liz and Barbara are sending is a powerful one (those entering the field—as well as library educators and librarian mentors—please take special note): librarians by definition need to be flexible, creative, entrepreneurial, and visionary to carry on the kinds of work done in technical service departments today.—CML

Academic library technical services departments are in a precarious position. On the one hand, they have always been the backbone of the library—the behind-the-scenes location where the work of ordering, processing, cataloging, and preservation of materials is done. On the other hand, the digital environment has become a threat to traditional technical services processes. The proliferation of vendors who are ready, willing, and able to take over many of these functions for libraries has forced most academic technical services departments to take a long, hard look at what services they have traditionally provided, how much it costs to provide them in this manner, and how much they would save if they took advantage of some of the outsourcing vendors are willing to provide. As a result of this process, massive restructuring of departments has become commonplace. Hierarchy is undergoing a "flattening" process, support staff are finding that they are being called on to do increasingly complex tasks, work groups are being formed, and librarians are reevaluating what they do best, what is absolutely essential, and what they can no longer afford to do themselves.

The advent of the digital, or "paperless" society, offers great advantages for the library user. First of all, the tradition of laboriously searching through card catalogs to find items has become a thing of the past. Online catalogs, or OPACS, have been providing access to library collections for approximately the last 20 years. Since the creation, in 1989, of the World Wide Web, libraries and library vendors have dreamed of a way to provide a seamless interface for their patrons—to allow them to search not only their own library catalogs, but other catalogs all over the world, as well as access full-text documents and explore the vastness of the Web. The possible utility of digital text has been proven. The problems of access, archival storage, and preservation are only now beginning to be explored.

For a long while, the concept of "publish or perish" dictated what scholarly information was available in paper format. Academic libraries were faced with the task of choosing the best possible books, journals, videos, and microtext to satisfy the demands of each academic department. The glut of printed materials forced many libraries to join regional consortia, and also to rely heavily on interlibrary loan. The ramifications of these decisions were twofold. First, by joining consortia, libraries acknowledged that they alone could not provide all the materials needed by their patrons, and that they would purchase selectively, according to the guidelines set up by the consortia. Second, interlibrary loan grew exponentially, to the point where many large libraries became net lenders instead of net borrowers.

Interlibrary loan has three great disadvantages: the cost, the time factor, and the potential unsuitability of the material. Cost can become prohibitive when it is necessary to obtain specialized material from a charging institution. In addition, although many patrons require their materials yesterday, the absolute quickest ILL turnaround approaches 48 hours, and an unusual, rare item can take a month to be obtained, if at all. Most libraries do not loan specialized or reference materials. Many are willing to make photocopies or fax needed material, but this is also time consuming and expensive. Finally, many patrons request items, based on the author or title or the scanty information provided by the cataloging record, hoping that they will contain the needed information. Many of these patrons are disappointed upon the receipt of the material because the information required is not in the texts that were ordered.

Enter digital publishing. With the widespread availability of the Internet, support for the transfer of digital information is becoming a reality. Glance through columns of "On the Internet," the *Chronicle of Higher Education*'s weekly listing of projects that involve digital and electronic information. Many of these projects are cosponsored by businesses and foundations, in cooperation with major universities and research institutions. One of the most intriguing projects is the Andrew W. Mellon Foundation's $700,000 grant to Columbia University Libraries to explore the implications of the electronic book on the research library.[1] By utilizing new, improved search engines on the World Wide Web, a patron can now locate the exact pieces of required information, from the privacy of home or office.

What is technical services' role in this transaction? First, the appropriate digital texts must be made accessible to the user. Accessibility requires an easy search mechanism on the library's OPAC, the storage and maintenance of large amounts of digital texts (either by acquiring electronic journal subscriptions or by accessing the appropriate online databases or Web sites), and a proficiency in delivering these texts to the patron's desktop, if necessary. This process is complex, to say the least. The acquisitions department is the most logical place to employ a local copyright and licensing librarian. This issue will be discussed further in the Acquisitions section of this essay.

How does this new role affect the academic library technical services environment? The traditional, conservative organizational structure must be revamped. Room must be made for creativity and innovation. New technologies must be explored and implemented. Today's rapidly changing digital scene requires libraries not only to choose appropriate technologies in a reasonable time frame, but also to wander into the "cutting-edge" stages of technologies. It is no longer possible to maintain the status-quo. If academic libraries do not embrace the new technologies, then they will be forced into a museum-type existence—good only to store archival materials of historic relevance.

A balance must be achieved and maintained between printed and electronic resources. A distinction must be drawn between which materials will continue to be purchased in paper format, and which materials will not. The dynamic nature of information must be explored. Which resources available on the World Wide Web are stable enough to be combined with the traditional library OPAC? What methods will be utilized to update links, and who will perform the updating? Who will provide new links? What methods will be used to index and classify these resources? This is a large task, and technical services staff are poised to tackle these issues in a way that academic reference departments may not be.

For the past 25 years, technical services departments have been undergoing continuous change driven by new technologies. The introduction of bibliographic utilities, such as OCLC and RLIN, and automated library systems created an entirely new functionality. Library staff once utilized to perform needed manual tasks, such as physically shelving cards in the card catalog, have been reassigned into entering bibliographic information online. Acquisitions and cataloging staff are reaping the benefits of years of hard work, by becoming proficient users of new technical services workstations at their desktops. No longer must staff run from terminal to terminal to access different online systems. Now it is possible to access the local OPAC, replete with full-text electronic databases, bibliographic utilities (such as OCLC and RLIN), a word processing program (such as Microsoft Word), a local UNIX system to access e-mail, and many other seamless options.

These integrated online systems come with a new set of problems for staff to resolve. How can staff be protected from the effects of repetitive stress injuries? Which staff can be relied on to produce accurate bibliographic records online? Which staff are capable of Web page development and maintenance? Which staff need more training and support? Which staff can train and support their fellow employees? Which staff would be better utilized as a liaison to public services and faculty?

Organizational Change

New technology increases the interdependence of technical services operations and fosters more interaction with all areas of the library, particularly with the reference department, circulation department, bibliographers, and systems staff. It is impossible for a technical services department to function well without adequate systems backup. Lines are becoming blurred among the computer center, interlibrary loan, technical services, and collection development areas, and there will necessarily be a continuous flattening of the hierarchy with the development of work teams and shared decision making among these areas. Organizational barriers will decline as functions become more decentralized and interdependent with integrated information systems. Continuous review of technical services processes and functions will be required in this changeable environment. The review process needs to combine a definition of goals and the inclusion of all staff. A phased-in approach for organizational change with good communication, appropriate staff development, and education will help to ensure success.

STAFF NEEDS

Librarians and staff need training to manage information, and to be flexible, adaptable, and innovative.[2] They need a working knowledge of new information structures, access points, and standards beneficial to the integration of new formats into the library. Depending on where work on electronic and digital files is completed, technical services staff need current knowledge of new hardware and software, including hypermedia and electronic format terminology. Most important, technical services personnel need to understand the underlying implications of new technology. How will better indexing techniques improve access to information? How will scanning tables of contents and graphics improve OPAC records? How will improving the structure and content of bibliographic records enhance retrieval?

Many staff members are being assigned higher-level work, which then requires an upward reclassification of jobs in the automated technical services environment. Work previously done at lower levels has either become automated, outsourced to a library vendor, or is not done anymore. Sometimes it is harder to stop doing old, established tasks than to implement new ones. Staff members feel a responsibility to continue established routines. This is where training and providing a broader view of library goals is required. Only by understanding the necessity for new routines and tasks will staff members feel comfortable and optimistic about the future. Library educators and administrators need to foster a spirit of creativity and encourage risk-takers to pursue careers in technical services.

ACQUISITIONS

Perhaps no other section of technical services has benefited more from the introduction of automated library systems than acquisitions. Verification of bibliographic information, preparation, transmittal and cancellation of orders can now be completed more efficiently. Electronic transmission of order and billing information between vendor and client is becoming commonplace. The automated process provides access to the library's own collection and the bibliographic records at many other libraries, by searching the database of a bibliographic utility or the files of other online catalogs via the Internet. Automated systems can provide budget, collection usage, and statistical reports useful to management and decision making

The relationship between library automation vendors and acquisitions staff illustrates how promptly vendors will respond to librarians' needs. The ordering and claiming process used to be quite time-consuming and costly, necessitating three and four copies of each transaction. Enter the Yankee Book Peddler (http://www.ybp.com). Yankee specializes in the provision of selection, acquisition, cataloging records, and complete shelf-ready processing. They serve as a secure, Internet-based, automatic network for serials claiming, payments, and renewals. Another excellent company is RoweCom (http://www.rowe.com). Payment is accomplished online with the use of a pre-approved digitized signature and BancOne.

The University of California at Berkeley has chosen RoweCom's Subscribe '97, stating that they save at least 8 percent of their serials budget by taking advantage of RoweCom's automated linkages to their OPAC. Other services provided by using online subscription services are approval and blanket orders, duplicate control, electronic ordering interfaces, bibliographic records, tables of contents, binding, stamping, and all other forms of preprocessing. Services like these make the role of the acquisitions librarian considerably easier.

Let's consider, however, the two biggest problems facing acquisitions departments today: reduced budgets and a glut of information in all formats to be purchased. Libraries cannot possibly collect materials in all subject areas; therefore they must pick and choose in accordance with their researchers' needs. This is not a new phenomenon. In 1962 Robert Downs stated

We are living in an era when the outpouring of print in all its forms has become enormous, pointing towards an acute

necessity for carefully defined acquisitions policies, specialization of fields among libraries, and cooperative programs for acquisitions . . . The laissez-faire philosophy
which university librarians are inclined to follow, attempting to achieve virtual autonomy in a wide area of knowledge and to serve all the needs of their clienteles without
reference to other institutions, probably calls for re-exami-
nation, although I am not optimistic that there will be any
radical change in the attitude unless or until a financial
pinch is felt.[3]

Thirty-five years later, the "financial pinch" has arrived.
With the option of purchasing materials in print, digital, or
microtext, and with the large license fees that come attached
to electronic information, library acquisitions budgets will
continue to be a pressing issue. Many academic libraries are
experiencing actual reductions in their overall budget, at the
same time that information costs (including serial prices) are
soaring. At the same time, new positions in acquisitions departments are needed, including a copyright and licensing
liaison, who will be responsible for making sure that the digital licensing fees paid by the library are fair and in good order.
    How will acquisitions departments survive the current
budget crunch? First, the need to acquire materials in a regional consortial arrangement is essential. Duplication of expensive titles is a luxury that most academic libraries can no
longer afford. Second, vendors like Yankee Book Peddler and
RoweCom should be investigated, and labor-intensive tasks
must be automated. Third, it might be beneficial to consoli-
date acquisitions and collection development under one roof.
In many libraries the bibliographic selection resides in units
separate from the acquisitions function. Communal decisions
must be made on which materials will be acquired, digitized,
or retrieved from other locations. Language "units" consist-
ing of a bibliographer and acquisitions staff should be considered. Finally, interlibrary loan and resource sharing should
become a priority function, as well as providing direct access
to fee-based, full-text journal retrieval services.
    Another area to explore in more detail is the gift and ex-

change function, relegated in most libraries to the acquisition department. Online sites such as the United States Book Exchange (http://www.usbe.com) provide all missing back issues at a cost of $7.00 each. A very colorful and innovative program at the University of Florida Libraries is another excellent example: ten journals are available for exchange programs with other institutions, museums, and associations. In this way the University of Florida receives over 1,000 journals and monographs monthly.

Bindery and preservation issues also fall under the rubric of acquisitions. In the same manner, preservation of digital materials should be handled by the acquisitions department. When all materials expenditures are handled in the same place, staff accustomed to managing budgets can be responsible for all purchases, both print and digital. Transfer of funds from the acquisitions budgets to the purchase of document delivery services will likely alter the amount of money available for the purchase of materials to be added to the collection. The processes associated with acquisitions, such as verification, ordering, receipt, and processing are the same as for interlibrary loan and document delivery, so these functions could be combined with acquisitions. This combination will facilitate implementation of "just-in-time" acquisition, with trained acquisitions staff determining whether their department, interlibrary loan, or document delivery will meet the customer's needs. Fee-based document delivery should be utilized when the material requested is unique and likely not to be useful for other members of the library community.

The role preservation plays in the overall role of the library will be dependent on the decisions made concerning the future directions for the development of the collection. For traditional printed materials, the use of library binding will remain the preservation process of choice. If fewer paper journals and monographs are purchased, binding will remain, but with a diminished volume of activity. Microforms will continue to play a role in the preservation of back issues of some items, especially newspapers, unwieldy printed materials, and materials from countries where acid-free paper is not an option. Cooperative and collaborative efforts will be the key to future preservation efforts of printed materials. Coordinated preservation projects have already been carried out under programs sponsored by SALALM (the Seminar on the Acquisition of Latin American Library Materials), the New York State Conservation Preservation Program, the National Endowment for the Humanities, and the Research Libraries Group Preservation Office.

Libraries are unlikely to eliminate earlier formats from their collections. These formats will exist alongside the information available in electronic formats. The ability to be able to use earlier formats that also depend on earlier technology may be difficult, if not impossible, to achieve and to resolve. The issues regarding ongoing usability of information requires much more discussion than it has yet been accorded.

Researchers require electronic access to full-text materials, when possible. Some items will continue to be available only in paper format, and these should continue to be purchased. Back runs of electronic journals should also be maintained, and licenses must be checked to assure that back issues of electronic journals will remain the property of the library purchasing them. Publishers have an incentive to publish electronically, thus avoiding the high cost of paper and printing. Reassessment of the scholarly publishing environment will be an ongoing concern.

The acquisition of access rights to digital information still needs to be resolved. Before digital libraries become a reality, the issues of copyright and licensing must be addressed or the available electronic data will be limited to those items not under current copyright or those produced to be available in the public domain. The Library of Congress, in collaboration with many stakeholders, is studying copyright issues in the electronic environment. The issues of copyright and licensing and other intellectual property issues associated with electronic documents may be some of the most difficult to grapple with, because of the impact on monetary issues.

CATALOGING

Cataloging materials has always been a focal point of technical services. Before the development of MARC (machine-read-able cataloging) in the early 1970s, it was extremely difficult to locate material by subject matter, or by any criteria other than author or title. The MARC format allowed catalogers to provide subject headings, local notes, serials holdings information, and much more. Keyword searching simplified and enhanced public usage of the OPAC. With the advent of keyword-searchable, full-text electronic documents, the dream of many olden-day catalogers has been fulfilled—texts that can be searched in many different ways, word by word. A bright future emerges—one in which all documents owned by a library could be scanned, indexed, and made available to patrons throughout the world via the World Wide Web. Yet, there are still many obstacles to this dream—foremost of which are the high cost of digital storage, the immense amount of time involved, and the lack of staff to facilitate such a project.

Coupled with the desire to provide increased access to library materials is the necessity for catalogers to incorporate changes in their practices that will reduce the cost of cataloging by improving productivity. More materials, both print and electronic, will require cataloging in a shorter amount of time. Technical services workstations equipped with labor-saving devices such as the Cataloger's Desktop and Classification Plus allow cataloging staff to access OCLC, RLIN (Research Libraries Information Network), CATSS (Catalog Support System) or other bibliographic utilities; subject headings and changes; classification schedules ; language and geographic codes; format information; the World Wide Web; and other library catalogs, as well as their own, at one PC terminal. Other cost reductions could include eliminating practices that do not enhance access to material, accepting cataloging from other libraries with minimal changes, and participating in cooperative cataloging efforts.

Shared cataloging is a highly specialized craft, one that does not lend itself well to outsourcing unless the materials to be cataloged are small groups of highly discrete information that no one locally has the expertise to catalog. Examples of outsourceable material would include those written in a language unknown to the local library staff, or materials with special archival significance which require extensive specialized research. Administrators are discovering that, although cataloging may look like an area where staff could be reduced and budgets extended, a well-equipped cataloging department is essential for implementing the indexing and classification of digital materials, as well as for maintaining the quality of an OPAC. Such recent fiascoes as the outsourcing agreement between the State Library of Hawaii and Baker & Taylor prove that taking the collection development and cataloging responsibilities out of the hands of local librarians is not in the best interest of the patrons being served, and that it is difficult to create a library profile that includes all the nuances a particular library needs, and allows a library vendor to satisfy a client.

Traditional descriptive cataloging will continue until the ability exists for software programs to search large text files efficiently. Inclusion of abstracts and tables of contents in catalog records will enhance the usability of the information, but may also increase the amount of time necessary to catalog it. The indexing of tables of contents might be more advantageous if purchased directly from the publisher. Blackwell North America, for example, has produced Bookscope, a CD-ROM database that includes searchable tables of contents, selected abstracts, and book reviews.

The enhanced capabilities of the OPAC (including linking to other databases and to the World Wide Web, and adding sound bytes and images to cataloging records) can only improve our standing with our patrons as premier providers of information. Many projects are now under way to catalog and index Web resources in a meaningful way. CyberStacks (http://www.public.iastate.edu/~CYBERSTACKS/OCLC.htm) is "a centralized, integrated, and unified collection of significant WWW and other Internet resources categorized using the Library of Congress classification scheme." The OCLC Internet Cataloging Project (http://orc.rsch.oclc.org:6990) is the "identification, selection, and cataloging of Internet-accessible resources through a coordinated cooperative nationwide effort between OCLC, colleges, university libraries, and other repositories of electronic information." Finally, the University of Michigan Digital Library Project (http://http2.sils.umich.

edu/UMDL/overview.html) "embraces the open, evolving, decentralized advantages of the Web and introduces computational mechanisms to temper its inherent chaos."

These projects (with the exception of the OCLC Internet Cataloging Project, which utilizes MARC fields exclusively) interpret cataloging rules with more flexibility and common sense rather than strictly adhering to the MARC format. The agreement on the elements for a core record for monographs, and the collaboration of the United States, Canada, Great Britain, and Australia in creating a record usable worldwide, mark a beginning of user-friendly cooperative cataloging—that is, more efficient and balanced cataloging which increases the access points desired by the end-user of the OPAC. Online catalogs will continue to provide users with the ability to select the depth of information that will meet their needs.

The role of catalogers is changing from one devoted primarily to cataloging of materials in the library, to one involved with the task of enhancing information access points for electronic documents, wherever they may be located. Many cataloging staff members are excited by the challenges presented in the evaluation and classification of Web resources, and are willing to pursue new methods of indexing and categorization more suited to electronic documents. Although many libraries will outsource their cataloging tasks to bibliographic utilities or consortia, cataloging as we know it will continue to exist and be refined in the years to come.

Until there are changes in the formats used in automated library systems, catalogers will occupy a pivotal role in the design and development of automated systems to support the researcher's quest for information. The two most commonly stated observations about the Internet are the vast amount of information it possesses and the lack of organization and reasonable access it affords. Catalogers' strengths in organizing information can assist in building bridges to these electronic resources and improving decisions concerning the creation and storage of digital information.

Some additional issues facing catalogers include the cataloging of materials in backlogs and materials in new formats, and the addition of new information to cataloging records.

Many large academic libraries have significant collections that have never been cataloged and, therefore, provide minimal or no access to the materials contained in them. Library catalogs available on the Internet could offer opportunities for shared cataloging information and reduce the amount of original cataloging for these materials. The diversity of formats will challenge catalogers to describe and provide access to the new forms of information. Format integration and the incorporation of new fields for electronic formats demand new approaches to catalog and location access. There continue to be issues regarding the number of bibliographic records required for multiple versions of materials, as well as continuing concern with the functional inaccessibility of materials that have been cataloged but still cannot be found. Examples include works published in groups and works cataloged or classified as part of a series.[4]

SERIALS

Serials play a significant role in the scholarly environment. Researchers in the science and technology areas usually indicate that serials are more important than monographs for their research. Publishers, researchers, librarians, and subscription agents are considering the implications of the migration to electronic journals and documents. The staggeringly high cost of some journal subscriptions has resulted in major changes in serials acquisition; double-digit rates of increase in serials prices have forced many academic libraries to maintain serial cancellation projects. These massive projects consume considerable staff resources as well as time. Some reductions in serial purchases can also be attributed to the transfer of funds to support document delivery.

Serial costs will rise for the next few years, owing to increases in foreign publishing , the cost of paper, and decreases in the value of the U.S. dollar. Libraries are exploring access alternatives to serial information. (*Editor's note: For an extensive discussion of these alternatives, please see Mary Cahill's essay in Part 3 of this volume.*) Generally access is made available through interlibrary loan and document delivery.

Currently no one source supplies full-text capability to a wide range of serial titles; however, the number of full-text serials is growing. Regardless of which combination of formats is chosen, the factors to be considered involve selection, receiving, cataloging, storage, and archiving—basically the same factors needed in handling paper serials. The difference lies in the increased use of technology and the implications for access through online systems.

CONCLUSION

The most challenging aspect facing technical services units in academic libraries today will continue to be that of keeping pace with the continuous changes in technology and information sources. All staff must be involved in discussions concerning strategies and the development of implementation plans for new methods to succeed. Organizational change will be necessary to shift old resources to provide new services. Fortunately, the inherent strengths of technical services staff for finding, managing, processing, and using electronic information holds great promise for the new academic library.

ENDNOTES

1. "Electronic Book Potential in $700,000 Columbia Study," *Library Journal* 24 (May 15, 1995): 1.

2. Peggy Johnson, *Automation and Organizational Change in Libraries* (Boston: G. K. Hall, 1991), 30.

3. Robert Downs, "The Implementation of Book Selection Policy in University and Research Libraries," in *Selection and Acquisition Procedures in Medium-Sized and Large Libraries*, ed. Herbert Goldhor (Champaign, Ill.: Illinois Bookstore, 1963), (Allerton Park Institute, No. 9), 8.

4. Sheila S. Intner, *Interfaces: Relations Between Library Technical and Public Services* (Englewood, Colo.: Libraries Unlimited, 1993), 40.

Additional Resources

Corbin, John. "Technical Services for the Electronic Library," *Library Administration and Management* 6(Spring 1992): 86–90.

The Emerging Virtual Research Library; ARL SPEC Kit 186 (Washington, D.C.: Association of Research Libraries, 1992).

Gorman, Michael. "The Academic Library in the Year 2001: Dream or Nightmare or Something in Between," *Journal of Academic Librarianship* 17 (March 1991): 4–9.

Levy, David M. and Catherine C. Marshall. Going Digital: A Look at Assumptions Underlying Digital Libraries, Communications of the ACM, 38(4) April 1995, 77–84.

Leonhardt, Thomas W., ed. *Technical Services in Libraries: Systems and Applications*, Foundations in Library and Information Science, vol. 25 (Greenwich, Conn.: JAI Press, 1992).

Saunders, Laverna M., ed. *The Virtual Library: Visions and Realities*. Westport, Conn.: Meckler, 1993.

Smith, Linda E., and Prudence W. Dalrymple, eds. *Designing Information: New Roles for Librarians*, Urbana-Champaign, Ill.: University of Illinois, 1993. (Clinic on Library Applications of Data Processing, 1992).

PART IV:

INFORMATION PROVIDERS

10

Making the Internet Manageable for Your Users (and Yourself)

Abbie Jan Basile

The case can be made that Abbie Basile is single-handedly making the Internet manageable in this chapter: she covers a huge amount of territory here on Internet reference and instruction issues and applications. I've already cribbed quite a bit for my classes from her suggestions.—CML

The thrill of victory, the agony of defeat. . . . Internet users can relate intimately to that phrase. Getting an e-mail reply from someone in Austria less than ten minutes after you sent your message, finding that obscure computing term in an online hacker's dictionary, locating census data for your county and state—it's all on the Net. Of course, getting lost in mile-deep menus and hierarchies, clicking your way into hypertext oblivion . . . those are possibilities, as well.

What role does the Internet play in the "recreated" academic library? Lacking a crystal ball, I base my answers on current uses of the Internet in libraries, as well as issues and options to be considered for your library's Internet services, present and future. Let me discuss these in three sections: librarians as Internet consumers, librarians teaching others to be effective Internet consumers, and librarians as Internet producers.[1]

The first of these sections is the "leanest," since most academic librarians are already using the Internet on a regular basis. I'll go into greater depth in the remaining two sections.

LIBRARIANS AS INTERNET CONSUMERS

Most librarians don't need to be persuaded to use the Internet in their work. They already use it heavily, some introduced to it by their users, some under pressure to do so from their peers and administrators, while others are out in front, leading the pack, well ahead of the never-ending tide of Internet newbies. They're creating Web pages, editing electronic journals, designing Internet credit courses for faculty, students, and their peers.

The majority of Internet-using librarians I meet and whose postings I read on various newsgroups and lists want to become more proficient as Internet consumers, often to increase their skills as Internet instructors. Others are desperate to use the Net but still lack access.

Not to use the Net in our information work is to deny users access to a wealth of information that, in many cases, continues to be free and fairly easily accessible. It can now be argued that the lack of Net access in any library is a form of passive censorship, that any librarian who has any financial resources to acquire materials and equipment needs to factor Net access into the library's budget—and *not* doing so is a grave disservice to his or her clientele.

At the same time, it's crucial to acknowledge that library-provided Net use often needs to be selective—responsive to the needs of the community to which the access is being provided. Internet-informed librarians are able to apply our expertise as evaluators, organizers, and teachers of information resources in making Net information available to our users. The lack of a Net connection in any library today is a serious shortcoming—even if the only connection is in the sole librarian's office. All librarians needs to have at least some grasp of what the Net consists of if they are to have any credibility in today's information industry.

Meanwhile, many of our users are out there surfing the

Net with wild abandon—coming to us with questions about a new Web site, or questions about finding an electronic mailing list in their subject area. How do we become effective Net consumers ourselves? Essentially by doing the same thing: by exploring the Net, crawling the Web, and throwing ourselves into the Net fray regularly. That's why that Net connection in the librarian's office is so important: it's not sufficient just to hook up a PC and say to library users, "Let 'er rip!" The librarian needs to be able to offer Net research and use guidance and skills just as for any other library resource. And for Net tools, experience is the best teacher. Acclimating oneself to Web browsers alone can be a time-consuming task, but it's necessary for all librarians to undertake it. This goes for every practicing librarian in academe today, from the entry-level cataloger to the library director. Within the year, you'll have egg on your face at some point, in some meeting, or in some user encounter, if you aren't at least conversant in Net lingo and basic topology. Get on your browser and ride—now.

LIBRARIANS TEACHING OTHERS TO BE INTERNET CONSUMERS

If listserv postings and conference topics are any indication of reality, it would seem that providing Internet instruction is becoming the ruling passion in academic circles these days. As with other instructional projects, the delivery of successful Internet instruction is dependent on a variety of factors, including, but not limited to, creating a cadre of capable instructors, having access to sufficient networked equipment, and engaging in ample planning and publicity. These factors should be familiar to librarians who have planned other types of instructional services.

CREATING CAPABLE INSTRUCTORS

Assessing Available Staff Resources

Unless you are a one-person operation, you probably won't want to take on teaching the Internet alone (if you *are* a one-person operation, we suggest you apply the following suggestions to yourself where appropriate). If you have an appreciable number of students and/or faculty needing Internet instruction, your library, as well as your sanity, will benefit from having an empowered, skilled, and enthusiastic group of Internet instructors. Be warned right up front about the Internet paradox, however: being an Internet expert does not necessarily a great Net instructor make. Rogue surfers may be able to get anywhere they want on the Net or the Web, but they may be wholly incapable of teaching others how to replicate their results (until they learn some instructional techniques).

The ideal Internet teacher not only has some idea of what is actually "out there," but also understands the way Internet tools work and is familiar with teaching methods (electronic and otherwise) and different teaching and learning styles. If you plan to offer sessions on specific subject areas, you may want to get your subject expert librarians into the pool of Internet instructors (about which we'll talk more later). In planning for staff Internet training you'll need to assess the staff's current level of teaching experience, their experience with and comfort using Internet tools, and their knowledge of subject-based Net resources.

It is usually a big leap from being a lone Internet user to standing in front of a room full of faculty and offering instruction on Web browsers, and thus identifying yourself as the resource person to whom they'll come for Internet help in the future. Allow enough time in your planning process for training future instructors to make this transition: give them time to investigate and use the tools they'll be teaching. Provide them with a solid Net reference work, such as Ed Krol's *Whole Internet Guide*, to reinforce what they've learned in the training sessions. (With the good guides, they might even read entire portions of it—egad!) It's handy to be able to put your hands on a detailed explanation of a tool or resource when you're by yourself in your office and something goes wrong.

You still need to get those instructors up in front of the room, however. An excellent confidence builder for new Internet instructors is team teaching. If possible, team up a novice Net user with a more experienced Internet teacher/ user. Having that other body in the room "just in case" does wonders for the new teacher's ability to execute successfully his or her portion of the instructional session. For those who are very apprehensive about moving from Net user to Net instructor, attending a few sessions as the hands-on rover or typist for the other instructor allows the newcomer to get a feel for the pace of the session and the types of questions and problems participants have. Eventually, the lines will become blurred between the novices and the "old hands" and, with any luck, you will soon have former novices teaming up with each other.

Beyond boosting confidence and skills, team teaching is a necessity for a hands-on environment if you have more than five or six folks show up (a pair of roller blades is helpful, too—but you'll still need multiple bodies to rove from machine to machine, kibitzing and de-glitching). Team teaching benefits the user by offering a better teacher-student ratio, and by giving students a mixture of teaching styles and approaches from which to learn. Additionally, instructors who are interested in peer evaluation of their teaching can gain that information from a colleague with whom they've taught.

Staff Training

There are several steps to take to increase your chances of a successful Internet training program for staff. Several of these have been duplicated in various staff training environments, while others are culled from a detailed e-mail message from Catherine Thomas, User Services Librarian at Columbia University, which outlines Columbia's comprehensive Internet staff training program.[2]

This is not a detailed list of "how-to" train the trainers (that is, which tools to cover and how), but it is a selective group of initiatives that encourage library staff to get involved and become active and enthusiastic Internet users.

- Create an electronic mailing list, newsgroup, or simple e-mail groupname for the Internet instructors and encourage them to use it to share their Net experiences, favorite sites, sites to avoid, questions, and ideas with the others in the group. The coordinator of the training could also post questions to the group to spark discussion among its members.

- Supply each instructor with an Internet reference source. The Columbia University Libraries' staff program places a selection of Internet publications on reserve for use by trainers and trainees.

- To keep trainees challenged and motivated to maintain and strengthen their Net skills, provide them with information on how to stay current on Internet resources, issues, and Net instruction ideas. Packets I have created with this type of information always are appreciated, since they pinpoint specific listservs, print journals, electronic journals, and Net sites that trainers can use to stay on top of Net resources and developments. If they find resources not mentioned in the materials you've provided, they can post that information to the group's online discussion forum, so that others can benefit from their discovery. This practice also serves as a reminder to others in the group (who may be slower in taking to the Net) that their colleagues are out there surfing and are finding relevant, helpful information.

- Encourage trainees to attend local Internet user group meetings. Many regions in the country now have a local Internet users group, which usually meets monthly and whose meetings you may want to promote to your trainees. These are usually informal gatherings where Net users from a variety of skill levels come to share and gather information. In the Cincinnati area, such a group is part of the local library consortium's interest group structure. The majority of its members are novice Net users but the informal nature of the meetings allows everyone to participate in discussion. Group members take turns demonstrating an Internet tool or site at the monthly meeting. The Columbia program also recommends attendance at such meetings.

- Encourage trainees to create Internet guides for a particular subject. This goal-oriented activity will help focus their Net exploration and will definitely strengthen their skills. Some of your staff may find their topic has already been covered elsewhere, while others may use another guide as a starting off point.

Since you are training your fellow colleagues, you will need to use your own judgment about which, if any, of these activities you mandate as a commitment to becoming an Internet instructor, and which efforts will be sufficient to encourage their participation.

EQUIPMENT AND FACILITIES FOR INTERNET INSTRUCTION

Optimal Internet instruction must take place in a hands-on environment. In-class computer use allows attendees to experience the pitfalls and problems that are inevitable in Internet use while the instructors are at hand and able to offer advice and detailed help. Of course, not all libraries have such facilities available.

If necessary, work out a cooperative agreement with departments on campus that have computer-equipped classrooms available. You could agree to offer instruction to that department's faculty first before using the room to give instruction to a wider audience. But the rule of thumb is: beg, borrow, or steal a campus classroom that has networked workstations. It will make a world of difference for you and your users.

One thing not to be overlooked is the effect the size of the classroom will have on your sessions. A room that fits the wish list below but only has eight workstations will require that you offer several sessions in order to accommodate any popularity your workshops gain. On the other hand, a large room with 40 workstations will require several rovers or helpers for the hands-on portion of the session. You'll also want to think about the traffic problems you may encounter with such a large group—for instance, the impact of having them all connect to the same resource at the same time.

My equipment wish list for an electronic classroom (or, "If I were queen of the universe, every electronic classroom would have . . . ") is as follows:

- a networked workstation for each workshop participant, with at least 32 MB RAM, all necessary helper applications available, and the most stable versions of various clients loaded.
- several laser printers to which everyone can send printing requests
- a networked workstation for the instructors, as specified above
- a ceiling-mounted or rearview projector
- a large writing surface *not* blocked by the projection screen
- a broadcasting system to control students' keyboards and monitor displays and to allow a variety of possibilities for projecting on the screen in front and onto all or some monitors
- a variety of lighting options, including note-taking lights, dimmer switches, and blackout window shades
- a document camera for use with written exercises or to be used as a backup with transparencies.

One hands-on tip that can be very successful is to address some of the individuals' questions and problems that come up in the class within a larger group discussion. Since many users have similar difficulties with the same tools, the full class discussion puts out many smaller fires in one step, and isn't that what group instruction is all about? This group summary of problems also allows the instructor to cover hints and tips that may have been omitted during the original instruction time.

For example, if you're covering three tools in one session, you could allow for hands-on use of each tool immediately after you've demonstrated and/or explained it. After that tool's hands-on time, you could plan for a three- to five-minute hands-on recap which would cover some of the problems the attendees experienced and might pass along good tips for getting out of trouble.

Here are some additional teaching tips for the electronic hands-on environment:

- Have at least one rover/helper for every 6–8 participants.
- Be prepared for many levels of questions, from modem access to ftp for compressed files.
- Have referral information ready (such as: phone numbers for the campus computing help desk and the reference desk).
- Stress the dynamic nature of the Net so everyone will be prepared for problems.
- Show your enthusiasm. Acknowledge the problems that will occur with Internet use but don't focus on them. This is fun stuff!
- Know the appropriate break keys for telnet sessions and pass this information on before hands-on time begins.
- Remember, no one knows everything about the Internet. People will be grateful for any information you pass along.
- Know how participants access the Net, so you're prepared for related questions and are familiar with commands and processes they'll be needing to use.
- Have a back-up ready for equipment/connection trouble (for example, overheads, boards, handouts with screen captures, presentation software with "dummy" online sessions).
- Be aware of heavy Net traffic times and plan your demonstrations accordingly.
- Stress the need for people to look at the text files that accompany the library catalogs' telnet sessions. These files contain important login/logout command instructions that may not be displayed once they're in the catalog.
- Double check any Internet addresses you use in handouts and demos.
- Know your room, its equipment and how you will access the Internet. Preparation plays a key role in an instructor's confidence.

PLANNING AND PUBLICITY

Structuring the Instructional Program

There are many possibilities for the content, length, and frequency of Internet instruction sessions. Your decisions will necessarily be based on your own preferences for instruction, as well as the variables discussed previously (such as available staff and room resources).

Sessions can be offered in one long instructional period, but here you must weigh the length of time required to cover the materials adequately versus user comfort and whether their schedules will accommodate a long block of time for workshop attendance. Many libraries offer a series of Internet workshops that take place several times a month or on a predictable schedule, such as every Tuesday afternoon. Dennis Dillon (from the University of Texas at Austin Libraries, where thousands of users have been taught to use the Internet) has noted that frequently offered, shorter Internet sessions seem to benefit learners the most:

> This allows the students to try out what they have learned, and then come to the next class supplied with both a firmer base of understanding, and with any questions that might have arisen during the interval.[3]

With the typical one-shot, 50-minute library instruction session packed to the gills with library services, search strategies, and sources, it is not an easy task to incorporate Internet resources into the game plan. Having Internet-related handouts ready for distribution may be the closest most of us will come to fitting the Net into course-related instruction. On the other hand, Mary Page and Martin Kesselman of Rutgers University make a strong case for finding room for Net resources in our other instructional sessions:

> Treating the Internet as something special and different just perpetuates the perception that it is difficult to use. Instead, librarians [at Rutgers] try to demystify the net-

work by melding discussion of subject-related resources on the Internet with subject resources already available at the library.[4]

This brings us to Internet workshops focused on a particular subject. Relevance of instructional content to a faculty member's research area is the best way we know to achieve high faculty attendance at library instruction sessions. Try scheduling a departmental Internet instruction session during a regularly scheduled department meeting time. Involve the collection development staff for the subject areas to be covered, and work with the department liaisons in setting up the session, both logistically and in terms of advance preparation with the department members. This is truly an ideal instructional situation, in which a Net expert, a teaching expert, and a subject expert are all present for the session.

Finally, you may decide to offer a credit course for Internet resources. A forum for such a course may already exist through your campus honors department, in an "experimental" college where new courses are tried out, or via your continuing education department on campus. Or a faculty member may be interested in developing such a course offering and the two of you can work toward creating a new class for that department.

In their discussion of teaching the Internet, Page and Kesselman highlight the California Polytechnic State University's Internet course, which meets for ten sessions and is offered for one credit. Students gain hands-on experience with resource discovery, as well as resource evaluation, something that should not be overlooked in the open, unlimited environment of the Internet.

Student assignments include oral presentations on three online library catalogs available on the Internet and an annotated bibliography on a research topic that includes at least fifteen relevant citations from various Internet resources, noting how the subject is covered in various resources.[5]

During the summer of 1995, the Miami University Libraries offered an intensive week-long course for one graduate
credit-hour through the School of Education. The course focused on using Internet resources in the K–12 classroom. Students were required to submit brief, "online diary" entries to
the class listserv, in which they discussed one to two Net sites
they would find valuable for use in their own K–12 class activities. Other assignments included a detailed evaluation of
two Web sites (including such aspects as how often the site is
updated, the purpose of the site, the completeness and source
of its information, and its organization and ease of use). For
their final projects, students designed a classroom activity
around a particular Net resource or service. All assignments
were posted to the class listserv.

There are three basic operating principles related to
Internet credit courses. First, put some calls out for syllabi on
appropriate listservs such as NETTRAIN and BI-L, as well as
checking with the ever-wonderful LOEX Clearinghouse[6] in
Ypsilanti, Michigan, to see what course syllabi they have on
hand. Never reinvent the wheel if there is one at hand to copy
or lift. Second, start off small. Don't try to cover all Internet-
related information, background, resources, tools, and subject areas, unless you have allowed for a very large time commitment in your schedule. A one-credit course may be a good
testing ground for your ideas, and from there a more grandi-
ose, comprehensive course can be designed. Third, try your
hand at offering "open" sessions to get a sense of what your
user population's experiences and skills with the Internet are.
This approach will also broaden your background as an
Internet instructor.

Delivery

Having looked at some of the broad issues of providing
Internet instructional services in your library, let's now look
at how you can use the Net to provide instruction and in-
struction-related services. For example, if you create your own
guides for your Net workshops (which usually ends up being necessary because of specific campus network scenarios

and variations in user needs and skill levels), you may want to make them available online via a library or campus-wide server. This service will allow remote users convenient access to helpful information. The same online availability could exist for workshop publicity, including course content, times/dates, instructor contact information, and endorsements from past attendees.

Instructional content can also be delivered over the network, as demonstrated by the University of Illinois at Chicago Library's E-Train listserv course. The entire content of the course is delivered through a listserv to which interested parties with UIC e-mail addresses may subscribe. The course, which is geared toward the UIC network environment, was first offered in 1994 and was repeated in 1995. Two lessons, delivered via e-mail, were sent out per week for eight weeks. The lessons are archived on the library's gopher, Web, and ftp site for ease of access for those who missed the course or are not affiliated with UIC. A four-person Internet Training Class Task Force spent two semesters planning and designing the course and preparing the course materials.

Rama Vishwanatham, co-chair of the task force, estimates that the course had 450 participants the first time it was offered and over 200 the second time.[7] A discussion group was created by library staff based on the assumption that E-train participants would want to join in online discussion about the course and their Internet explorations. (Since the group was not heavily used, it was discontinued for the second E-train class.) Vishwanatham notes that the day-to-day administration of the course and its listserv were not difficult, but that others who plan on presenting instruction in this way should be prepared to deal with connectivity issues, such as the state of the campus networking plan and to what extent faculty will have network access in their offices.

Having identified a need to address additional Internet topics and issues, and having seen a positive response and increased Internet use from the first two offerings, the UIC task force is working on an advanced class called E-train II. This course will cover topics such as the World Wide Web, creating home pages, connectivity issues, and dealing with

multimedia files. The task force will deliver this new instruction via a Web page for the course. Publicity for all of these
courses was facilitated by campus-wide online communication forums, such as UIC's Campus-Wide Academy, as well
as by traditional print sources, such as campus newspapers
and newsletters.

Online instruction can also be delivered via the tool you
are teaching, such as via Web pages for World Wide Web instruction. If you don't get caught up in the glitz of creating
the coolest Web page ever (and trust us, it's better that you
don't!), you can create some pretty straightforward pages
using HTML or an HTML editor. These pages can cover general information such as Web terminology (for example, a glos-
sary with links to graphs of Internet usage, visual depictions
of how the networks on the Net are interconnected, or links
to artists' paintings as an example of the term "hypermedia").

You can also have pages and URLs that address the difference between the text-only browsers (such as Lynx) and the
graphical, full-bells-and-whistles browsers such as Netscape.
Additional instructional Web pages may offer links to various subject sites on the Web, software archives for easy acquisition of helper applications (such as JPEG), and guides on
how to use HTML to create Web pages. The possibilities are
practically limitless and pretty exciting once you begin.

As a means of focusing your instructional Web pages, you
may consider constructing an online system that clearly follows the outline for your in-class session (almost like using
presentation software). All connections to sites or tools you
want to demonstrate and discuss could be easily located
within your pages. An advantage for your users is that the
page and its information and resources will be accessible long
after they leave the workshop.

Regardless of whether you offer in-class or online instruction, for credit or non-credit workshops, the key to successful
instruction is (and this will not be news to many of you) confident, competent, adaptable instructors who have seemingly
unending enthusiasm for the Internet. Even in an online instructional setting, the voice and tone of the messages distributed by the instructor will greatly influence the learner's

attitude toward the Net and toward the library and its instruction staff.

It is important to let our users know that their use of the Internet will not be hassle-free and to present them with possible problems they will encounter. But even this seemingly negative information can be framed as an attempt to give them a realistic view of the network and to reinforce in their minds that many of the difficulties they encounter will not be caused by anything they have done. It's just the Net. At the same time you're pointing out the problems, you can offer alternative solutions—and you can solicit other solutions from the class as an interactive assignment. This kind of supportive, realistic encouragement goes a long way in turning people on to the Internet.

Librarians As Internet Producers

Internet tools exist that can help us, the information organizers extraordinaire, design and maintain online systems that directly respond to the needs and desires of our specific user populations. Using them, librarians can take control of an overall information system's design, screen layout, and screen wording. By listening to user and staff input, employing careful thought toward design principles, and applying the knowledge we have of our users, librarians can make their resources more easily accessible and understood by their patrons.

For instance, libraries can use Web software to create an overall information access system that includes connections to the local OPAC and networked databases, local information (such as library policies, staff information, library instruction schedules, and publicity for special events), local campus resources and the Internet—which can be presented via screens and menus developed by library staff.

TO SERVE OR NOT TO SERVE: ISSUES FOR PROVIDING ACCESS TO INTERNET RESOURCES

A variety of options is available to libraries for the provision of access to Internet resources. On one end of the service spectrum a library can opt for providing access to external Internet resources only. In other words, no Web server is maintained by the library. Instead, the initial starting point for the user is always another institution's or organization's home page or main menu. This scheme, like anything else, has both advantages and disadvantages. By not running an in-house system, the staff does not have to concern itself with system design, maintenance, or content selection. Nor will staff have to maintain the various links and connections found on the pages or menus, a process that can easily consume large amounts of time, especially if not done on a regular basis. (I used to set aside four to six hours every week for fixing problem links on the Miami University Libraries' Internet menus. This was in addition to the two hours each week that a student worker spent moving through our Internet menus and identifying the items which were not functioning.) In such a scenario, however, if the library does not have a server, the necessary, time-consuming, and often tedious work of quality control is instead left to someone else. The only link information that the library needs to maintain is the single connection to the top level of the other Web server.

One of the drawbacks of not maintaining a server, however, is that the library has no control over the frequency or quality of the maintenance. Frustrations may arise when resources listed on the screens are links to nowhere because a directory path has changed, a site has relocated to another machine, or the service simply no longer exists. Lacking the ability to correct these problems (because the errors exist in remote files that aren't accessible to library staff), the library and its users will be very dependent on the level of commitment to quality control by the providers on the other end. The library will also lack input into the inclusion of new Internet resources on the system.

Depending on how many listservs and newsgroups you read, you could easily come across 20 new sites each day. To read an announcement of a new resource, connect to it, deem it useful for your users, and then not be able to provide them with easy access to it is very vexing. Also, even if a new item is added to the "outer-controlled" system, you may not be happy with the decision regarding its location within the structure—a structure which, it is worth noting, you hope will be as stable as possible, since you don't want menus, sections, and labels changing so frequently that it's impossible to remember where resources are located.

To return to the topic of instruction for a moment, being able to teach the Internet using a locally designed and locally maintained system makes a world of difference. A large influence on your Internet workshops will be the existence of any library-administered Internet services, such as a Web server. Information resources and help screens can be added and the system designed based on user input gathered from instructional encounters. The situation is ideal when you can instruct others in the use of a system of which you have thorough knowledge because of your role as a system maintainer and/or designer.

Obviously, then, a library that chooses to point to an external server must be discerning in selecting that server and fairly undemanding. Investigation should be made into the server provider's system, delving into such issues as frequency of maintenance and addition of new items, stability of system design and structure, length of time the system has been available, and possibility for input into resources and structure.

Some libraries point to well-known, long-established (in Internet terms) systems, such as the home page for Netscape. Other libraries may decide to choose a more locally maintained system, such as a nearby school's Web page. But systems that best fit the criteria for quality, reliability, and renown are often the busiest and most popular systems, so initial access can be slowed considerably by the volume of connections.

Let's set the soapbox squarely on this page and proclaim the benefits of library-run Internet services and encourage librarians who have not already done so to start down the road toward Internet independence. Academic libraries all over the country are running World Wide Web servers to provide access to local and global information as well as easy access to library services. Much like the previous discussion of whether to administer and maintain your own Internet services locally, a library can do a little bit with Web services for its users, or it can do a lot.

OPTIONS FOR WEB SERVICES IN LIBRARIES: A FICTIONAL CASE IN POINT

The Web is the hot topic of the day, and in order to stay on top of library technology trends and to keep up with their users' demands, the (fictional) Casey Library's humanities reference department wants simply to provide access to the Web and its resources. Networked workstations with graphical Web browsers and the full complement of helper applications will be made available in public searching areas for patron use. Bookmarks will be maintained by librarians and a home page, which is running on a remote site, will be selected. True, some effort in selecting, organizing, and maintaining bookmarks is required and there is some hassle involved with connecting to a remotely stored home page.

So, the humanities reference staff decide to create a departmental home page which will include links to sites formerly listed in the bookmarks. Yes, staff have to learn HTML and some decisions and compromises must be reached about the design of the home page, but overall this approach is seen as advantageous since the page will allow them to make information available about their department, its staff, services, hours, and the like.

Here's where things get interesting. This reference department has counterparts in other units of the Casey Library system. Several of the other departments have begun to create their own home pages too. So, after much talking up of the Web, approval-getting by administration, and equipment purchasing, the library system as a whole decides to mount a Web server. Now, that's a project: challenging because of the balance that will need to be struck among various library departments and their ideas about system design, exciting because of the control library staff will now have over their electronic information system and the way it delivers information to their users, and a bit scary since there's always the chance that the users aren't going to like the end result or even the idea of this new service.

Having gone down this road, I have some suggestions. First, many libraries that undertake this type of project have convened a task force or team to oversee the design, implementation, and sometimes even the ongoing maintenance of the Web system. Populating the team with staff from a variety of departments should help the final product be shaped by the activities and needs of both staff and users of the libraries. This team's role could be defined as the sole creator of Web pages, although they would be smart to gather extensive input from their colleagues. The scenario eliminates the need for large-scale staff training; but, since the Web is the talk of the town, creating library Web pages may appeal to many of the staff.

In our hypothetical example of the Casey Library, the other reference departments will definitely want their home pages included in the system. Collection development staff may also be interested in creating Web pages for their subject areas and interlibrary loan may want to take a stab at online ILL forms.

STAFF ISSUES

In such a scenario, where possibly large numbers of staff have a high level of involvement, some continuity and training issues will need to be addressed. For instance, you may want to take measures to ensure a certain level of visual and structural consistency across various subject-based pages. One way to attain system uniformity is to have staff use a preconstructed template for their pages, which will also take a lot of the guesswork out of HTML for the uninitiated.

No group wants their system to look like a patchwork quilt, but getting staff to agree on a Web page template is no easy thing. Something as simple as a single, identifiable graphic, be it a logo or a striped bar, may go a long way toward continuity and eliminate the debate over the specific elements a universally used template would contain.

Since staff will need to have accounts on the computer where the Web server software resides, staff training must include not only HTML, but some basic instruction on how staff will transfer their HTML files to that computer and at least some basic coverage of the computer's operating system (such as UNIX). If some staff choose to create and edit files in that system's environment, then thorough training on system editors (such as UNIX's pico or vi) will also need to be covered. The purpose of the training should not be to make them UNIX masters, but to provide the skills that will open their eyes to available possibilities. As Michael Ridley of the University of Waterloo Library states, "The goal is not to have them become system experts but to enable them to be creative and innovative with the technology within the information needs context."[8]

SYSTEM CONTENT

Back at the fictitious Casey Library, we now have trained staff who are about to create an administration-supported Web server. Resources and services for inclusion come very close to being limited only by staff time and the purpose of the system. Local library information, such as staff and departmental phone and office numbers, information about the instruction program, names of collection development and departmental liaisons, maps and floor charts of the libraries, as well as an overview of the print and nonprint resources are just a few of the "about the libraries" items that come to mind. Specific departments may develop Web-based information, such as scanning in documents from special collections or providing ILL forms online.

Staff could add the resources they would like to have accessible through the system, such as the OPAC, online databases, connections to remote resources (such as library catalogs from around the world), and, of course, Internet resources. This last item is a huge addition to the system, not just because of the global nature of the Internet, but because the beauty of the Web is its ability to connect users easily to Net resources regardless of the Internet tool required for access.

Let's not omit a plug for one of the most exciting areas for library Web applications—the possibilities it offers for faculty and library staff collaboration. Collection development and departmental liaison staff can work with faculty to create course-specific Web pages, which could include links to local library and Internet resources relevant to student work in that class.

PROTOTYPES AND FEEDBACK

So now the library creates a prototype of its Web system and makes it available in test mode to gather feedback from its internal and external user populations. The library was able to move quickly on creating the system since it decided not to collect hard data first on what users expect and want from their system. Instead, the group decided to base their system design decisions on the cumulative knowledge they have gathered about their users from past reference and instructional experiences.

This approach is advocated for two reasons: user input can still be gathered but the data will be focused on reactions and comments on the prototype; and, if enough time is allotted for revisions after the test period, it should not be difficult to make changes based on user reaction. Web systems are much more accommodating toward revisions, than, say the gophers of the past, which were fairly hierarchical.

One more thing regarding system feedback: placing an HTML forms-based comments box prominently on your Web page will help gather feedback easily and from a wide group of users. It will also indicate to your users the library's commitment to client-centered services.

The bottom line is that the Web is a tool and, like other tools, it can be used with basic skills to produce quality, usable information products. With more advanced knowledge, one can produce works of outstanding quality—in our context this quality would allow us to enable our users to access local and global electronically based information in a well-designed, library-based, user-centered environment.

SYSTEM MAINTENANCE

As of this writing a trend regarding the administration of library Internet services is beginning to appear. In the recent past, most Internet services were maintained by one person or a team, who (after gathering staff input one hopes) designed, selected, and maintained the Internet portion of the library's online services. Recently, however, talk at many and various institutions has turned to incorporating the selection, collection, and maintenance of Internet resources into the established workflow and departmental divisions that handle collection management for other types of library resources.

Proponents of the latter scheme believe that this "mainstreaming" of Internet resources empowers librarians by giving them the opportunity (some would say mandate) to incorporate the Internet into their collection development activities. This distribution of workflow also makes Internet collection development a manageable task, since no one person or team is responsible for everything related to the Internet.

CONCLUSION

The Internet presents librarians with significant opportunities and challenges in the areas of instruction, electronic resource planning, staffing models, and user services. Internet-based technologies offer us the opportunity to control our electronic services, which is no small thing. So often we can only acquire or gain access to electronic resources that some other party has already designed and marketed for a broad library audience. Informed by our knowledge of our individual user populations, and their skill levels and research needs, and guided by an awareness and interest in information organization, we can use this new technology to define our library's online environment.

From an instructional standpoint, the control of the electronic landscape gives us the ability to alter that definition based on new resources and services and changing user needs, not to mention the great satisfaction of teaching a system maintained and designed by local librarians. This powerful new role requires a commitment to learn new skills, to stay well informed on the rapidly changing electronic information landscape, and to stay ahead of our users' needs.

But, clearly, what's gained far outweighs the required input of time and energy. Management of our electronic services affords an exciting opportunity to gain an intimate understanding of the design and content of our systems—systems that we'll be teaching others to use. Through our instructional activities we gain an even richer understanding of the people who use our systems, and the way they access and utilize resources in an online environment.

So the rewards for our efforts are really threefold and interdependent. By controlling our electronic milieu, we gain an enhanced understanding of our patrons and how they use our resources. This insight—much of it gained through our instructional efforts in class and at the reference desk—combined with system design and management activities enables us to create new and revise existing services based on new user data, new resources, and developments in information technology.

ENDNOTES

1. The author thanks Louis Rosenfeld for his useful suggestion to divide the chapter into these three sections.

2. In response to a listserv posting by Thomas, in which she briefly described her staff training efforts, I asked her for a fuller description of her program and was sent a lengthy, very informative e-mail message from which this information is excerpted.

3. Dennis Dillon, "An Internet Experience: Electronic Information Training Program at the University of Texas," *Library Issues* 14 (1994): 3.

4. Mary Page and Martin Kesselman, "Teaching the Internet: Challenges and Opportunities," *Research Strategies* 12, no. 3 (1994): 162.

5. Page and Kesselman, 164.

6. University Library, Eastern Michigan University, Ypsilanti, MI 48197 [Online] at LOEX@online.emich.edu

7. My thanks to Rama Vishwanatham who kindly granted me a telephone interview regarding the E-train listserv course mentioned in this chapter.

8. Michael Ridley, "Innovation and Implementation: Adopting and Managing World-Wide Web Services in Academic Libraries" (paper presented at the Second International WWW Conference 1994, Chicago, Ill., October 1994).

11

Lessons Bull Durham Taught Me: Reference as the Show

Ed Tallent

Ed Tallent's essay on reference teamwork should be required course reading for all public service wanna-bes as well as refresher material for anyone starting to feel the first flickerings of reference burnout. By the end of the chapter you, too, might be thinking of trades and free agencies that would change your place of work for the better.—CML

As a boy, my dream was to play second base for the Boston Red Sox. I was the ubiquitous no-hit, good-glove ballplayer on my Little League team (second base was a good position for me because I did not have a strong arm). But in Little League I learned the value of teamwork—I found that although I wasn't going to be Ted Williams at the bat, there was still a valued place for me on the team. Our coach made each of us feel valued, and instilled in us a pride for ourselves and for the team. The team worked because it molded together a variety of skills and temperaments. No one of us alone could win a game, and there were no triple plays made by solo players. But when we played well together, we were unbeatable.

I eventually traded one dream in for another (although if

the Sox call tomorrow I am available), and now, as a reference librarian at Harvard I grapple with the realities of providing reference service in the late 1990s. I, like every other practicing reference librarian, am constantly on the brink of being overwhelmed by content, formats, patron demands, and progress. Print plus microformats plus imagery plus CD-ROM plus tapeloads plus Internet subscriptions plus Web browsers: it seems like we're thrown a new curve each day of our professional lives, and time for batting practice diminishes as the drop on the ball gets lower and lower. Fortunately, my Little League background, supplemented by repetitive screenings of Bull Durham (the definitive baseball movie for our time), allows me to apply a ballplayer's perspective to the information service issues I face in the library, and it's clarified many of them for me. Bear with me as I make some comparisons between playing the all-American sport and providing academic reference.

PUT ME IN COACH (FOR THE GOOD OF THE TEAM)

There are 25 players on a major league team, with a variety of specialties. Some can hit, some can field, some can run, some can pitch and throw, and a happy few can do nearly all of it well. Some play one position, while others can play several. There are pitchers who start and others who relieve. There are pitchers who close the game and batters who pinch-hit. There are a few utility infielders. They are all pieces of a puzzle that constitutes a team.

What makes the team run? There is a manager, a person with authority, wisdom, experience, and a vision for the team. Good managers communicate all of these assets to their players and their coaches. The good manager uses his coaches wisely, delegating according to their strengths. Coaches provide much of the connection between the players and the manager. Coaching is ongoing constantly. Think of the first- and third-base coaches. There is never a time during a game when they are not on the field. They are an integral part of the action. The players are trained to have clear indications of the expectations: they watch for signals from the coaches on plays that might be on and if they should run or not. There is constant communication, from the coaches to the base-runners, from the dugout to the outfielders, from the catcher to the pitcher, from the manager to the coaches. Everyone needs to be on the same page for the team to succeed. A common goal—winning—unites them. In baseball, that common goal is obvious, but it is less so in today's reference work.

Teamwork is certainly not a concept alien to reference librarians. Many of us have worked in a variety of team environments. In most reference departments there has traditionally been a head of reference (the manager) and perhaps one or more assistant heads, unit heads, or coordinators, each with intermediate responsibility for some specialized area within reference. Also typical to traditional reference departments has been a blending of educational backgrounds and subject specialties: a good team has usually provided some subject depth in the major fields served by the reference department.

This is changing in the emerging new academic library. Some changes are subtle, some are stark. One of the major shifts has been to a specialization in and accent on formats ("electronic resource librarians" as compared to humanities specialists, for instance) rather than content. In fact, there is such a dizzying array of formats that no one member of the reference team can be expert in accessing them all. Thus we have had to abandon a commitment to content and subject in favor of assisting users simply to access information in the myriad ways we and publishers of the information make it available. Some would say this change is analogous to baseball's practice of using the widely detested designated hitter.

The practice of having a head of reference, or coach, is also changing in some libraries. Teams have taken over completely at some institutions, and there is no hierarchical head of a reference unit—only equal peers on the team. The question of who calls the plays comes to mind, but the practice is for the team to come to agreement on what its work will be and how they will achieve it. Imagine how this would work with the New York Yankees . . . imagine how it works in libraries. . . .

Teamwork, too, seems to have been transmuted in some of the new reference configurations. Whereas in the past the members of a good team supported and backed each other up as needed, new teams appear to be arrangements of individuals with clearly demarcated responsibilities, with the collective sum of the individuals defining the team, rather than a spirit of shared purpose and common goals. Come to think of it, this has nearly a one-to-one correspondence with what's going on in major league baseball today.

WHAT'S YOUR AVERAGE, SON?
(THE 55 PERCENT REFERENCE ACCURACY POINT)

Statistics are, of course, dangerous. They are, like everything else, also relative. In baseball, a batter who got on base 55 percent of the time would be on the cover of *Sports Illustrated*, Wheaties boxes everywhere, and Letterman two nights a week. Alternatively, a second baseman who fielded 55 percent of the balls hit to him would find his face on the manager's dartboard. The numbers need context.

So, too, in reference. There are, certainly, some reference librarians who provide too little or inaccurate service. And then there are those who overwhelm students with too much information, too many sources. These poor students are so blitzkrieged they are fearful of ever approaching a reference desk again. The overkill reference librarian, like the hot dog grandstanding ball player, acts from his or her own ego, rather than responding to the needs of the student or the game.

ALL THOSE EMPTY SEATS
(NON-USE OF REFERENCE SERVICE)

As the summer progresses and teams are in the running for the playoffs, attendance at the contenders' stadia tends to increase. Yet even teams with good records can have near-empty ballparks some of the time. We can ask ourselves in reference: if we are providing such a necessary service, why do so many people not make use of us? Why do so many people define "knowing how to use the library" as the ability to find a book?

One of the answers to this last question is that we have made it so darn difficult to locate a book. Catalogs have not been terribly user-friendly. Library signage is often not adequate. If the signs a catcher gave his pitcher were as obscure as the Library of Congress Subject Headings are to most normal people, the average ERA in the major leagues would hover somewhere in the vicinity of 27.

The other major factor affecting the attendance in our reference rooms, is, of course, remote access. More and more of our users are accessing our catalogs and online databases remotely and bypassing the reference room, making a beeline from their dorms and offices right to the stacks and the circulation desk instead. This is great progress—if they are actually getting what they need for their research. It's hard to believe, however, that they are getting *all* they need, considering the comparatively minuscule amount of information that's available either full-text or bibliographically online.

WHERE HAVE YOU GONE JOE DIMAGGIO?
(THE TGIF PHENOMENON)

Whereas Ernie Banks would say "Let's play two," we typically staff reference desks on weekends as minimally as possible. Yet weekends are when our fans (students) have the most free time to come to the ballpark (get their research done). At a high-use time, we leave students to the mercy of their peers at the circulation desk.

ALUMINUM BATS (PING!)

Who can help but get depressed watching a game where aluminum baseball bats are used? Yes, they last longer and provide more power than wood, but lost is the evocative sound and feel of the ball cracking against a Louisville Slugger. At computer workstations in our reference rooms and from homes and offices, many researchers are using aluminum bats these days and getting easy hits: finding information of some kind online has become much easier and faster than ever before. As in T-Ball, with electronic resources you will almost always make contact with the ball. The problem is all those "pings" we're hearing—as graduate students hit one out of the information ballpark with WWW browsers, locating the latest Brad Pitt or Madonna home page, while they neglect to use many of the printed indexes and abstracts that lead to sources vital to their research.

THE FIRST BASE DUMPING GROUND

One of the worst comparisons that can be made between reference and baseball is that, in some benighted libraries, reference is the place where staff end up because they don't fit anyplace else ("Aw, anybody can play first base—just put the old codger there"). Reference has not been thought to be a challenging position in some institutions. Fortunately, this idea is dying out rapidly, as the tasks expected of reference librarians proliferate and everybody in reference must have MVP potential just to keep up.

REVITALIZING THE SHOW

Baseball has undergone a transformation during the 20th century, and some fans would say it's not been for the good. They may contend that the emphasis is more on big business and lucrative self-promotion than on the game, and football is fast gaining ground in the hearts of diehard American sports fans.

Well, reference and the reference setting are also changing in the new academic library. The proliferation of information and access methods, combined with heightened patron expectations, can make reference a highly stressful place to work. Much of the change occurring, however, is refreshingly productive and stimulating. Gone are the days when reference rooms were simply quiet study areas. Learning and research is increasingly interactive and collaborative. Conversation is constant (and not just among the reference librarians)—students are working together. Reference librarians are providing proactive reference service, approaching patrons and asking if they need assistance. Electronic information arcades are staffed by roving librarians and library assistants, actively seeking out users in need of assistance. Librarians provide e-mail and teleconferenced reference, consult with teaching faculty via the Internet, and construct interactive library skills home pages and even classes on the Web. The new reference room is a complex, multilevel, technologically demanding environment.

WHAT'S THE LINEUP OF LIBRARIANS?

Over time, a reference department may respond to the ebb and flow of information needs and formats, but there is a constant common to all reference scenarios: the reference staff must possess certain qualities to be effective. They must be outgoing, good communicators, tactful, constant learners, patient, and have a good sense of balance and a well-developed sense of humor. They will attempt to maintain a user's perspective of the library, and will direct programs and services that are user-centered.

The new reference department will be staffed by individuals who love to teach and are comfortable with technology, or at least not afraid of it. As in baseball, there are archetypical players.

The Leadoff Hitters

We will need players who will get things started, librarians who will be constantly experimenting and setting the table for new reference ventures. These librarians will challenge us and question the way in which things are done. They may be irritating to be around sometimes, but a winning team needs them.

The Contact Hitters

Second in the lineup, this is the type of player who keeps things going. This person does the little things that lead to success: making that contact with an academic department, getting that handout completed, figuring out why that Internet connection is not working.

The Designated Hitters

Having enough people to staff the reference desk will still be a challenge. As we are in a period of demographic shifts, it would be foolish not to take advantage of the skills more senior colleagues in reference possess. Some of them may not have highly developed technical skills, but they could offer training in classic and still valuable reference sources, provide a bridge from the past to the future, and maintain a status as the department's reference experts.

The Cleanup Hitters

Cleanup hitters drive in the runs. They are the people in the department who galvanize all of the plans and possibilities and bring everything together. These people are the doers—and the ones who get others in the department to be doers, too. Like the leadoff hitter, they believe that experimentation is good and there are no failures, just learning experiences. Just like the cleanup hitters, these librarians put people in the reference seats. They are the good teachers that draw the students in. They are able to pull that program together, get organized quickly for a class, and provide dynamic reference quality leadership.

The Students of the Game

One of baseball's weaknesses these days (as with all sports) is that the collective memory of the participants is diminished. Only the latest commercial venture is recalled. The reference department needs people who understand how the academic bureaucracy works, who have the contacts and the history, and who are able to appreciate the combination of the new and the old.

The Closers

Decisions will have to be made. Priorities will have to be agreed on, so we will need managers who will not be afraid to make a decision. When the ball is in their hands, we will feel confident of success. There is a strong element of trust there. These "closers" will also possess the inner strength to come back after a bad decision and try again. They will be supportive of risk taking and will not look at errors as something bad. Just as a closer maintains the win, these library closers will see to it that the work of the above types is not wasted. The combination of skills will be exploited to its fullest.

CONCLUSION

The main lesson Bull Durham—and a lifetime's study of the game—has taught me is that everyone on the team has something to contribute. In good reference departments, even though much of our work is based on text and databases, words and numbers, indexes and bibliographies, in the end the success of the venture depends on the people who make up the team.

12

Librarian-Teachers and the Virtual Library

Esther Grassian

Successful teachers in the recreated academic library will be experts at experimentation in an environment that encourages new ideas and methods, as Esther Grassian describes in her essay on librarian-teachers. In addition to discussing how academic librarians may approach teaching in the future, Esther emphasizes two prerequisites for creating effective public services in all libraries: the need for risk-taking and the need for administrative support for that risk-taking.—CML

THE UCLA COLLEGE LIBRARY

In the old card catalog days it seemed as though mountains would crumble before there would be major changes in libraries. For the most part, physical library surroundings were fixed. Librarians and library administrators deliberated long and hard before making changes. There were lengthy debates, for example, whenever someone suggested changing the location of a reference book. The academic reference librarian's primary function was to sit at the reference desk and answer questions. These responsibilities could not be changed by adding instruction unless instruction could be fitted in around the reference librarian's "real" responsibilities.

Now, change is our constant companion. The question is not so much "Will there be another change?" as "What is the latest change and how do I learn about it?" As the pace of change increases, librarian-teachers also ask "How can I keep learning these changes quickly enough to be able to turn around and teach them to my users?" The Internet and the "virtual library" hold us spellbound today, as they grow, intertwine, and mutate at a geometric pace. Librarian-teachers and others frequently write and publish material on teaching the Internet, in books, in hard-copy magazines and journals, and on the Internet itself. Let us sharpen the focus now and look at teaching and the virtual library.

WHAT IS THE "VIRTUAL LIBRARY"?

Can we teach the "Virtual Library"? Can we use it to teach? The 1989 edition of the *Oxford English Dictionary* (OED) defines "virtual" as "That which is so in essence or effect, although not formally or actually,"[1] and in relation to computers as "Not physically existing as such, but made by software to appear to do so from the point of view of the program or the user."[2] Most OED definitions of "library" refer to collections of books or other physical objects such as films, "gramophone records," and so on.[3] Though there is no direct reference to "virtual library," one definition of "library" may apply—"a great mass of learning or knowledge."[4] The virtual library has also been defined as "a metaphor for the networked library"[5] and as "remote access to information or the contents of libraries housed electronically and deliverable in real time."[6]

In 1995, *College and Research Libraries News* reported that Stanford University is "attempting to invent the electronic equivalent of the Dewey decimal system for the Internet,"[7] and that "Stanford's four-year effort is designed to create a 'virtual library' by providing Internet users with a seamless interface to . . . information services and collections on the Net."[8] How user-friendly will the Stanford University "seamless interface" be? Will it and other digital library projects[9] eliminate the need for instruction in critical thinking about electronic resources, as well as their effective use? If instruction is still needed, what form(s) will or should it take? In what ways will it be new or different? Most important, what are the key issues in instruction, no matter what form it takes? At this point it is difficult to say whether or not digital library projects will result in a decreased need for instruction. One can only hope that this will be the case, although it is hard to believe that such projects will completely eliminate the need for instruction, in spite of the fact that a number of academic institutions mounting these projects (and other electronic products) have moved in this direction by joining together in a consortium.[10]

Of course, commercial producers are not included in this consortium, and commercial vendors' products often form an important part of the virtual library. So, if we still need to teach effective use of resources in spite of digital library efforts, as it seems we may, our instruction will take a variety of forms, some of which may be unknown to us at present. Yet, librarian-teachers have had years of experience in using and adapting instructional formats to teach the use of libraries and library resources, and are well prepared to face this new "call to arms."

Miriam Dudley began the current "bibliographic instruction" (BI) movement in the early 1970s with her well-known, self-paced workbook, designed to teach basic skills to large numbers of college students quickly and easily.[11] Workbooks became a popular and widespread means of instruction in libraries. They not only provided a cheap, reasonable means of instruction, but their very creation and use encouraged librarians to think about and develop other forms of instruction.

AND NOW THE WEB

During the ensuing 25 years, librarians have been teaching print reference sources, the OPAC, CD-ROMs, locally or centrally mounted databases, and lately, Internet resources, including telnet, ftp, e-mail, gopher, and World Wide Web (WWW or Web). We have taught all of these in a variety of ways—in one-shot classes, integrated into other classroom instruction, or stand-alone; through formal courses, video-tapes, computer-assisted instruction (CAI), point-of-use guides, and handouts. We have done demonstrations and hands-on instruction. We have developed paper exercises, tutorials, and workbooks. In the virtual library we have also used help screens, online tutorials, gopher sites, and now we are seeing instructional Web Pages designed by librarians, and using new features, such as frames. The Association of College and Research Libraries (ACRL) Instruction Section and the Coalition for Networked Information have even developed a "meta-instructional" Web site, in a joint project to identify, review, and select exemplary Web-based Internet education materials.[12]

Paper, video, and CAI instruction require varying amounts of time, money, and effort to produce. It is also expensive and time-consuming to revise video and CAI when they become dated, even when it is possible to do so. Now, with all of that experience and with a body of both theoretical and practical literature in hand, we come to the "virtual age" prepared to be flexible and open to new instructional formats.

OPACs have help screens as do various software packages. Generally this form of instruction is equivalent to reading a manual in electronic form and does not allow for any form of interaction. Some OPACs allow "comments" from users which staff then respond to on a one-on-one basis, or as to a listserv.[13] Although these interactive exchanges may be archived and available to all users, many may not want to (nor know how to) take the time and trouble to search the archive. Then, too, archived answers to questions may be accurate at the time a question is answered, but answers may be different as enhancements are made, databases are added or dropped, or database coverage or searching capabilities change.

Not long ago gopher seemed to offer an instructional solution. Gopher sites could be set up fairly easily, and menu-driven gophers could lead users to help in the form of tutorials. Indeed, from 1992 though 1994, when gopher was in its heyday, librarians bravely and eagerly began teaching the Internet and making use of its potential as a teaching tool. But even as the library instruction world developed learning and teaching strategies for gopher, another Internet tool—the World Wide Web—swiftly superceded gopher's rudimentary instructional use and took its place. Many, if not most, of the gopher sites developed by libraries just a few years ago have already become defunct; in some cases they have been transformed into Web pages.

The Web was little known or used a short time ago, yet it has exploded into our consciousness to such a great extent that major newspapers now have regular features on it, or refer to it throughout the paper. Once a week, the *Los Angeles Times*, for example, devotes most of its Business Section to cutting-edge technology stories. Rarely do these stories appear without one or more URLs ("Uniform Resource Locators" or Web addresses). In fact, URLs are now becoming a part of our collective unconscious, as they appear widely in advertising movies, television shows, radio programs, and other products, from beer[14] to books.[15]

On the Web, where hyperlinks and client-server architecture meet, is where our instructional paradigm shifts once again. Instruction within the virtual library now can take graphic, audio, and/or video forms, as well as text, all within one "location," interwoven or as separate elements. Interaction can be built into any Web Page. Web Pages can offer "in links" to the same page or "out links" to other pages, all of which can be revised and updated quickly and easily.

The instructional pendulum is already swinging back to the point of origin for the current BI movement, the workbook, but in a modernized and expanded form to take advantage of evolving Web capabilities. Soon someone will probably develop an electronic workbook, where users can see video clip segments of instructional sessions, try the modeled action on their own, replay the video if necessary, and even complete a test or questionnaire designed to measure outcomes, all from their own workstations. Or they may listen to a lecture accompanying PowerPoint or other software slides, or ftp an instructional guide or handout, complete an online exercise or questionnaire, and get feedback on the results—again, all from their own workstations.[16]

Indeed, it is the evolution of Internet resources and tools such as the Web that poses the most pressing problem of teaching and the virtual library—how to cope with this swiftly mutating environment and yet stick to basic principles of good instruction. The answer?

We must make a paradigm shift in the way we plan, implement, and evaluate virtual library instruction, and we will need to rely on our 25 years of teaching experience to develop new instructional techniques and identify tried-and-true techniques that can be applied in the virtual environment. What are good instructional principles for planning, implementation, evaluation, and revision, and in what ways are they different in the virtual environment?

PRE-PLAN

To paraphrase a well known real estate adage, the three most important factors in instructional planning for the virtual environment are "audience, audience, and audience."[17] But who are our users now? For years we have known our audiences. In a physical library setting, where most of us have been teaching the virtual library up until now, we have found it fairly easy to identify the library's community of primary users.

In academic libraries, for example, primary users are usually faculty and students (and often, staff). Academic libraries typically target these users as their primary instructional audience, and build their instructional planning around them. Libraries often distribute printed needs-assessment surveys to their primary users, or conduct in-person focus groups of primary users to help determine instructional needs. In the classroom, librarians in all types of libraries have dealt with defined groups, generally at a homogenous stage and within a defined age range, which could be broken down, for example, as primary school–age children (K–6), young adults (7–12), adults (college students to senior citizens).

In the virtual library, on the other hand, our audience could be anyone, anywhere in the world with access to a computer hooked up to the Internet. So, the first and most important step is to decide who will be our primary instructional audience. Every other step in instructional planning for the virtual library hinges on this critical decision.

Once we have identified our primary constituency, we may want to clarify our goals and objectives by writing "teaching development policies" for this group, as we have done with collection development policies, and restrict our instructional efforts to that level.[18] In fact, for most libraries, the reality of shrinking or stable resources will probably dictate focus on "core instruction" for our primary instructional users and additional instruction will be added only as we can afford the time, energy, and funds to implement it.

If we do this, we should understand that instructional service gaps will appear, especially as much of our virtual library becomes available to an ever-expanding global audience. In this event, it is easy to imagine "instructional entrepreneurs" popping up, whose sole business purpose will be to translate instruction into many different languages and provide instruction for the virtual resources of a user's choice, at any level the user chooses. At least one OPAC vendor[19] also offers users search and display options in a number of languages, including Finnish, French, and Russian, and this is a trend which will probably continue.

PLAN

Once we have decided on our audience, we can follow the same basic instructional planning steps utilized in instructional planning for the physical library, although means for accomplishing these steps may differ greatly. It is most important, first, to determine reactively or proactively whether there is a need for instruction or if indeed help vehicles (such as digital library projects, new-and-improved Internet tools, or improved vendor help) have eliminated this need. Once we have determined that there is a need for instruction, it is essential to define the need in writing. This assessment should lead naturally to the process of setting goals and objectives to meet the defined need. We can then design content and format (the means of implementing instruction), deliver instruction, and finally, evaluate and revise based on our program goals and objectives. Most of these steps are standard practice for BI librarians in their own institutions and have been documented more fully elsewhere.[20]

DETERMINE NEED

Librarians have been able to determine needs reactively through analysis of reference desk interactions, as well as electronic "comments," e-mail reference questions, or e-mail requests for help. Librarians also use print surveys and in-person focus groups as proactive needs-assessment measures. Interactive forms on Web Pages will allow us to continue reactive needs assessment in the virtual library, and expand it to proactive needs assessment. In addition, we will be able to take proactive needs-assessment steps by surveying our users electronically or by establishing electronic focus groups.

DEFINE NEED

Once we have determined a need, we must define it within the context of five elements: the institutional setting, the library setting, existing or planned instruction programs, available or obtainable resources (including staff), and audience.

What are the institutional and library settings? What are the goals and objectives of existing and planned instructional programs, and will any of them meet the identified need? It may take some time to document existing and planned BI programs, including goals and objectives, as well as form(s) of evaluation and revision, as sometimes these elements are tacitly assumed and are not documented.

Furthermore, it may be difficult to obtain precise information on available resources, such as appropriate hardware and software for preparation, as well as delivery, network connections, data lines, phone lines, modems, working copy machines, clerical help, additional instructors, appropriate lighting, and classroom space for in-person instruction. These resources may or may not be available, or may be at a premium because of high demand from other programs. It is far better to develop several alternative approaches or fallback positions in case there are no additional resources to be had. Teaching the virtual library, though, offers us an opportunity to rethink our instructional approaches, alter our goals and objectives, and grab the imagination of our users and administrators as never before. The education world in general is waking up to the fact that enormous changes are both possible and probable in a virtual environment, including virtual schooling for children, for example.[21] We in libraries are at the forefront of change in the electronic information world. We must keep running just to keep pace or we will be left far behind.

SET GOALS AND OBJECTIVES

With parameters of the instructional need in hand, the next step is to develop measurable goals and objectives to meet the need. What do we hope to accomplish? How and when do we hope to accomplish it? What measurable criteria will we use to determine success or failure in terms of the outcomes of instruction?

DESIGN CONTENT AND SELECT FORMAT

While our goals and objectives may outline the content of instruction clearly, selecting or designing the format is quite another matter. Virtual instruction is different from—and more challenging than—in-person instruction. We need to anticipate users with highly diverse learning styles, varying levels of expertise, and even varying levels of language facility. In a live group session, it would be possible to determine skill levels and language facility fairly quickly, if not learning styles. Unlike a live session, it would be quite difficult, and certainly not cost-effective, to do random pretesting in virtual instruction, as even users among our intended audience may fluctuate from minute to minute. In fact, we may very well draw much greater numbers of users virtually (including those who have never used a physical library) than we have previously in the physical environment.

How can we forestall problems in working with an audience that fits certain minimum requirements (for example, undergraduates enrolled at our institution), yet that has varied and indeterminate skill levels? Under these circumstances, the virtual instructor should anticipate questions of all kinds from all levels of users. Even with basic or "core" instruction, we would be well advised to build in stages of training and various forms of training, and allow the user to choose her or his level and style preference, perhaps through a series of interactive questions or a short diagnostic pretest. A user-centered, self-directed approach should also allow the user to choose to repeat an instructional segment or to decide for himself or herself whether to go on to the next level or go back to a previous level.[22]

According to recent research, it is possible for programs to "learn" from users' responses.[23] In fact, we can now envision using or developing intelligent agents that will "notice" that a user needs help and offer or deliver instruction accordingly. Or programs might be designed where simple "triage" based on search results would allow the system to suggest a level of instruction to the user, who will then choose where to start and what to learn.[24]

Some form of interaction and some means of getting "live" help are also crucial elements of an effective virtual instruction program. Interaction can come in the form of interactive forms or "chat" sessions, or even interactive help screens or the ability to provide "comments" via e-mail and receive responses. E-mail reference addresses and toll-free phone numbers are good means of providing virtual aid, and are good uses of the electronic medium. Interactive forms on Web pages also offer excellent possibilities for reference questions and diagnostic testing, as well as evaluation of outcomes.[25]

TEST INSTRUCTIONAL MATERIAL

Before implementing instruction—that is, making it available on a widespread basis—it is extremely important to test it on naive users and continue to revise and simplify until it is at its most basic level. Software developers always build in time for beta-testing and often postpone release dates until bugs have been eliminated. Librarians developing virtual library instruction need to allow some time for testing and revision as well. Of course, software vendors can usually dictate when new software releases will be available. For librarians, on the other hand, severe time pressures will play a large part in determining the speed at which this testing and revision process takes place. If we are to release new versions of virtual library software or databases, however, we must balance speedy release with the immediate need for reliable and efficient help.

IMPLEMENT INSTRUCTION

Ideally, instructional enhancements will be released only after beta testing has been completed and necessary revisions have been made. Means of program implementation can also vary. For those without access to the Web, distance learning and paper instructional guides may be other effective approaches, especially when combined with the option of e-mailing reference and informational questions. In fact, electronic distance education (EDE) offers an excellent means of reaching users in scattered and remote locations for classes (and it may closely resemble traditional one-shot instructional sessions in the physical library). Research has proven that this resemblance is true for EDE programs in general, however, only when the content has been well defined, the instructor is well prepared and well organized, and the medium is used effectively.[26]

EVALUATE OUTCOMES AND REVISE

Evaluation, particularly outcomes measurement, is also of vital importance, and should be a built-in component of instruction efforts. If our instruction is virtual, evaluation can be a virtual activity as well. Posttests that measure learning and the incorporation of critical thinking can be administered virtually via interactive forms, but again, distribution will take much careful planning and preparation.

The revision process, too, can take a virtual form, through the use of listservs, e-mail, and newsgroups, whereby one can work with immediate or distant colleagues on ideas and draft program revisions.

THE LIBRARIAN-TEACHERS

But how do we develop and deliver these new forms of instruction? It is important to keep in mind that librarians working at the cutting edge often find themselves balancing on the edge of a razor—trying to fulfill their ongoing responsibilites while at the same time planning for new environments, new users, and new or unknown technology. These people need support in the form of release time for creative investigation and problem-solving. They need clerical support and they need the freedom and encouragement to meet with their colleagues, virtually and physically, by attending conferences and by spending time making good use of listservs and newsgroups. They also need encouragement to form partnerships with other groups and individuals on campus (within and outside the library), as well as groups and individuals at other locations (both within and outside the library profession). They need support in developing grant proposals and using innovative teaching techniques and software. We need to show them our appreciation for the risks they continue to take and even the mistakes they make in doing so.

CONCLUSION

The critical issues for librarians learning and teaching the virtual library, then, will be the ability to define the audience, the range of implementation methods available, the obtainability of instructional resources, and the presence of an environment that welcomes risk-taking. Most important, risk-taking librarian-teachers need support, encouragement, and appreciation for their bravery. The pioneer's life can be thrilling, but it is not easy.

BASIC STEPS IN PLANNING AND DELIVERING INSTRUCTION

Prerequisite: Decide on the audience

1. Determine need

2. Define need

3. Set goals and objectives

4. Design content and select format

5. Test instructional material

6. Implement instruction

7. Evaluate outcomes and revise

ENDNOTES

1. *Oxford English Dictionary*, 2d ed., s.v. "virtual."
2. Ibid.
3. Ibid., s.v. "library."
4. Ibid. Neither the 1989 edition of the *Oxford English Dictionary*, nor the two 1993 supplements have a definition of "Internet" as we know it.
5. Laverna Saunders, "The Virtual Library: Computers in Libraries Canada," *Computers in Libraries* 12 (December 1992): 71.
6. Saunders, "The Virtual Library," 71.
7. Mary Ellen Davis, "News from the Field," *College and Research Libraries News* 56 (April 1995): 231.
8. Davis, "News from the Field."
9. Beth Gaston, "NSF Awards Digital Libraries Press Release," http://www.informedia.cs.cmu.edu/Info-News/nsf/oz.html. The National Science Foundation has awarded $24.4 million to fund six digital library projects, at the Carnegie Mellon University, the University of California, Berkeley, the University of Michigan, the University of Illinois, the University of California, Santa Barbara, and Stanford University.

10. A 1995 e-mail message Jacqueline Wilson stated that

Leaders of fifteen of the nation's largest research libraries and archives and the Commission on Preservation and Fitness today signed an agreement that pledges collaboration toward the establishment of a National Digital Library Federation. . . . A primary goal of the Federation is the implementation of a distributed, open digital library accessible across the global Internet. . . .

In support of that goal, the Federation will establish a collaborative management structure, develop a coordinated funding strategy, and formulate selection guidelines to ensure conformance to the general theme of U.S. heritage and culture. The Federation also will adopt common standards and best practices to ensure full informational capture and guarantee universal accessibility.

11. Miriam Sue Dudley, *Chicano Library Program* (Los Angeles: University of California Library, 1970); Miriam Sue Dudley, *Workbook in Library Skills: A Self-Directed Course in the Use of UCLA's College Library* (Los Angeles: University of California Library, College Library, 1973).

12. Some examples include Information Literacy Skills Workbook, http://www.uwp.edu/library/toc.html; Library Research at Cornell: A Hypertext Guide, http://www.library.cornell.edu/okuref/research/tutorial.html; Shortcuts Express Homepage, http://library.nmsu.edu/projects/tutorial/express.html; Purdue University Libraries Tutorials, http://thorplus.lib.purdue.edu/tutorials/pluto/index.html; UCSD Science and Engineering Library—Electronic Classroom, http://schplib.ucsd.edu/electclass/classroom.html; ACRL/CNI Internet Education Project, http://www.cwpu.edu/orgs.cni/base/acrlcni.html; and The World Lecture Hall, http://www.utexas.edu/world/lecture/.

13. The University of California's MELVYL system, for example.

14. For example, Imported Beer of the Month Club, http://www.tdmedsign.com/hops/club.htm.

15. For example, Amazon.com.Books, http://www.amazon.com.

16. The Internet Hunt now seems a distant memory. But in its time, it was another good example of how a librarian was among the first to step forward and teach use of the Internet by encouraging distant learners to answer treasure hunt–type questions. Rick Gates started the Internet Hunt in 1992. Hunt questions were intriguing, yet seemed impossible to answer until the answers, and, especially, the search strategy, were posted. Past Hunts are archived by the Coalition for Networked Information.

17. The three most important factors in real estate value are said to be "location, location, and location."

18. This is a variation on Mardikian and Kesselman's proposal that libraries develop "access development statements" as opposed to "collection development statements." Jackie Mardikian and Martin Kesselman, "Beyond the Desk: Enhancing Reference Staffing for the Electronic Library," *Reference Services Review* 23 (Spring 1995): 21–28.

19. VTLS (Virginia Tech Library System).

20. Association of College and Research Libraries, Bibliographic Instruction Section, *Sourcebook for Bibliographic Instruction* (Chicago: ALA, 1993).

21. Odvard Egil Dyrli and Daniel E. Kinnamon, "Preparing for the Integration of Emerging Technologies," *Technology and Learning* 14 (May–June 1994): 95.

22. "Research Assistant," a computer-assisted instruction program developed by Ann Bevilacqua, provides an excellent model of this approach. For further information on "Research Assistant," contact:

Upper Broadway Bodega Software
Ann Bevilacqua
6934 Mohawk Ln.
Indianapolis, IN 46260
Phone: 317–253–7948
E-mail: 71303.3401@compuserve.com
ABevilac@Velcome.IUPUI.edu

23. In 1994 Roesler and Hawkins cited research done by Tom Mitchell and his colleagues at Carnegie Mellon University regarding an intelligent agent that helps schedule meet-

ings. Marina Roesler and Donald T. Hawkins, "Intelligent Agents: Software Servants for an Electronic Information World (and More!)" *Online* 18 (July 1994): 30. More recently, some Web sites that use intelligent agents have become quite popular, for example, Firefly (http://www.firefly.com/), which matches people with similar interests in music.

24. Nicholas Negroponte, *Being Digital* (New York: Knopf, 1995):102. "The idea is to build computer surrogates that possess a body of knowledge both about something (a process, a field of interest, a way of doing) and about you in relation to that something (your taste, your inclinations, your acquaintances). Namely, the computer should have dual expertise, like a cook, gardener, and chauffeur using their skills to fit your tastes and needs in food, planting and driving. When you delegate those tasks it does not mean you do not like to prepare food, grow plants, or drive cars. It means you have the option to do those things when you wish, because you want to, not because you have to." *Ibid.*:151.

25. These e-mail reference/information and interactive form approaches will require that library staff commit to short turnaround response times, and be prepared for an overwhelming response when the world can beat a path to our doors. We can take effective proactive steps, though, by pressuring OPAC vendors to include interactive help screens, tied to an e-mail address and an archive of Frequently Asked Questions (FAQs). Or, we might even consider creating or asking vendors to create, a new help category, "Frequently Requested Instruction" (FRIs), with lots of choices and levels of user-friendly help.

26. Michael A. Burke, "Designing Effective Electronic Distance Education Programs for K–12 Staff Development," *Clearing House* 67 (March–April 1994): 236.

ADDITIONAL RESOURCES NOT CITED IN NOTES

Coalition for Networked Information: Network Services, http://www.cni.org/services.html.
Duda, Andrea L. Guides to Using the MELVYL System, http://www.library.ucsb.edu/melvyl/.

Nickerson, Gord. "The Virtual Reference Library." *Computers in Libraries* 13 (May 1993): 37–39.

"Stanford Creating Digital Dewey for Internet." *College and Research Libraries News* (April 1995): 231.

VTLS Inc. Web page, http://www.vtls.com/index.html.

Wilson, Jacqueline. "National Digital Library Federation Agreement Signed." lauc-list@uci.edu (5/16/95).

13

Virtual Library Instruction: Training Tomorrow's User Today

Pat Ensor ·

Pat Ensor's essay discusses some of the same issues Esther Grassian raises, only from the perspective of those being taught rather than those doing the teaching. The two essays combined give a 360 degree discussion of "virtual instruction."— CML

As we hurtle ever faster into the electronic age, the academic librarian's conception of instruction must be reexamined. This is true for instruction to an even greater extent than many other areas of librarianship. We can know from day to day that what we do at a reference desk is still relevant and meets many needs successfully because we interact with library users directly. In areas of technical and access services, we know that purchasing and making printed materials accessible, and gaining access to more electronic resources, are still useful endeavors because we can measure their use.

When looking at instruction as it takes place in and through academic libraries, however, we have far less assurance that what we are doing is successful and meets user needs. This is something inherently more difficult to determine because of the character of most of our instruction interactions. What we traditionally define as library or bibliographic instruction has tended for the most part not to be interactive.

Our instruction programs tend to consist primarily of classes where one library staff member (or at least no more than a few) teaches a group of students. The instruction program also typically produces printed handouts (perhaps signage, too); may have great responsibility for designing help and information screens with electronic products; and perhaps has created one or more computer-assisted instruction presentations. The vast majority of these efforts are not interactive and include few or no attempts to determine how successfully they meet their intended goals. In fact, it may be unclear what those goals are.

All of these tendencies were questionable enough in the age of print; in the age of electronics, they are a pathway to complete irrelevance for library staff involved in instruction. But if electronic resources offer more challenges, they also offer more possibilities. It is unclear, for instance, whether the most gifted of library instructors could ever have incited widespread enthusiasm for the research process and a list of books that would be useful for a business class.

But we now work in a time that brings us an electronic phenomenon we literally could not have foreseen a few years ago—a worldwide application of hypermedia concepts accessible through fun and exciting interfaces, otherwise known as the World Wide Web and its graphical user interface browsers. We do not have to drum up interest in this; all we have to do is display it. In fact, the world is not waiting for libraries to lead the way in this area. Instead, we have to convince the world that libraries are relevant to an interest in electronic information.

Not only do electronic resources automatically incite interest, they also contain keys to instructing more successfully—the ability to design the item being used in such a way as to make it easier and/or more informative, and the ability to know much more about how people interact with the resource. This is where promise and opportunity lie.

TERMINOLOGY AND THE BASICS

The terminology that will be used in this chapter for the topic of instruction is important, and it is time we examined what we call this process, in light of the electronic future. To call this function in libraries "bibliographic instruction" is to label it immediately irrelevant to the virtual library. "Bibliographic" means something that pertains to the writing of books, and it needs to be clear that instruction in a library is no longer limited (if it ever was) to telling users how to use printed books. "Library instruction" is a far more understandable and commonsense term, and at least it can be stretched into the electronic age—here it is used to denote instruction in using resources that are owned by a library, or made available under a library's auspices—that is, through a library contract and/or on a library computer.

If librarians want to make clear their involvement in instructing people in the use of electronic resources of the future, it may well be time to change the name of this process to "information instruction." What meaning is there in the concept of library instruction for someone who may interact with a library system without ever coming into the library? Janice Simmons-Welburn speaks of the need for "post-bibliographic instruction," and although ultimately this important concept should not be called something defined by what it is not, at least it is another way of making clear that we must move beyond the "bibliographic."[1]

Instruction is also defined to include the full range of methods of teaching a user: from printed handouts, to classes, to help screens, to the system design that makes something easier to use, to one-on-one interaction at the point of use. Our definitions, and our minds, must be expansive to keep up with the electronic future.

Abigail Loomis and Deborah Fink have done an excellent overview of the tasks involved with instruction in the virtual library and of the audiences for which instruction will be done.[2] They break down the essential content for instruction in the virtual library by asking four guiding questions. Users of electronic systems need to be able to answer the question "where am I?"—that is, to orient themselves, choose relevant resources, and navigate them effectively. They must also know "how do I do it?"—the mechanics of how to use the specific resource they've chosen.

"What am I trying to do?" is at the heart of the research process, just as it is for more traditional print-based research. A search strategy is, of course, of vital importance in any kind of research process, but is even more important (especially with respect to vocabulary) in the use of electronic information gathering. Even fairly sophisticated users have great difficulty grasping the concept that most computer systems will only look for exactly the terms they enter in the computer. In contrast, much of the serendipity of print-based research came from humans browsing terms and knowing that, although an item refers to a topic that is apparently unrelated to the main subject of interest, it might be desirable for retrieval. Some computer systems try to address this computer limitation in a variety of ways, but they are not in widespread use in libraries.

Finally, Loomis and Fink encourage users to ask "What do I do with it?" They make the excellent point that librarians can no longer afford to shy away from dealing with how patrons store and manipulate the information they've retrieved electronically. This is part of the process of managing information. In looking at the audiences for instruction in the academic virtual library, Loomis and Fink don't see the types of users changing much. The primary change to be noted among students (and that should be affecting instruction programs already) is the increase in the diversity of the student population—cultural diversity, a variety of ages, a range of life experiences, and (an increasingly important factor) many levels of computing experience.

The implication of Loomis and Fink's work is that future library instruction-needs assessments must expand far beyond who is majoring in what, and include the cultural mix, numbers of nontraditional students, and assessments of computing experience. The virtual library may attract more faculty interest in library instruction as faculty become aware of all that is available electronically. It may also make them more amenable to receiving instruction themselves, Loomis and Fink note, since their resistance to the idea that they need instruction may be overcome by the obvious newness of these resources. There are pitfalls, too, however, since the nature of the virtual library means that evaluative skills are even more important for users to have, and faculty may resist the extent of library involvement that is needed to teach these skills adequately.

Loomis and Fink briefly note the growing importance of consideration of the remote user, primarily to conclude that more research and development is needed in this area. More and more of our users are at remote locations, but do we know how many and what proportion of our audience they represent? They also include in their consideration of audiences for instruction a group that is all too often forgotten—library staff. Library instruction programs tend not to be closely entwined with what is usually called staff training, but the two need to come ever closer in implementing the virtual library. Well-trained staff who are comfortable with change and new technologies are essential in instructing users, and libraries must support adequate training and practice time.

Loomis and Fink are not as concerned with providing a survey of current methods of instruction in dealing with electronic resources; their work is well supplemented by an article by Kelly L. K. Collins and Sharon Nelson Takacs called "Information Technology and the Teaching Role of the College Librarian."[3] Collins and Takacs note past survey results that have shown user preferences for one-on-one instruction and, indeed, this is the most effective way of teaching. However, they feel one-on-one instruction will not reach large populations, so they survey other methods of teaching information technologies. They briefly discuss peer instruction, group instruction, computer-based presentations, and supporting materials, noting the advantages and disadvantages of each. This gives a pretty good idea of what has gone on in library instruction for electronic resources. It's time to move beyond traditional limitations and conceptions of library instruction, though, and into the future. The virtual library demands more from us than endless hours spent producing reams of paper handouts and an infinite number of verbose lectures relaying the wonders of computers. It also calls for more than being physically bonded with a particular building. We must reconceive what we want to accomplish in instruction and imagine new ways of doing it.

WHAT ARE WE TRYING TO DO?

Loomis and Fink present a range of content areas for teaching about the virtual library that most librarians would probably agree are desirable to cover, but how does that relate to current and future library instruction practice? And does it truly meet user needs, or does it just seem like it should? Or, even worse, does it only meet our ideas of what their needs should be? It's time to decide that we are doing library instruction to meet user needs, not librarian needs.

WHATEVER WE'RE TRYING TO DO, ARE WE DOING IT WELL?

The everyday library instruction practitioner may well argue, and even believe, that users', especially students', information needs are being met by the instruction they receive; one cannot possibly know this, however, unless one evaluates user knowledge levels or interacts substantially with each student one instructs. There is a woeful shortage of research to show clearly that any given library instruction program accomplishes any worthwhile end. The recent library instruction literature is filled with studies that equate students' opinions of a library instruction presentation with genuine evaluation. Even articles that evaluate methodologies appropriate to instruction in information technologies offer contradictory evidence—for example, does it help to have a projected computer presentation or not?[4] One recent article, comparing the effectiveness of four methods of instructing students on PsycLIT, found that the only method that made a significant difference in student performance was a video created by PsycInfo![5] Might it not save us time if we all just bought this video? Another study seems to demonstrate that library instruction does make a difference—specifically, a "canned" computer projection presentation and an audiotaped narrative about OPAC searching was used with one set of students, while another set received no instruction.[6] The students who viewed the presentation did better on exercises than those who did not; however, even this study may have been affected by nonviewers being mostly freshmen who also had less computer experience, compared to primarily upperclassmen with more computer experience. And even if the results are accepted, the improvements were obtained with a presentation that did not depend on the presence of a librarian, rather like the PsycInfo video case cited above.

Tom Eadie's *Library Journal* article of 1990 and his follow-up paper printed in *Research Strategies* in 1992 have not been convincingly contravened by any of the responding papers or discussions. He doubts "the value of bibliographic instruction, understood as instruction programs for library users that are delivered on a schedule and in anticipation of questions that have not yet been asked."[7] He feels that some of the tasks named as justifications for instruction are better accomplished at the reference desk, and he convincingly questions several traditional rationales for library instruction. One rationale Eadie refers to as "cost effectiveness" raises questions that are even more vital in the age of the virtual library than they have ever been before. The contention, belied by Eadie, that "group BI is a more cost-effective use of a librarian's time than one-on-one of [sic] reference service" rests on the concept that most library instruction classes are effective in actually teaching students something substantial. In fact, as Eadie points out, we do have evidence that the best instruction is done one-on-one with motivated learners—and this is not a description that fits most library classroom situations. In an age of incredibly fast-paced change and vast growth in the knowledge that could be taught, is a lecture that results primarily in 30 students knowing there are bathrooms on every floor of the library really worthwhile?

WHO GETS TO DECIDE WHAT USERS NEED?

Overwhelmingly strong existing patterns in deciding what users need in library instruction can best be summed up by a quote from an unassuming but important article by the editor of this volume: "[librarians] want to teach not what their students want and need to learn, but what the librarian wants to teach them."[8] LaGuardia discusses an approach to library instruction for undergraduate students based on assessing their needs by listening to what is asked at the reference desk. She describes classes that do not involve sitting in a classroom and learning about bibliographic concepts, but that spend active class time learning and practicing real library skills, using computerized resources, identifying some items about their research topic, and finding them (or not finding them) in the library.

The past few years has seen a sudden rise in library literature devoted to total quality management, continuous quality improvement, and customer service in libraries—and applications to reference service have recently been made.[9] An area notably lacking coverage in these discussions is instruction. Many librarians assume so automatically and unquestioningly that they can best decide what students need to know that they've never stepped back to consider it objectively. This failing has been true of print-based instruction, too, but it is even more ludicrous in the time of the virtual library—many of us know much less about some areas of electronic research available through our own libraries than our students do and the pace of change is incredible, yet we still linger in the delusion that we can control an area of knowledge and hope to teach those controlling concepts to others.

In one very prescient article in 1985, Keith Stanger considered applying the concepts of market research to deciding whether library instruction was meeting user needs, and he concluded that it was not.[10] Most of us would accept the general statement that students need to locate useful materials more easily in the library, but much of our library instruction seems to lose sight of that need. As Stanger notes, "It is one thing to score high on a library skills test . . . and quite another to actually use this knowledge to find materials."

A recent welcome recognition of the imperative for change in academic library instruction is found in Janice Simmons-Welburn's paper on alternative models in instruction in the face of downsizing. What she calls post-bibliographic instruction " . . . must be focused on the pragmatic concerns of the information seeker" and " . . . is driven and contextualized by the rapid changes in information technology."[11] Her paper is a must-read in this age of trying to work smarter, not harder, with fewer resources. Broad assessments of student populations can still be informative for library instruction programs, but we need to include much more in these assessments than how many students are in each subject area and at what academic level. There is evidence that effectiveness of library instruction could improve if such factors as level of computing experience and cultural heritage were taken into account; these factors should also be considered in needs assessment.

HOW MUCH CAN WE TEACH?

Instruction librarians have long bemoaned the difficulty of teaching the research process, or the literature of a field, or whatever they thought best to teach, within the typical "50-minute hour" class period. In practice, many have realized that the answer to this challenge is not to find more ways to cruise through increasing amounts of information per minute, but to focus on what is important and to try to cover only a few things. In the age of the virtual library, however, it is time to see this not as a miserable stopgap that is the best we can do, but to embrace it and learn to see it as a blessing. Many of us also complain about how much there is to learn in the new world of electronic resources and how fast it changes.

This fact makes it even more imperative that we accept, and teach our students and faculty, that this is the way it is—electronics have brought us tremendous advantages in revolutionizing the information universe, and this universe will not hold still so we can know it and teach it. It is the number of resources available and how fast they change that make it even more ludicrous to think that the world of research can be covered in one or two class sessions. (Although full-length courses can support a realistic hope of covering much more material, they will touch the lives of only a fraction of the students contacted in brief, one-shot sessions.) We cannot teach everything, and we must accept that.

So, what should we teach? Before this is decided, one must get a reasonable perspective on the place that any given library instruction class can take in a student's life. To think that this is the one library class they're going to get in their five years of school, therefore they must be taught the research process, critical thinking, and how to use a few CD-ROM products, plus how to find periodicals, and where the copiers are, is completely self-defeating. Information overload can be boring, intimidating, frightening, off-putting, or all of the above. Even if one knew that this was the only chance a student had in his or her learning career to be instructed about the library, overload would still be ineffective.

There is now some recognition—beyond the knowledge that level of motivation plays a part in learning—that affective factors play a part in learning. (Yet many librarians still act as if they don't know that library instruction not tied to a specific assignment is a big waste of time.)[12] Information overload does not contribute to an emotional state of readiness in a student to learn about the library, or to enjoy using it in any way. There needs to be more study and consideration of how librarians can address student feelings about the library. We also need to know more about what students do with what they do learn, since this might also give us a better perspective on what we can accomplish in a limited amount of teaching time.

One study looks at patterns of CD-ROM searching among a group of students after they received instruction about it.[13] The students generally needed to learn the minimum amount to let them fulfill their assignment; over half of them were then short-term searchers and only 4 percent continued to be habitual database searchers. Much attention can be directed toward what we think students ought to learn, but even what we try to impart using that approach will be less effective if students perceive it as irrelevant.

HOW USER NEEDS SHOULD AFFECT CONTENT

Of course, the best way to find out what someone needs is to ask him or her—what a heretical concept! Despite all the concerns in library instruction literature about critical thinking, conceptual models, and the sacred research process, students would probably identify themselves as needing to know things more like how to use PsycLIT and how to find journal articles. As Joanne Bessler noted in an 1990 article, "Perhaps patrons do know what is good for them. Perhaps it's time for librarians to stop trying to teach patrons and to focus more effort on listening."[14] The future of library instruction was also addressed very well along these lines in a conference on rethinking reference in academic libraries. As James Rettig noted, "Each user will shape and reshape the information landscape to meet individual needs. . . . [w]e academic librarians must get beyond their [sic] current impasse on the 'To BI or not to BI?' question and recognize that its answer is almost always individual and situational."[15] Of course, the total content of teaching should not be determined by what pupils already think they need to know, since there are resources available of which they're not aware but that might be useful to them, whether they think so or not. A course in library instruction concepts certainly has time to introduce the whole research process, critical thinking and all the rest, but one-shot classes will probably be much more successful at really helping students if the focus is on getting them to the information they need, not telling them about a rigid research process which may have almost nothing to do with their individual needs.

If we have comparatively little time with a given class of students, why not try to ensure—by asking the students what they want to find out about—that some useful information will be imparted? A few such class conversations, with demonstrations and active involvement included, will tell the librarian much more about any common items students want to know, and information they need will definitely be communicated to them. Even if only an hour is all that is available, that still does not mean that tons of information should be crammed into the session, giving students all they'll need

to know about library research in the next four years. It is
much better to motivate them to get started, give them a better chance of succeeding in their initial uses of the library, and
then let them develop their own conceptual models and research processes. Anything we can also impart about dealing
with the fast pace of change in electronic resources and how
to learn and work on their own will be invaluable to them.

Many opportunities should then also naturally arise for
telling students about resources with which they're not already familiar. A frequently underdone part of the academic
library instruction program is outreach.[16] Electronic resources
seem to draw in quite a few new users with little or no pro-
motion; if they're being heavily used, why work hard to bring
in more people? Although there is certainly a point to making
sure that the library not advertise in a way that seems likely
to draw more people than it can possibly handle, on the other
hand, undoubtedly many students, faculty, and staff on all
campuses haven't the faintest idea that all these new electronic
resources exist, let alone what they can do. In fairness to them
and their information needs, libraries need to make greater
efforts to ensure that word gets out widely about electronic
resources. The electronic world not only brings libraries new
resources, it brings new ways to advertise them. Librarians
should have in their outreach "bag of tricks" Web pages, both
from the library and from other campus areas, as outreach
avenues.

Any e-mail broadcast abilities that are available and acceptable on campus are also possible avenues. Any group of
people using campus computer facilities are a likely audience
for computer facilities in or through the library, so computer
labs are a good location for print or, if possible, electronic advertising.

INSTRUCTION'S PROMISE FOR THE FUTURE: DOING THINGS THAT WORK

Library literature has shown for years that lectures about library resources do not facilitate patrons' use of the library to
satisfy their information needs. There is not even any certainty

that computerized demonstrations of electronic library resources come close to accomplishing that goal. And a point certainly not to be lost is that even if they are successful in most cases, the vast majority of people using academic library resources, especially electronic ones, will never have a library instruction session.

So what are we to do about contributing to our users' success in using the library? We must begin by not assuming that instructing someone to use a badly designed system is the place to start in our considerations. Our part should begin much earlier: instruction librarians must be more heavily involved in system design, both in working with vendors and in making changes in in-house systems where that is possible. This involvement must be based on getting user opinions about systems, not on what a librarian thinks is easy or difficult to use. As much of the literature that questions the value of instruction points out, some of our time might also be better spent questioning our own ways of doing things in libraries—for example, we shouldn't just create a card catalog in electronic form because that's the way we've always done things.

Some of this literature goes to the extreme of recommending stopping mass instruction and putting as much time as possible into one-on-one work. The overriding importance of one-on-one encounters should not be discounted, as they generally are, by saying "but of course we can't reach everyone that way." We can't reach everyone with organized instruction either, and a busy reference desk undoubtedly involves just as many instructional encounters, if not more than, an active instruction program. What's more, invaluable intelligence can be gained at the reference desk about what should be covered in an instruction program. If academic libraries are going to continue to do some group instruction and to develop some tools aimed at a mass audience, it would be best to put those efforts into something that is continuously capable of being assessed for its usefulness. This does not mean rigorous assessment suitable for research study all the time, but it does mean having largely interactive sessions where instructors can receive feedback about what's working and what's not. It also means a responsibility for doing evaluation that involves pretesting and posttesting whenever any new approach is used.

The "new" approach to instruction for the moment is active learning, and it does hold the promise of being a method that actually works.[17] Those who ask "what do I drop from the hour so the students can have time to be active?" are stuck between models: active learning involves completely rethinking the material covered. It's better for students to learn a few things thoroughly about the library than it is for them to sit through classes that cover 50 things from which they learn nothing.

One form of active learning that holds a great deal of promise is collaborative learning.[18] Anyone who has worked in an electronic resources area knows how students frequently group together to use products, and how much more receptive they are to learning and communicating with each other than with a librarian instructor. Collaborative learning involves grouping students and giving them activities in and/ or out of a class session to increase their involvement in their own learning. Although one 1994 report did not find evidence of greater learning after a use of collaborative learning in library instruction, many complex factors feed into assessment of collaborative learning, and more research needs to be done in this area.[19] Students may be better prepared to learn within the library when technology has been more widely acknowledged in their campus experience.

There is a strong movement to incorporate technology into the classroom; librarians need to make sure that access to library technology is considered part of this picture, since what students learn in their "real" classes is what is most credible and important for them.[20] Another very promising approach to teaching technology that goes beyond the library's concerns is a concept developed at Augustana College called Technology Toolbox.[21] Although developed by the library, this instruction manual and the classes based on it include campus computing resources beyond those of the library. The concept is that instructors whose students have gone through this process will know that the students have a grounding in the use of the basic computing skills needed on their campus. Expand this concept to use computer-assisted instruction (CAI), and there are some truly exciting possibilities.

Computer-assisted instruction, a method tried by many academic libraries with at least some degree of success, is a promising method that needs much more exploration to maximize its utility. Next to one-on-one assistance, this is the form of instruction exciting the most interest in patrons as shown in several studies; it is another excellent way of reaching users at their point of need for instruction.[22] Development and maintenance of truly useful computer-assisted instruction is very time-consuming, however, and involves great personnel resource investments. It may be decided that the expenditure of time and money is worth it, but there needs to be more rigorous testing of what is accomplished by any given CAI application.

Something not usually considered when evaluating CAI projects, however, is how useful they can possibly be, based on how they are being made available. CAI could be a tremendously useful way of reaching remote users, most of whom will never be reachable by classes (no matter how they're taught) or by printed handouts (no matter how wonderful). Yet, if months of effort are put into creating a CAI package that can only be used on a handful of machines in the library itself, that effort is wasted. The cost far outweighs the possible benefits.

On the other hand, efforts put into using the World Wide Web to convey library information and instruction make that material available remotely, possibly to the whole world! Exploring connections that can be made through the Web is currently the most profitable direction for libraries. Hand-in-hand with this direction is the fact that printed instructional materials need to be assessed even more carefully than ever before for costs and benefits. Remote users may never have any opportunity to receive these, and even for those who do receive them, are they truly helpful? Does every single library have to do its own handouts for each product? A tremendous amount of effort goes into essentially redesigning vendor handouts without any idea of whether library-produced handouts are useful at all, let alone whether they're more useful than the vendor ones.

THE VIRTUAL LIBRARY PATRON OF THE FUTURE

At some point in the next five years, many libraries will need to assess the point at which they have more users from outside their buildings than inside them. Primary attention cannot then remain fixed on dealing with patrons in a building. Now we address primarily those who come in the building and consider the others a sideline; but this is no longer appropriate, and the next trend we foresee is an entire redesign of instruction for the virtual library.

ENDNOTES

1. Janice Simmons-Welburn, "Alternative Models for Instruction in the Academic Library: Another View of the Upside of Downsizing," in *The Upside of Downsizing: Using Library Instruction to Cope*, ed. Cheryl LaGuardia (New York: Neal-Schuman, 1995), 15–23.

2. Abigail Loomis and Deborah Fink, "Instruction: Gateway to the Virtual Library," in *The Virtual Library: Visions and Realities*, ed. Laverna M. Saunders (Westport, Conn.: Meckler, 1993), 47–69.

3. Kelly L. K. Collins and Sharon Nelson Takacs, "Information Technology and the Teaching Role of the College Librarian," *Reference Librarian* 39 (1993): 41–51.

4. Linda G. Ackerson and Virginia E. Young, "Evaluating the Impact of Library Instruction Methods on the Quality of Student Research," *Research Strategies* 12 (Summer 1994): 132–144.

5. Dorothy F. Davis, "A Comparison of Bibliographic Instruction Methods on CD-ROM Databases," *Research Strategies* 11 (Summer 1993): 156–163.

6. Nancy L. Buchanan, Karen Rupp-Serrano, and Johanne LaGrange, "The Effectiveness of a Projected Computerized Presentation in Teaching Online Library Catalog Searching," *College and Research Libraries* 53 (July 1992): 307–318.

7. Tom Eadie, "Immodest Proposals: User Instruction for Students Does Not Work . . . " *Library Journal* 115 (October 15, 1990): 42–45; Tom Eadie, "Beyond Immodesty: Questioning the Benefits of BI," *Research Strategies* 10 (Summer 1992): 105–110. (Responses to this paper follow on pages 111–121.)

8. Cheryl LaGuardia, "Renegade Library Instruction," *Library Journal* 117 (October 1, 1992): 51–53.

9. Donald G. Davis, Jr., and James P. Niessen, "Negotiating the Passage from User Demands to Needs," *Journal of Academic Librarianship* 20 (July 1994): 140–141; Christopher Millson-Martula and Vanaja Menon, "Customer Expectations: Concepts and Reality for Academic Library Services," *College and Research Libraries* 56 (January 1995): 33–47.

10. Keith J. Stanger, "How Responsive Is Bibliographic Instruction to the Needs of Users?" *Reference Services Review* 13 (Fall 1985): 55–58.

11. Simmons-Welburn, "Alternative Models," 17.

12. Diane Nahl-Jakobovits and Leon A. Jakobovits, "Bibliographic Instructional Design for Information Literacy: Integrating Affective and Cognitive Objectives," *Research Strategies* 11 (Spring 1993): 73–88; Thomas G. Kirk, "College Libraries and the New Technology," *College and Research Libraries News* 55 (April 1994): 196–197.

13. Bruce A. Leach, "Identifying CD-ROM Use Patterns As a Tool for Evaluating User Instruction," *College and Research Libraries* 55 (July 1994): 365–371.

14. Joanne Bessler, "Do Library Patrons Know What's Good for Them?" *Journal of Academic Librarianship* 16 (May 1990): 76–77. (Responses to this paper follow on pages 78–85.)

15. James Rettig, "To BI or Not to BI? That Is the Question," in *Rethinking Reference in Academic Libraries*, ed. Anne Grodzins Lipow (Berkeley, Calif.: Library Solutions Press, 1993), 139–151.

16. Lynn Westbrook and Robert Waldman, "Outreach in Academic Libraries: Principle into Practice," *Research Strategies* 11 (Spring 1993): 60–65.

17. John A. Mess, "Use of Roleplaying in Bibliographic Instruction," *Science and Technology Libraries* 14 (Winter 1993): 105–118.

18. Jean Sheridan, "The Reflective Librarian: Some Observations on Bibliographic Instruction in the Academic Library," *Journal of Academic Librarianship* 16 (March 1990): 22–26; Marjorie Markoff Warmkessel and Frances M. Carothers, "Collaborative Learning and Bibliographic Instruction," *Journal of Academic Librarianship* 19 (March 1993): 4–7.

19. Diane Prorak, Tania Gottschalk, and Mike Pollastro, "Teaching Method and Psychological Type in Bibliographic Instruction: Effect on Student Learning and Confidence," *RQ* 33 (Summer 1994): 484–495.

20. J. Christopher McConnell, "Technology and Teaching in Academia," *Reference Librarian* 39 (1993): 31–40.

21. Jeanne R. Davidson, "Computer Technology: Pandora's Box or Toolbox?" *Research Strategies* 12 (Summer 1994): 182–186.

22. Ann Bevilacqua, "Computer-Assisted Bibliographic Instruction," in *Bibliographic Instruction in Practice: A Tribute to the Legacy of Evan Ira Farber*, ed. Larry Hardesty, Jamie Hastreiter, and David Henderson (Ann Arbor, Mich.: Pierian Press, 1993), 67–76; Bruce Leach, "Computer-Based CD-ROM Tutorials: Providing Effective On-Demand Instruction," *CD-ROM Professional* 6 (July 1993): 113–114, 116–117; Shannon Azzaro and Kaye Cleary, "Developing a Computer-Assisted Learning Package for End-Users," *CD-ROM Professional* 7 (March 1994): 95–96, 98–101.

PART V:

INFORMATION SEEKERS

14

Challenges and Opportunities in Reaching the Remote User

Ilene F. Rockman

Librarians have been working with remote resources for many years, ever since the earliest computer networks and databases were created. We're very used to accessing information remotely and handing it over to grateful patrons at a desk or in a classroom. But the natural progression of such access to remote information is, of course, being able to capture that information remotely and deliver it remotely, so patrons can use our services from anywhere on Earth and literally never have to enter the physical library. Ilene Rockman discusses the needs of this growing clientele of remote users and how we can anticipate and fill those needs.—CML

As libraries continue to look ahead to the creative enhancement and expansion of their collections and services, the needs of the external (remote) user cannot be ignored. Traditionally, libraries have focused on the internal user. Yet, if the mission of the library is to be visionary and anticipatory, it is clear that the needs of all types of users must be addressed in an inclusive statement, such as the following:

- to create environments conducive to discovery and learning
- to provide information appropriate to the needs of users, equitably and efficiently
- to develop methods for the timely and expeditious delivery of information resources
- to assist all users with the transformation of data into knowledge
- to support the need for information anytime, anywhere, and in any format

To serve the needs of the remote user adequately, a library must seriously examine the four S's:

- services—the types of instructional materials and programs offered
- staffing—the range of competencies and the partnerships with nonlibrary personnel to address the technical needs of remote users
- security—attention to the protection, integrity, accuracy, and reliability of data to be accessed and delivered
- (infra)structure—the ability to deliver information through a variety of network configurations and typologies

Librarians have studied the impact of, and written extensively about, remote access, including the evaluation of user searching behavior.[1] These reports have conflicting conclusions ranging from no impact on in-house library attendance based on remote use of library catalogs during off-hours, to the impact of "invisible" users who may confound the library's ability to deliver "high level personal service."[2]

Some libraries have measured the impact of remote users by counting network connections to World Wide Web servers, while other libraries have quantified remote use through such statistics as increased book circulations, interlibrary loan requests, electronic suggestions, demands for telereference services, electronic registration for library workshops, and requests to download or export library information files. Often, libraries consider remote access as a supplement to, rather than a substitution for, in-house library services.[3]

SERVICES

Services to any, and all, remote users change the concepts of time and place. Libraries may provide remote services to their local clientele who may be located in classrooms, laboratories, offices, or residences. Concomitantly, libraries may also assist nonsite, primary clientele during times when the library is open or closed. These geographically dispersed individuals may be alumni, friends, emeriti faculty and staff, students admitted (but not yet enrolled) in a college or university, or employees of a sister campus institution or branch library. Consideration may also be given to those users who have no affiliation with a host institution, but have a need for accessing a remote collection of information resources. Wielhorski identifies and summarizes the following general categories of remote users:[4]

- affiliated campus users (traditional students, faculty, staff, administrators)
- affiliated off-campus users (these include research center personnel, distance education students, and users at institutions within the same university system)
- unaffiliated local (community) users
- unaffiliated distant users (anyone with Internet access)

All of these individuals may compete equally for services (accessible ports or reference assistance), whether they use the library system consistently or on an infrequent, part-time basis. The one common denominator among all of them is the embracing of technology. Although they may be novices or sophisticates, they do possess an increased need for service (such as clear online help screens, full-text databases displayed online, document delivery to e-mail boxes or fax machines, self-service circulation check-out and renewal functions, telereference services, access to downloadable image files, subject guides to Internet resources, or network-accessible multimedia learning tools available online or deliverable to an electronic mail account). It can be safely said that both levels of users share an increased need for technical assistance as they wrestle with the variety of telecommunciation challenges and retrieval tools in this fast-paced, ever-changing electronic environment.

Paying for Services

Due to the costs of delivering subscription-based information, such as full-text sources, equitably to local and remote users, libraries have embraced a strategy of collaboration with colleagues to stretch their precious materials budgets. One example of collaboration is the pooling of resources to employ a cooperative group purchase for multiple, discipline-specific online databases. By pooling dollars, and sharing common network ports, maximum access to these online resources can be achieved.

Within the 22 campus libraries of the California State University system, maximum returns on investments have been realized. Equal access to databases has been made available to both local and remote users, whether they reside in an urban, suburban, or rural environment. Key to the success of the project is the leveraging of funds to redesign subscription payment plans in order to gain educational discounts on the cost of access to, and fax or Internet delivery of, full-text documents. In addition, collaborative agreements also made possible the procurement of necessary software, Ethernet-equipped workstations, printers, and scanners to transmit image-based documents over the Internet. This "strength in numbers" group purchase approach permits increased access to information for all users, especially those in remote locations, and is possible due to library and vendor agreement on the number of simultaneous users, selection of electronic databases, and predictable fixed costs.[5]

Another example of economic collaboration supportive of the library's service mission to increase access to information involves the private sector and both the K–12 and higher education communities.[6] These projects include

- Mississippi 2000, a joint project among the state of Mississippi, Bellsouth Telecommunications, Northern

Telecomm, IBM, Apple Computer, and ADC Telecommunications to link two universities with four secondary schools and a local educational network.

- California Research and Education Network (CALREN), funded by Pacific Bell in 1993, to promote the creation and development of new high-speed data communication projects. One such product is the Distributed Learning Resources Project of Project DELTA (Direct Electronic Learning Teaching Alternatives), which focuses on the design, implementation testing, and demonstration of an integrated, high-speed, networked multimedia learning environment among several campuses of the California State University system. Content delivered through Project DELTA initiatives ranges from the transmission of digitized biology slides to multimedia courseware in art history.
- NYNEX, New York, which focuses on distance learning in upstate New York among Cornell University, Syracuse University, and the Air Force Research Center.

Additionally, the strides made by cooperative efforts between librarians in California and New York through the Consortium for Educational Technology for University Systems (CETUS) may prove to be useful to other librarians facing challenges in determining the appropriate level of library resources to deliver, the integration of information competence into education programs, the broad applications of the principles of fair use of copyrighted works, and the delineation of learners' responsibilities in acquiring the necessary tools and applications needed to access information resources transmitted through library outreach programs.[7]

Distance Learning

As the number of students desiring access to higher education increases while budgets do not support the addition of new faculties or facilities, and as demands for continuing education or extended education opportunities for working professionals continue to grow, universities are developing creative solutions to address these challenges. One such solution is distance learning, a form of instruction in which the student and instructor are separated and instructional materials are delivered electronically. Traditionally, this form of learning has included mail order correspondence courses and book- or video-based independent learning resources in which students usually work at home, receiving instruction through print or audiovisual materials, educational television broadcasts, or a combination of these or other methods.[8] However, with rapid advancements in telecommunications capabilities, distant learning has been transformed into a much more widespread form of teaching and learning. Also known as off-campus or extended campus learning, newer initiatives include the ability of users to share digitized resources over a network, while collaborating with each other or with their instructors electronically using computer conferences or electronic mail technologies. Distance learning may involve a number of delivery systems, including

- two-way, full-motion, interactive voice and video presentations, which provide face-to-face interactions between teacher and students
- one-way networks that broadcast video instruction to a large number of locations, handling questions through audio hookups or fax machines.[9]

Students enrolled in individual courses or degree programs through distance education still need access to library resources, as well as library instruction programs to learn how to analyze, evaluate, and apply critically both print and electronic resources to an information need. One library has taken the position that whatever the mode of distance instruction, and wherever the clientele may be, library resources must be available. Elements of library support include courier and electronic document delivery, electronic journals, full-text databases, reference assistance and instruction, cooperative arrangements with other libraries for collection access, cooperative development of databases, and strategies that emphasize access as well as ownership of resources.[10]

The services of the library will, no doubt, increase as the number of distant learners increases. Librarians who plan and deliver services to these remote users will not only need to be comfortable with technological change, but will need to possess the characteristics of flexibility, adaptability, patience, willingness to learn from mistakes, and willingness to take risks. Effective distance teaching and learning will require rapid access to resources on-demand in a variety of telecommunication modes. The library must also be able to support students and faculty at times and locations convenient for them, rather than for the library.[11]

The Downside

Despite the excitement generated by the infinite service possibilities of delivering information anytime, anyplace, any way, and to anyone, there is also a downside to remote service. Lynden notes that "one of the first disadvantages is the clutter or crowding which has occurred on the Internet."[12] The amount of information available is staggering, as the number of World Wide Web sites, Internet providers, and users continues to explode. This rapid acceleration makes it a challenge for librarians to stay current with not only the sites and content of Internet-accessible resources, but also with the optimum methods for applying learning theory to systems design. Users need to know not only the basic cognitive mechanics of connecting, locating, and retrieving desired information, but also the higher-order learning skills of how to apply, analyze, synthesize, evaluate, and transform these data into knowledge. All of these tasks must be communicated attractively, easily, and accurately through the network.

In addition, the issue of response time is of paramount importance. Remote users are impatient, especially when a cost is associated with the network connection, or time restrictions affect the ability to download files of information. Moreover, remote users are often demanding of technical assistance for the preprocessing and postprocessing of data (decompression of files, displaying or printing of information).

Creative Solutions

All of these issues and challenges are yet to be fully resolved. In the meantime, librarians have taken the liberty of providing creative solutions, such as the placement of instructional materials (for example, handouts and cheat sheets) on the network. Text materials are reformatted to accommodate the image and visual capabilities of placement on library home pages for access through the World Wide Web.

At the University of Cincinnati's Engineering Library, for example, over 500 incoming freshmen are trained through the Engineering Library's home page.[13] This strategy permits the library to provide instruction without having to add staff. Located on the home page are electronic reserves, new book lists, links to the online catalog, subject guides to resources in the library and on the Web, and a comments/feedback section.

Universities have found, however, that remote access to home pages through dial-up telephone lines can pose special challenges.[14] Convenient point-and-click browser programs (such as Netscape or Explorer) are not as easily accessible remotely, as they are through direct campus network connections. As a result, users must invest in special serial line internet protocol (SLIP) or point-to-point protocol (PPP) connections in order to take advantage of the graphical user interface (GUI) capabilities of the World Wide Web through remote telephone connections. This added functionality, which permits the downloading of graphics and images, keeps remote users connected longer, thus creating a contentious environment for those sharing port access through a dial-up modem pool.

In summary, the provision of both material and programmatic services to remote users is fluid and ever-changing. New types of users are emerging, often possessing a diversity of skill levels. Expanded service roles for librarians may include telereference services for handling queries in a batch or online environment; user interface and front-end design of resources for easier and more convenient access to information by both novice and experienced remote users; selection and acquisition of electronic and multimedia resources for network delivery; creation and/or development of multimedia instructional guides for access and use of information resources; collaboration with network administrators for easy authentication, validation, or identification of remote users; and design and development of increased self-service options, such as electronic forms for comments and suggestions, reference queries, interlibrary loan requests, or delivery of print library resources. Libraries have begun to document these services to provide further guidance to those sites considering such offerings.[15]

STAFFING

Service to remote users requires a library to rethink traditional job descriptions and staffing models. Rather than employing individuals for reference or subject expertise alone, libraries are wise to consider hiring personnel not only with instruction and collection development skills, but also with technical and graphic design expertise.

At the Albert R. Mann Library of Cornell University, remote users may contact the reference desk with questions about selecting the correct database to access through the library's single Gateway system, and also with telecommunication questions related to the installation, use, connection, printing, and saving of records.[16] Librarians at Cornell University, as well as at other libraries, are challenged to provide high-quality reference, troubleshooting, and consulting services to remote users. These librarians must match user queries to a variety of print and electronic resources (including bibliographic, numeric, graphic, and full-text databases; image archives; and World Wide Web sites for multimedia learning materials).

Just as library users may benefit from training guides and online tutorials, so may library staff members. At a minimum, both users and library employees should be competent and successful in accessing, retrieving, displaying, and manipulating a variety of robust information sources and formats.

Some libraries, such as the Hillman Library at the University of Pittsburgh, have recognized the need for collaboration between librarians and academic computing professionals, and have included side-by-side library offices for both groups better to assist local and remote users. Librarians in this setting conduct reference interviews, analyze user queries, advise users on database content, and educate users about access points. Computer specialists work hand-in-hand with librarians to troubleshoot technical questions related to equipment, network access, and the downloading or manipulation of data.

At the Pennsylvania State University Libraries, a pooling of staff expertise has resulted in an effective model for Internet instruction as a joint project between the library and the computer and information systems office, building on the strengths of both organizations.[17] Other libraries may choose to employ systems librarians, electronic resource librarians, or technical experts who are not librarians. New positions may be created, or existing positions may be reevaluated and redefined as they become vacant.

Whatever the local decision, it is clear that traditional staffing patterns and job descriptions may not be adequate to meet the needs of the present and emerging population of remote users. Therefore, libraries need to determine if it is better to develop the in-house library expertise to diagnose and advise users on complex technical problems related to hardware and software platforms, or if the work can be assigned to local computer professionals to provide this support.[18]

SECURITY

Reports in the popular and scholarly press note an acute rise in the number of malicious attacks on the Internet.[19] Not only does this intrusive behavior add to the proliferation of network traffic, but it poses serious threats to direct access to needed information. Malevolent, mean-spirited hackers and crackers (those individuals who deliberately break into computer systems to cause damage and wreak havoc) focus their attention on the Internet. The relative ease of access through remote log-ins or modem pool lines contributes to their ability to steal password files, block the delivery of information, infect networks, and deny service to others.[20]

According to experts at the Computer Emergency Response Team (CERT) based at Carnegie Mellon University, these attacks are increasing. Since 1988, CERT has responded to over 3,000 Internet security incidents, some emanating from libraries. For example, in August 1994 computer hackers caused a two-hour shutdown of the 41–member libraries of the Ohio Library and Information Network (OhioLINK), a statewide academic network and Internet gateway.[21]

Because of system vulnerabilities, some libraries have chosen to disconnect temporarily from the Internet (thereby avoiding the problem of user authentication and password verification) to protect their data and, instead, provide access only to their local clientele from within the library.[22] This extreme measure is ironic in an era where remote access to resources is commonplace, and library resource sharing is a way of life.

Other libraries have chosen to work with their systems personnel to change access configurations in an attempt to block potential security holes and known bugs in operating systems or systems utilities that are more pronounced when exposed to a remote login prompt. Gene Spafford of the Purdue University Computer Science Department observes that security will always be inversely proportional to convenience.

To avoid such problems, some universities have developed network connection policies. Such documents note the consequences of network abuses, and the proper use of network resources. Other libraries have taken steps to install firewalls to deter unauthorized access to network-accessible resources. All of these attempts are stop-gap measures, since it is difficult to safeguard completely data on the network.

(INFRA)STRUCTURE

Remote users are at a complete disadvantage if a reliable, high-speed, easily accessible, wide area network infrastructure is not in place. The emergence of ATM, or asynchronous transfer mode, can serve to meet the needs of present and future remote users quite well. As a set of international standards for high-speed digital networks, ATM permits the transmission of massive amounts of data (interactive video, sound, image, animation, multimedia, computer data, text, and the like) at blinding speeds and simultaneously over a single network. ATM reduces the data into common digital bits, processes them, and then reassembles them into video, voice, or data signals. Currently the cost of ATM is extremely high, and unaffordable to most educational institutions; within the next few years, however, ATM should be more affordable to libraries, and able to be used at the desktop.

One of the chief benefits of ATM over other technologies, such as high-speed dial-up, Ethernet, or Integrated Services Digital Network (ISDN), is its scalability. Unlike ISDN (which can carry voice, data, and video over the same narrow-band communications channel), ATM is flexible and scalable. As the network grows and expands, so does ATM. In addition, it is fully interoperable with existing wide area network environments such as fiber distributed data interface (FDDI), which was developed to permit communication between large computers and peripherals over an optical fiber network. Furthermore, ATM can handle complex applications ranging from geographic information systems to videoconferencing. It provides a better platform for bandwidth-intensive applications, and better performance than T-1 or T-3 speed frame relay systems. In addition to ATM, librarians are also following the developments in mobile data networks and wireless technologies. These may include personal data assistants and wireless modems used in conjunction with cellular telephones and laptop computers. Early experiences show great potential, although some users note that the slow speed of wireless modems can affect the ability of learners to connect conveniently to WWW sites.

The importance of sufficient bandwidth cannot be underestimated. The growth of high bandwidth connections that will provide users with access to interactive digital video and audio capabilities will increase libraries' opportunities to reach and teach remote users.[23]

CONCLUSION

Reaching the remote user will continue to be a challenge for libraries as services (instructional programs and support materials), staffing (levels and competencies in subject fields, material types, and technical configurations), security (accessibility and reliability of data), and infrastructure (network bandwidth capabilities and scalable technologies) remain key elements of a library's service mission. No longer does remote access simply mean dial-up access to an online catalog. Today's remote users expect access to include the full complement of information resources, including multimedia databases and World Wide Web resources from anywhere, at any time, to any place. There is no doubt that information technologies, and the role of the library, will continue to evolve and change the way users obtain and create new knowledge. Librarians need to be comfortable with this change, while they position themselves to take proactive roles in managing to meet the present and future needs of the remote user. The basic trends are clear: more users, greater distances, increased distribution of computing power, growing bandwidth requirements, heightened need for information competency, and more user-to-user communication.[24]

ENDNOTES

1. Paul Heller, "Remote Access: Its Impact on a College Library," *The Electronic Library* 10 (October 1992): 287–289; Larry Millsap and Terry Ellen Ferl, "Search Patterns of Remote Users: An Analysis of OPAC Transaction Logs," *Information Technology and Libraries* 12 (September 1993): 321–343; Ernest A. DiMattia, Jr. "Total Quality Management and Servicing Users through Remote Access Technology," *The Electronic Library* 11 (June 1993): 187–191.

2. Elizabeth Dow, "The Impact of Home and Office Workstation Use on an Academic Library" (Ph.D. dissertation, University of Pittsburgh, 1988); Sally Kalin, "Support Services for Remote Users of Online Public Access Catalogs," *RQ* 31 (Winter 1991): 197–213.

3. Lois M. Bellamy, John T. Silver, and Mary King Givens, "Remote Access to Electronic Library Services through a Campus Network," *Bulletin of the Medical Library Association* 79 (January 1991): 53–62.

4. Karen Wielhorski, "Teaching Remote Users How to Use Electronic Information Sources," *Public Access Computer Systems Review*, 5, no. 4 (1994): 5–20. [Online:] at gopher info.lib.uh.edu, port 70, or http://info.lib.uh.edu/pacsrev. html

5. Ilene F. Rockman, "Editorial: Affording Electronic Resources: Collaboration Is the Key." *Reference Services Review*, 23, no. 1 (1995): 3.

6. Teri Phalen Cassell, "Telco Projects in Education," *Syllabus* 8 (June 1995): 10–12.

7. Alexander L. Slade, *Library Services for Off-Campus and Distance Education*. Englewood, Colo.: Libraries Unlimited, 1996.

8. *Information Resources and Library Services for Distance Learners: A Framework for Quality* (Seal Beach, Calif.: The Trustees of the California State University, 1996). This is a joint project of the California State University, the State University of New York, and the City University of New York. It is also available in an electronic version on the home page of the Consortium for Educational Technology for University Systems (http://www.cetus.org).

9. John Walsh and Bob Reese, "Distance Learning's Growing Reach," *THE: Technological Horizons in Education* 22 (June 1995): 58–62.

10. "Final Report of the Use of Electronic Instructional Technologies" (San Luis Obispo, Calif.: California Polytechnic State University, Academic Senate Curriculum Committee, January 27, 1995), 4.

11. William M. Plater, "The Library: A Labyrinth of the Wide World," *Educom Review* 30 (March–April 1995): 38–41.

12. Frederick C. Lynden, "Remote Access Issues: Pros and Cons," *Journal of Library Administration* 20, no. 1 (1994): 19–36.

13. Dorothy F. Byers and Lucy Wilson, "Library Instruction Using Mosaic," *Proceedings of the 16th National Online Meeting* (Medford, N.J.: Learned Information, 1995), 47–52.

14. David L. Wilson, "Internet@Home: Many Colleges Poised to Improve Off-Campus Access to Computer Networks," *Chronicle of Higher Education* 41 (June 16, 1995): A20–A22.

15. *Providing Public Services to Remote Users*, ARL SPEC Kit 191 (Washington, D.C.: Association of Research Libraries, 1993).

16. Susan Barnes, "The Electronic Library and Public Services," *Library Hi Tech* 12, no. 3 (1994): 51.

17. Sally Kalin and Carol Wright, "Internexus: A Partnership for Internet Instruction," *Reference Librarian* 41/42 (1994): 197–209.

18. Wielhorski, "Teaching Remote Users How to Use Electronic Information Sources," 11.

19. David L. Wilson, "'Cracker': A Serious Threat," *Chronicle of Higher Education* 40 (August 17, 1994): A23–A24.

20. Ilene F. Rockman, "Editorial: Hackers and the Reference Librarian, or Is There a Firewall in Your Future?" *Reference Services Review* 23, no. 2 (1995): 5.

21. "OhioLINK Tightens Security after Hacker Causes a Network Crash," *American Libraries* 25 (October 1994): 806–807.

22. Len Arends and Lori Witmer, "Campus Combats Hacking Troubles," *Mustang Daily* (California Polytechnic State University) 58 (May 12, 1994): 1, 5.

23. Wielhorski, "Teaching Remote Users How to Use Electronic Information Sources," 5.

24. D. M. Soon, "Remote Access: Major Developments in 1995," *Telecommunications* 29 (January 1995): 57.

15

Is Anyone at Home? Remembering Our In-Library Clients

Caroline M. Kent

If the academic library of the future were a question of "either/or"—if we were going entirely into an online environment, or if necessity forced us to stay entirely within the realm of print—many of the most pressing issues facing us would be moot. We would not have to learn new systems (weekly, or so it seems) while retaining our expertise in the old, we would not have to house print collections as well as store mammoth databases, we would not have to find the money to acquire a multitude of formats. Of course, none of us would sacrifice the research future to such an overly simplistic, short-sighted quick fix—choosing entirely "either print or electronic" is not a realistic option. The reality is that we will be working with both print and electronic resources for the foreseeable future. And who will be using those resources? We've heard quite a bit about the remote and distant user up to this point. In this essay about in-house clients, Carrie Kent reminds us where our bread-and-butter clientele will be for many years to come.—CML

A few years ago, while I was sitting at a reference desk at Harvard University, I was approached by a graduate student who asked me to assist him in untangling a mangled citation, an act that, although made easier by my experience, turned out to be relatively straightforward. I obliged, determined the location of the journal in our libraries, and sent him on his way. It had not been a difficult or challenging task, and, up to this point, had been a relatively unnotable interchange. But as he turned to leave, the student suddenly turned back and wistfully said, "I've been waiting all my life to find a reference librarian like you." Then, ducking his head in embarrassment, he left.

I was stunned by the remark. For some time after, I used this story as an example of the sorry state of reference staffing in many of the Harvard libraries. But as time has passed, and I have gained knowledge of many other academic reference departments and what is happening in them, I begin to wonder if Harvard is so terribly unusual.

I now routinely question my teaching colleagues and friends about their library experiences both here and at other institutions. Among the many positive remarks made, the two negative remarks that I frequently hear are, "There was no one around to help me," and "The person behind the desk was clearly not a real reference librarian." And that brings me to a simple and rather shame-faced observation: We are removing our most highly trained and experienced personnel from our reference desks, and—guess what!—our students and faculty know it, and are not happy about it.

WHAT DO WE EXPECT OF OURSELVES, AND IS THAT OUR PROBLEM?

The sad part is, of course, that we did this not because we necessarily wanted to, but because we felt compelled to. It is no secret to any public-service administrator that reference and research librarians are having to do too much; the breadth of activities expected from them is at an unprecedented level. We still expect them to demonstrate skill with all the tools and services required by print media, but now we also demand an equally large set of skills associated with online and networked resources. They must accurately and politely answer simple and complex reference queries, in person, on the phone, on the network.

They must teach, both one-shot classes and for-credit courses. They must serve as liaisons with the faculty in areas of service, teaching, and collection development. They must select materials, not just for the reference collection, and not just those in print, but materials for all parts of the collections in all formats. Oh, and let us not forget that we also expect them to handle any time-critical computer issues that arrive for our patrons, as well as change the paper in the copy machine when there is no one else around to do it.

They handle problem patrons shouting at the library assistants, urinating in the stacks, exposing themselves to innocent freshmen. They handle normal students gone berserk at exam times, and irate faculty demanding impossible data files at impossible times.

They create bibliographies, both printed and online. They build home pages and help design system interfaces. They constantly annotate and interpret the library through the work of their colleagues in cataloging and collection development.

They serve on library committees, on academic committees, on American Library Association (ALA) committees. They attend workshops and conferences, and write articles, books, and reviews . . .

All of the above might lead the reader to think that this is an essay on "burnout" in reference librarians. But it is not. It's not that I don't care about the mental health of reference and research librarians, but I must care about our users just as much. And I am led to ask the question: In the midst of all of these activities, how much time can reference and research librarians give to the "in-house" client, that person who, in the case of academic libraries, may be paying a large tuition to get good, direct, face-to-face service, whose research depends on access to research tools, both human and material.

WHO IS THE ACADEMIC IN-HOUSE CLIENT?

I define the academic in-house "clients" or users as the persons who expect to be able to receive fast and accurate help by walking into their library, with "their" library being defined as the research entity supported by their tuitions and the endowments of their academic institution. There are, of course, many library pundits who continually predict that somewhere in the not-so-distant future there will be no legitimate need for most people to come to a physical place called the library.

Although I am a firm believer in the progress and value of digitization and network-accessible resources, I disagree with the premise that in the near future there won't continue to be a great many "in-house" users. There are a number of reasons that lead me to feel this way.

First, there will always be nondigitized materials. Not only will certain of the large, retrospective collections that have little common value but deep research value remain in older print formats, but the print medium remains, as a very "highly computerized" professor recently confided to me, the finest and most dependable archiving method yet available.

There will always be students and faculty who, either always or sometimes, prefer face-to-face contact with the person helping them with their research processes. There will also continue to be, for many years, people who are not yet fully comfortable with any "digital library." And there will always be people who want to study, talk, do research in, and just plain think in the "library place"—the physical space that we have and will continue to design such that these activities are properly supported.

Many of our users will often, if not always, choose to have their reference questions answered via e-mail or phone, have their photocopies delivered directly to their microcomputers or fax machines, their books by intercampus delivery service, and so forth. But if my experience (which leads me to believe that there will also remain many people who want to walk in our front door and receive those same services) is correct, then we shall have to be prepared to continue to meet those demands in the best way possible.

DEFINING SERVICES AND SERVICE PRIORITIES FOR THE IN-HOUSE CLIENT

In my opening paragraphs I listed a number of activities, all or some of which are now regarded as appropriate activities for reference and research staff. These activities include answering reference/research queries using both printed and automated reference materials; teaching library-use and research classes; developing curricula for teaching programs and credit-bearing courses; maintaining faculty contacts; doing book selection and collection development; troubleshooting a wide variety of microcomputers, software, and peripherals; creating bibliographies (both in print and online); creating Web home pages; handling patron issues; managing staff; serving on in-house, local, and national committees; writing articles, books, reviews; spending extensive time on learning new systems and sources; and attending workshops, subject-related seminars and courses.

Very few people would question that any of the listed activities (short of problem patrons and filling copying machines with paper) are not in countless ways additive, in the long run, to an individual's ability to become a better research advisor. But how do we staff reference desks and offices when we are engaged in these countless valuable and complex activities? Very few of our institutions are currently engaged in creating larger staffs; most institutions are going through reengineering or downsizing projects. How in the world, then, are we going to provide research services to the patrons of both our digital and our physical libraries?

SOLUTIONS

The single, most expensive activity that a reference/research librarian can engage in is one-on-one contact with a library patron; however, for in-house patrons, one-on-one contact is at the heart of why they choose to come in to use our services.

Central to finding the correct solutions to the dilemma of intensely conflicting demands is being able to answer two questions:

- What do our library users need?
- What do they expect of us?

The answers to these questions will vary from academic community to academic community. Levels of commitment to teaching and research, the size of a library's collections, differences in subject orientation, differences in the types of students that attend our institutions—all of these factors and more change the answers that any one of us might arrive at.

User-needs assessment of some form is an exercise that all libraries should periodically engage in. This could mean a large, scientifically constructed user survey, or a series of "focus group" meetings with different groups of faculty and students, where the returned information is more qualitative and anecdotal. The ideal would be to engage in a certain amount of each sort of data collection.

Once we know the answers to our two questions, we can then engage in *thinking* about what we do. This seems self-evident, but most of us have very little time to spend really thinking, alone and in groups, about what it is that we do. We tend to react, and our services often reflect that. Ideally, we should think in groups—that is, we should engage in strategic planning. This is not always possible, but we must resist the temptation to avoid serious, inclusive planning efforts that "take too much time." No one model of service works well in more than one institution. We must be able to adapt models to suit our circumstances, and that requires thought and planning.

Listed below are some possible solutions to evolving service to our in-house users. All of these ideas, or some combination of them, would find appropriate locations:

- Give users easy access only to less expensive support staff. Make contact with a reference librarian possible only through an appointment.
- Limit the hours that easy, walk-up access is possible.
- Categorize your users, and put restrictions on what sort of service you offer any one category.[1]
- Break down patron requests by ease of predicted an-

swer, and create different services to satisfy different need levels.

- Radically increase the amount of classroom teaching done; theoretically, the more students handled with a more efficient student-teacher ratio, the better off we'll be.
- Create "specialties" in our reference/research positions, so that not everyone is expected to participate fully in all activities.
- Restrict or cut back on reference and research staff members' activities.

Each of these ideas has both its proponents and its adversaries. I'm not advocating any one as an ideal solution, but the financial facts that most of us face demand that we at least consider these options in our thinking.

THE MOST REASONABLE OUTCOME

Most academic libraries will find the most reasonable solution to the in-house service dilemma by using modified forms of several of the ideas in the previous section. If restricting the number of services or the hours that a particular service is offered results in a more substantive, balanced approach to service, it might be well worth doing. We must be careful that we evaluate and reevaluate what we do constantly. Flexibility and the ability to be self-critical are increasingly important characteristics in public service staff and administrators.

Bringing reason and control to what we do is often quite difficult for us. Most good reference and research librarians are good because they care about all of the patrons' conflicting needs, and work not to have to say "no" or put restrictions on what they offer. Most reference librarians would rather work themselves to distraction and burnout than restrict their activities. For that reason, inclusiveness in the planning process is very important.

CONCLUSION

We are of the greatest use to our patrons when we think about what they need, about what they have asked for, and about how we feel about the services we offer. In a world where everyone is discussing networking and our digitized future, we must be careful to protect those users who do not fit the pattern of the digital library. In times of great change, protecting the things that already work is often quite difficult.

As a group, we have little to fear if we listen to our in-house patrons, and if we remember why we are doing what we do. Good reference and research librarians have a passion for what they do, and that passion finds a good home in both the old and new ways of executing our service imperative.

ENDNOTE

1. Charles A. Bunge, "Potential and Reality at the Reference Desk: Reflections on a 'Return to the Field,'" *Journal of Academic Librarianship* 10, no. 3 (1984): 130.

ADDITIONAL RESOURCES

Biggs, Mary. "Replacing the Fast Fact Drop-In with Gourmet Information Service: A Symposium." *Journal of Academic Librarianship* 11, no. 2 (1985): 68–78.

Ford, Barbara J. "Reference Beyond (and without) the Reference Desk." *College and Research Libraries* 47 (September 1986): 491–494.

"The Future of Reference Service [Panel discussion at Univ. of Texas, Austin]." *College and Research Libraries News* 49, no. 9 (1988): 578–587.

Lipow, Anne Grodzins, ed. *Rethinking Reference in Academic Libraries*. Berkeley, Calif.: Library Solutions Press, 1993.

Martin, Rebecca R. "The Paradox of Public Service: Where Do We Draw the Line?" *College and Research Libraries* 51 (January 1990): 20–26.

AFTERWORD

The New Renaissance Librarian

Cheryl LaGuardia

The concept that echoes through the pages of this book is unmistakable: change is constant, the only constant is change. With this as a given, it seems as if we librarians are engaged in the endless pursuit of trying to pin down and organize concepts, ideas, images, and sounds that alter and transmute in our very hands, while we attempt to classify and control them in order that humanity may sensibly get at and use them to their advantage.

Traditionally, librarians have been good at classifying and controlling—with our classification systems and controlled vocabulary. Our part in civilization has been to maintain order amid chaos: a subject heading for every book, and a book for every subject. Qualities that are valued in our profession have included a high degree of intelligence, a good memory, neatness, a good sense of method, and a sense of humor to keep all this order and method in perspective.

This approach has worked quite well up until recent years, when the arrival of the Internet and its mass contents and appeal began to challenge our notions of research as well as our ability to access information coherently. The scope of what's available to researchers now can genuinely overwhelm even the most scholarly and sophisticated among us. It's not possible to categorize and compartmentalize all the material that may be at your fingertips from across the globe one day, and then may have disappeared without explanation the next. We may always have taken as a given the basic fact of change, but none of us bargained that change would accelerate at the pace it has within our lifetimes, particularly in the realm of information access.

In different ways, all the essays in this book address this whirlwind change we're experiencing—it's obvious you're going to talk about change when you're "recreating" a library. The key element that makes this change bearable—that makes it work and allows for progress—is acceptance of it. The term several of these authors use to discuss this acceptance is "flexibility."

The old adage about the oak tree (that stiffly resists the wind until it breaks in a gale force) compared to the willow tree (that bends in the wind and survives) applies very aptly to effective libraries and effective librarians. Flexibility is a major asset for both library staff and buildings: as Jim Rettig points out, buildings that incorporate flexibility in their basic design will serve their institutions much better much longer than inflexible, fixed designs. So, too, will the flexible among us prevail long after the adamant and unchangeable have broken under the waves of change and been left behind in the wake of progress. Hazel Stamps makes this point repeatedly in her interview about staff: the one common characteristic she looks for in all candidates today, no matter what the job, is flexibility.

It's a compliment to say that someone has a Renaissance mind; it implies that he or she is well rounded and well versed in the arts, sciences, and literature. Many librarians may be said to have Renaissance minds: one of the things that first drew me to the profession was meeting so many librarians with wide interests and broad, yet specialized knowledge. Librarians as a whole continue to be among the best-read, best-informed creatures on earth.

As difficult and challenging as it is to work in the demanding environment that is today's academic library, it is fortunate that a new kind of librarian is being forged. It is a Darwinian struggle, to be sure, for the survivors of the infotech battles of this century will emerge into the new millennium as New Renaissance Librarians: well-educated professionals with a facility for creating and learning new systems rapidly, always open to new possibilities.

One of the questions that remains to be answered about our profession is whether in future we will be a group of subject specialists, with narrowly defined areas of expertise, or whether we will be generalists in a variety of formats and subjects. Or will we, as Sherlock Holmes opined, cram our heads full to the extent that at some point for every new thing we learn another chunk of knowledge is lost to us? Is this the case now?

The issue of who and what the New Librarian will be is too large to tackle and discuss fully here. Fortunately, the larger discussion will take place in another volume of the New Library Series: *The New Librarians*, by Kenneth Carpenter and Caroline Kent.

AUTHOR BIOGRAPHIES

Abbie Jan Basile has been designing and maintaining Internet services and teaching Internet workshops since 1992. She is presently information services librarian at the Folsom Library, Rennselaer Polytechnic Institute, in Troy, New York. She was previously an electronic services instruction librarian at Miami University in Ohio, where her responsibilities included designing and maintaining the Libraries' Internet Resources menus and overseeing the implementation and design of the libraries' World Wide Web front-end system. She helped establish and chair the Library and Information Technology Association (LITA) Internet Resources Interest Group. Before that she was an assistant librarian in the reference department of the University of Michigan Graduate Library, where she coordinated the online and CD-ROM search services and established the library's Internet instructional services. She received her M.L.S. from the School of Information and Library Studies at the University at Buffalo in 1991.

Stella Bentley is dean of libraries at Auburn University in Auburn, Alabama. She was previously assistant university librarian for collections and information services at the University of California, Santa Barbara, and before that she directed collection management and development at Case Western Reserve University. Bentley has been a member of the Research Libraries Group (RLG) Collection Management and Development Steering Committee, has served as the chair of the Association for Library Collections and Technical Services (ALCTS) Library Materials Price Index Committee, chaired the University of California Collection Development Committee and the University of California Computer Files Committee, and is the current chair of the ALCTS Scholarly Communication Discussion Group. She earned her M.L.S. and Ph.D. at Indiana University.

Mary Cahill is head of interlibrary loan and document delivery at Schaffer Library, Union College, in Schenectady, New York. A past president of the Eastern New York Chapter of the Association of College and Research Libraries (ACRL), Cahill now serves as chair of the Committee on Interlibrary Loan of the Capital District Library Council. She is engaged in research on the economics of just-in-time access in undergraduate libraries and the impact of this economic model on library instruction, as well as on how electronic journals are changing traditional interlibrary loan and local resource sharing. Cahill earned her B.A. from Edgecliff College of Xavier University and her M.L.S. at the State University of New York at Albany School of Library and Information Science.

Richard DeGennaro is the senior library advisor to JSTOR (a digital journal archive). He was formerly Roy E. Larsen Librarian of Harvard College. He has also served as director of the New York Public Library and director of libraries at the University of Pennsylvania. He has been a member of the Commission on Preservation and Access, on the Research Libraries Group's (RLG) board of governors (serving as chair in 1984–1985), was president of the Association of Research Libraries (ARL) in 1975, and president of the American Library Association's (ALA) Information Science and Automation Division, and has served on many committees, councils, and advisory boards. DeGennaro is an internationally recognized authority on library and information technology and library management. He is widely published and has carried out many consulting assignments. He was awarded ALA's Melvil Dewey Medal in 1986, named Academic/Research Librarian of the Year by the Association of College and Research Libraries (ACRL) in 1991, awarded an honorary doctorate by Wabash College in 1991, and received distinguished alumnus awards from Wesleyan University and Columbia's School of Library Service. In 1993 he was the recipient of ALA's Hugh C. Atkinson Memorial Award.

Pat Ensor was appointed head of information services at the University of Houston Libraries in 1992, and was acting assistant director for public services there from February to November, 1994. She was previously coordinator of electronic information services at Indiana State University for over eight years. She has been involved in selection and service, including instruction, for electronic information for ten years. Pat has published numerous articles in the electronic information field, covering OPAC usage, information standards, online searching, and CD-ROMs. She is the author of *CD-ROM Research Collections*, and coauthored *CD-ROM Periodicals Index* and *CD-ROM Collection Development: A Practical Guide*, as well as editing the book series Key Guides to Electronic Reference. She is a regular columnist for *Technicalities* and is book review editor for *TER: Telecommunications Electronic Reviews*, the first electronic publication of the Library and Information Technology Association (LITA).

Esther Grassian is a self-described "mostly harmless" reference/instruction librarian in the University of California, Los Angeles (UCLA) College Library. She has been involved in library instruction since the early 1970s. She has served as vice-chair and chair of the California Clearinghouse on Library Instruction (CCLI), South, and has been curator of CCLI South's Depository since 1980. She has taught UCLA's undergraduate "Library and Information Resources" course seven times, and in 1989, co-proposed a "User Education/Bibliographic Instruction" course for graduate students in the UCLA library school. Grassian co-taught the course in 1990 and taught it on her own in 1993 and 1995. She has also co-compiled a sample bibliographic instruction course syllabus for a library school course, and, in 1994, was asked to serve as a National Endowment for the Humanities panelist/reviewer in the area of library instruction. Her publications include chapters in *Learning to Teach* and *The Sourcebook for Bibliographic Instruction*, both published by the Association of College and Research Libraries (ACRL) Bibliographic Instruction Section in 1993. In 1995 she was named Librarian of the Year by the Librarians' Association of the University of California, Los Angeles, for her work in developing and implementing Internet training programs for UCLA Library staff and users. She is currently past-chair of the newly renamed ACRL Instruction Section.

Caroline M. Kent is head of research services at Widener Library, Harvard University. Over the past 20 years she has worked in public and technical services at Harvard, Massachusetts Institute of Technology and Brandeis University libraries. In her 14 years at Harvard, she has developed, implemented, and managed a variety of reference and research service programs. Her book *The New Librarians* will be part of Neal-Schuman's New Library Series (forthcoming 1998). She is also coauthor of *The Gateway Library: Reinventing Academic Libraries* (forthcoming 1999 from ALA Publications) and a coauthor of *Teaching the New Library* (Neal-Schuman, 1996).

John Kupersmith is Internet services librarian at the Washoe County Library in Reno, Nevada. Previously he spent 12 years at the University of Texas (UT) at Austin General Libraries, where he was responsible for the user interface and public service aspects of the locally developed online catalog/database/full-text system, initiated the library's gopher, and coordinated online searching. Kupersmith also has an extensive background in library user education and reference work at UT Austin and the University of Pennsylvania, has served as an adjunct faculty member for the Association of Research Libraries' (ARL) Office of Management Services (OMS), and is co-designer of the OMS Training Skills Institute. He is the author of "Technostress and the Reference Librarian" (*Reference Services Review*, Summer 1992) and has taught several workshops on technostress management. Kupersmith holds a B.A. degree from the University of Washington, an M.A. in

English literature from Brown University, and an M.L.S. from Rutgers University.

Cheryl LaGuardia is coordinator of the Electronic Teaching Center in the Harvard College Library. Previously she worked in various public and technical services at the University of California, Santa Barbara, and at Union College in Schenectady, New York. Since 1992 she has written the column "CD-ROM Reviews" for *Library Journal*. In 1996, the Reference and Adult Services Division (RASD, now Reference and User Services Association) honored her with the Louis Shores–Oryx Press Award for her reviewing. LaGuardia serves on the editorial review boards of several library publications. Her published work includes *The CD-ROM Primer* (Neal-Schuman, 1994) and *Teaching the New Library* (Neal-Schuman, 1996). Since 1995 she has served as a judge for the Association of American Publishers Professional/Scholarly Publishing Awards Competition. The Nelson A. Rockefeller College of Public Affairs and Policy at the State University of New York at Albany recently honored her with their 1996 School of Information Science and Policy Distinguished Alumni Award.

Liz Lane is director of the New York State Library (NYSL) in Albany, New York. Previous to that she was principal librarian for collection acquisition and processing at NYSL. She has over 25 years of experience in academic and research libraries, including work in both public and technical services. She currently serves as president of the New York Library Association's Academic and Special Libraries Section. Lane received a B.A. in history and political science from the College of St. Rose and an M.L.S. from Syracuse University.

Susan Lee is associate librarian of Harvard College for planning and administrative services. Her primary responsibility is for the financial and budgetary programs, as well as for facilities, library computer networking, and human resources. Before coming to Harvard in 1989, Lee was associate director for administrative services at the University of Connecticut Libraries, and previous to that she spent ten years as a college library director and adjunct professor in management. Her many publications and presentations, as well as classes and consultation projects, have focused on library management with an emphasis on organizational change, strategic planning, and human resource development. She has a B.A. and an M.A. from Long Island University, an M.B.A. from Nichols College, and the M.L.S. and D.A. from Simmons College.

Clifford A. Lynch is the executive director of the Coalition for Networked Information (CNI) in Washington, D.C. He was previously director of the division of library automation at the University of California (UC) Office of the President, where he was responsible for the MELVYL information system, one of the largest public access information retrieval systems in existence, and the computer internetwork linking the nine UC campuses. He held various positions at UC from 1979 to 1997. Lynch has also been involved in a wide variety of research and development efforts in the application of advanced technologies to information management and delivery, including work with computer networking, information servers, database management systems, and imaging technologies. Lynch received his Ph.D. in computer science from the University of California at Berkeley. He participates in several standards activities (including the NISO Standards Development Committee). He has published extensively and serves on a number of editorial boards. He is also a director-at-large for the American Society for Information Science.

James Rettig is university librarian at the University of Richmond. Formerly he was assistant dean of university libraries for reference and information services at the College of William and Mary in Williamsburg, Virginia, where he has been involved in planning a much-needed and fervently hoped-for major expansion and renovation of the library facility. In his previous position as head of the reference department of the Main Library at the University of Illinois at Chicago he helped oversee planning or a major renovation of that library building. He has written and spoken widely on reference issues. From 1981 until 1995 he edited and wrote the "Current

Reference Books" review column in *Wilson Library Bulletin*. In 1992–1993 he served as president of the American Library Association's Reference and Adult Services Division (RASD, now Reference and User Services Association). In 1988 RASD honored him with the Isadore Gilbert Mudge Citation "for distinguished contributions to reference librarianship"; in 1993 the American Library Association presented the G. K. Hall Award for Library Literature to him for *Distinguished Classics of Reference Publishing* (Oryx Press, 1992); and in 1995 RASD honored him with the Louis Shores–Oryx Press Award for his contributions to the reviewing of library materials. He has a B.A. and an M.A. in English from Marquette University and an M.A.L.S. from the University of Wisconsin at Madison.

Ilene Rockman is associate dean of library services at California Polytechnic State University, San Luis Obispo. Her 20-year career has included service in school, public, and academic libraries. Her experience has included reference and instruction, collection development, acquisitions, cataloging, circulation, systems and networking, staff development, and administration. She participates in activities of the American Library Association, and serves on the editorial boards of *RSR: Reference Services Review*, *RQ*, and *Library Administration and Management*. Her articles have appeared in *Library Journal*, *Library Trends*, *Journal of Library Administration*, *RQ*, *College and Research Libraries*, *College and Research Libraries News*, *Reference Librarian*, *RSR: Reference Services Review*, and *Education Libraries*.

Hazel Stamps is senior human resources program administrator for the Harvard College Library. She has worked at Harvard University for over 34 years, having spent the last 23 years working in personnel at the Harvard College Library.

Barbara Stewart is presently Latin American Cataloger at the University of Massachusetts, Amherst. She has worked in a variety of libraries, having been director of the Green Tree Pennsylvania Public Library, head of the Automotive and Welding Library at Houston Community College, head of reference at a public two-year college and graduate school library on the Texas/Mexico border, head of technical processes at Cambria County Public Library, and Latin American Cataloger at the University of Pittsburgh. Her book, *The Neal-Schuman Directory of Library Technical Services Home Pages*, was published in August 1997. She has written and spoken widely on a variety of technical services, Latin American collections, and Web issues.

Ed Tallent is coordinator of research instruction at the Harvard College Library, and coauthor of *Teaching the New Library* (Neal-Schuman, 1996). In his 14-year career he has been head of reference at Lamont Library, Harvard University, as well as reference and instruction librarian at Cornell's Uris and Olin libraries. He coauthors *Library Journal*'s "CD-ROM Reviews" column with Cheryl LaGuardia.

John Vasi is associate university librarian for administrative services and planning at the University of California, Santa Barbara, where his responsibilities include space planning, budget, and systems. Before that he worked with building- and space-planning-related matters in libraries at the University of Colorado and the State University of New York at Buffalo. He has published a number of articles and essays on the topics of ergonomics, ADA access, and rehabilitating library spaces for technological use. Vasi is past president of ALA's Library Administration and Management Association (LAMA), and has also chaired LAMA's Buildings and Equipment Section and Equipment Committee.

Index